**The Proceedings of The Conference
on Biblical Interpretation
1988**

THE PROCEEDINGS OF THE CONFERENCE ON BIBLICAL INTERPRETATION

1988

BROADMAN PRESS
Nashville, Tennessee

© Copyright 1988 • Broadman Press
4260-05
ISBN: 0-8054-6005-5
Printed in the United States of America

EDITORIAL PREFACE

This book contains the papers presented at The Conference on Biblical Interpretation, April 25-27, 1988, at Ridgecrest Baptist Conference Center in Ridgecrest, North Carolina. The conference was sponsored by the six seminaries of the Southern Baptist Convention.

The papers in this collection have been edited with a light hand so that the book might be produced in time to be available at the Southern Baptist Convention meeting in June, 1988. No effort was made to bring the papers into conformity with one standard of style or grammar; rather, we have chosen to let each author's work stand substantially as it was written. Of course, we have corrected errors of spelling and sometimes altered the order of words when clarity was thanks stake.

Some papers presented special difficulties. J. I. Packer accepted the invitation to speak at this conference after he was already heavily committed to similar duties elsewhere. Because of this circumstance, Dr. Packer was unable to prepare formal papers. Instead, he spoke from rather detailed and extended notes. Typescripts were made from the audiotapes of his addresses, and it was the editor's task to develop manuscripts for inclusion in this volume by comparing the typescripts with the notes. It is hoped that the results accord with both the views and high standards of J. I. Packer, though of course only the editor is responsible for any miscommunications that may result because of this process. In addition, several papers by other authors contained graphs, charts, or other illustrations. Due to our production schedule, we were not always able to include these aids. Finally, John Hewett's response and Jerry Vine's sermon were prepared from audiotapes; therefore, the papers have the flavor of oral communication.

This volume is the second of a projected three-volume set. The first volume was *The Proceedings of the Conference on Biblical Inerrancy, 1987*. Broadman Press anticipates publishing the third volume which will be entitled *The Proceedings of the Conference on Biblical Imperatives, 1989*.

ABOUT THE AUTHORS

James T. Draper, Jr., is pastor of First Baptist Church in Euless, Texas.
Ken Hemphill is pastor of First Baptist Church in Norfolk, Virginia.
John Hewett is pastor of First Baptist Church in Asheville, North Carolina.
Richard Jackson is pastor of North Phoenix Baptist Church in Phoenix, Arizona.
Robert Johnston is dean at North Park College and Theological Seminary in Chicago, Illinois.
Walter C. Kaiser, Jr., is professor of Old Testament and dean at Trinity Evangelical Seminary in Deerfield, Illinois.
Kenneth A. Mathews is professor of Old Testament and semantics at The Criswell College in Dallas, Texas.
Grant Osborne is professor of New Testament at Trinity Evangelical Seminary in Deerfield, Illinois.
James I. Packer is professor of historical and systematic theology at Regent College in Vancouver, British Columbia, Canada.
Jon Stubblefield is pastor of First Baptist Church in Shreveport, Louisiana.
Daniel Vestal is pastor of First Baptist Church in Midland, Texas.
Jerry Vines is co-pastor of First Baptist Church in Jacksonville, Florida.
John D. W. Watts is professor of Old Testament at The Southern Baptist Theological Seminary in Louisville, Kentucky.

CONTENTS

1. **When Awe-Full Is Wonderful** 13
   Richard Jackson
2. **The Challenge of Biblical Interpretation: Creation** 21
   James I. Packer
   Responses: Kenneth A. Mathews 34
              John D. W. Watts 41
3. **Hope** 47
   Daniel Vestal
4. **How We Interpret the Bible: Biblical Interpretation
   and Literary Criticism** 51
   Robert Johnston
5. **Interpreting the Old Testament** 65
   Walter C. Kaiser, Jr.
6. **The Matchless Love of God** 93
   Jerry Vines
7. **The Challenge of Biblical Interpretation: Women** 103
   James I. Packer
   Responses: John Hewett 116
              James T. Draper, Jr. 122
8. **Lord, Stir Us Again** 129
   Ken Hemphill
9. **Interpreting the New Testament** 137
   Grant Osborne
10. **Biblical Interpretation and Theology: Bringing
    the Bible to Life** 169
    Robert Johnston
11. **What Is the Gospel?** 183
    Jon Stubblefield
12. **The Challenge of Biblical Interpretation:
    Eschatology** 191
    James I. Packer

13. Interpreting the Bible: God's Word for Our Day 205
    Panel Discussion
14. Workshop Summary 221

The Proceedings of The Conference on Biblical Interpretation
1988

1
WHEN AWE-FULL IS WONDERFUL
1 Timothy 3:16
Richard Jackson

Introduction

Someone living close to Niagara Falls could possibly, over a period of time, grow so accustomed to the magnificent beauty and force and power of nature that he could look at the awesome scene with something close to indifference. Likewise, a resident of northern Arizona could forget the awe-inspiring reasons why every year thousands of people go out of their way to gaze upon the splendor of the Grand Canyon. In such cases, it is not so much that "familiarity breeds contempt," as it is that "familiarity breeds callousness." What once we considered a thrill and a privilege just to behold becomes commonplace, and we take it for granted. The object of our one-time admiration has not changed . . . we have.

When it comes to a mighty waterfall or a beautiful river-carved canyon, such an indifference is sad and regrettable, but hardly dangerous in any sense of the word. Not so in another area of our lives to which all of us are susceptible. Regardless of where we live geographically, those of us who love and serve the Lord Jesus through the local church, which is exactly what He calls us to do, live continually with the risk of falling into a spiritual indifference that is, indeed, dangerous. It not only has a crippling effect on our development but also can cause a creeping paralysis that leaves us literally worthless in the kingdom work. Like the familiarity with the waterfall or the rock formation, it does not happen overnight. The change in our attitude is gradual, sometimes almost imperceptible. And, interestingly enough, the more active we are in the life of the church, the greater the danger.

We read the Word so often that we forget that it is holy. We celebrate the Lord's Supper on a regular basis, and we forget the solemnity and holiness of the occasion. We preach at least three times each week, and we forget that this "foolishness of preaching" is the holy assignment by which God has chosen to save the lost. If we are not careful . . .

> the choir members start to think their major goal is to hit the right notes at the right time;
> the ushers believe their job is simply to hand out bulletins;

the Bible Study teachers think they had better cover so much material in so much time and not offend anyone in the class;

Somewhere along the way we reduce everything that goes on "in the name of Jesus" to a merely human act. God deliver us from ever losing "the wonder of it all"!

There was a little boy in Bible study class who had been listening intently to all the teacher was saying about God's marvelous acts in creation and in the life of Jesus. Finally, in an attempt to express his awe, the little fellow said, "God just wonders me!" May God give us back whatever it was in our childlike spirit when first we came to Christ (which is the only way any of us came) that made everything we learned a wonder, a marvel, and a delight. In this computer age, if we are not careful, we will start to have "computer minds," and before you know it, we very casually believe that if it doesn't compute then it doesn't exist. If we can't touch it, taste it, smell it, or hear it, it isn't there.

That is not the kind of faith we have. There is a great deal of mystery and awe in the Christian faith. Everything about it is startling and unexplainable. As a matter of fact, the apostle Paul, whom even nonbelievers admit was a master of logic, expression, and rhetoric, found himself speechless and finally simply said, "Thanks be unto God for His unspeakable gift!" (2 Cor. 9:15)

Is it possible that we have become so familiar with all the words of our faith that we have lost the wonder of our faith? Have we forgotten that what we have in Christ Jesus is that priceless, unspeakable gift that is more valuable than all the dollars we may accumulate the rest of our lives, more valuable than any Nobel prizes, Rhodes fellowships, or Congressional awards that we may receive? It is said that Raphael's masterpiece of the Christ-Child and His mother could not be bought for $5,000,000. Do we understand that the Christ alive in us makes $5,000,000 an embarrassing, paltry sum?

There is a wonder and a mystery that runs continuously through every event of the Christian faith.

> From that night in Bethlehem when the sky should have been dark but was ablaze with the glory of God to that noonday in Jerusalem when the sky should have been bright and was blackened with the judgment of God, there was mystery.
>
> From the early days of His life when Jesus confounded the wisest men of Israel to His last day on earth when He commissioned some of the simplest men of Israel, there was mystery.
>
> From the moment when the Holy Spirit descended like a dove on Jesus in the Jordan River to the moment the Holy Spirit descended like a flame of fire on Jesus' disciples in the upper room, there was mystery.

As a matter of fact, in Paul's letter to the believers in Ephesus, the first nine verses of chapter 3, Paul mentioned the word *mystery* three times: "The mystery was made known to me" (v. 3); "My insight into the mystery of Christ" (v. 4); "The mystery hidden for ages in God, who created all things" (v. 9).

In our text, Paul gave a synopsis of this mystery in just one marvelous verse. In fact, this verse is one of the most precious verses we have because it is believed to have been one of the hymns of the early church. "By common confession great is the mystery of godliness:

> He who was revealed in the flesh,
> Was vindicated in the Spirit,
> Beheld by angels,
> Proclaimed among the nations,
> Believed on in the world,
> Taken up in glory" (1 Tim. 3:16).

Be careful! This is the very thing we are talking about. We are so used to hearing what we consider to be the "basic facts" about our Lord Jesus that we tend to skim right over them and lose their wonder. If we can read right past those six truths and *feel* no sense of awe, much less be *filled* with it, we are in grave danger of being far from where we need to be. Let us consider those six divine truths. Do we *really* understand what they are telling us?

First, notice this:

> Revealed in the flesh and vindicated in the Spirit.
> Seen by angels (who are nearest the throne of God) and preached to Gentiles (who were far from God).
> Believed on in the world and taken into glory.

In the Greek manuscripts, these phrases are in the language of poetry. It is as though the hymn were a three-stanza poem of contrasts, expressing the six-fold mystery of godliness. The word *mystery* here means "revealed truth, that which was once concealed, but now stands openly revealed." They were things that were hidden and so concealed that reason could not discover them. Even now, though they are revealed, they involve matters so vast and so profound that not even the most brilliant scholars pretend to comprehend them fully.

Mystery #1: Incarnation

"He who was revealed in the flesh . . ."

The apostle Paul began with the impossible-to-comprehend fact of God's coming in the flesh . . . God Incarnate. Jesus Christ's human form and nature were real. Paul, one of the most learned men of his day, could not begin to grasp how the infinite God of the universe could be wrapped in flesh and filled with blood and held together by bones and ligaments and muscles and still be God Almighty but he believed it.

This is a good place to start as we attempt to determine if we have lost some of our awe, our wonder. Every year when we stand beside the cradle of Bethlehem, are we simply enjoying a nice story, or do we find ourselves uncontrollably sinking to our knees in awe of Majesty lying in a manger? What is Christmas to you these days? Someone has said, "Whatever else Christmas is, it is wonder's response to something bigger than life."

Mystery #2: Vindication

"Was vindicated in the Spirit . . ."

This refers, of course, to the fact that it was the power of the Spirit that justified everything Jesus claimed or did. He was tempted in all points, yet lived above sin. He performed mighty acts and proved His claims again and again. Then the ultimate vindication—sinful man judged Him guilty of blasphemy and put Him to death, but God reversed the verdict and vindicated Him by the power of the Spirit when He raised Him from the dead.

Is Easter no longer filled with awe for us? Have we so long sung, "Up from the grave He arose," that we have forgotten that ours is the only faith in the world that has a risen Savior? Have we come to take that so for granted that we no longer realize that if it were not for this fact, we would of all men be the most miserable? Do we stand before the empty tomb with the same attitude as the neighbor of Niagara Falls has when he beholds that masterpiece of nature?

Mystery #3: Exaltation

"Beheld by angels . . ."

Yes, the angels saw and worshiped Christ before He came to earth, but with His incarnation, they beheld God as never before. Oh, to be sure, they had seen His justice and power and wisdom and sovereignty; but in the incarnation of Christ Jesus, they saw love and tenderness and condescension. They knew Him to be holy, for that was their song, "Holy, Holy, Holy." But they did not know Him to be essential love as they knew it when they saw that "He spared not His own Son, but delivered Him up for us all."

When they saw God in the flesh, they ministered to Him, watching around His cradle, getting word to Joseph to warn him to flee, caring for Him in the wilderness, one of them strengthening Him in the garden of Gethsemane (Luke 22), and finally one of them rolling the stone away from His grave (Matt. 28) while two others sat at the foot and the head of the place where He had lain.

Have we lost the wonder of all that and think of it as we think of Rumpelstilskin or Rapunzel? This truth should bring us so close to the angels that we thrill to share with them our common focus: Our gazes meet on Jesus our Lord. We have one common love, one common loyalty, one common Lord—and wonder beyond wonder—those who waited on our Lord now minister to us! They love the members of the body for the sake of the Head. Do we have the audacity to take that for granted?

Mystery #4: Proclamation

"Proclaimed among the nations . . ." "Preached unto the Gentiles . . ." (KJV)

Until Christ came, *nothing* was preached unto the Gentiles. They were dogs and barely worthy of any crumbs. But Jesus changed all that. Jesus is the exclusive possession of no race and of no country. He is the Messiah of the nations, of the whole world. The angels did not proclaim, "Joy to the Jews!" rather their message was, "Joy to the world!"

If we take this for granted and fail to stand in awe of this one point of the divine mystery, we are ingrates, undeserving of such love. When Jesus' arms were outstretched on the cross, they encircled all of us. If it had not been for His love that included even those of us who are "dirty dog Gentiles," we would be living in a world without hope.

Mystery #5: Verification

"Believed on in the world . . ."

This is such a beautifully simple statement, and yet it houses a miracle. When Jesus died and rose again and ascended into heaven, the number of His followers was 120 (Acts 1:15). All they had to tell was a story about a Galilean carpenter who had died as a criminal on a hilltop and whose grave was empty. Their story was so strange, no one could imagine that anyone would believe it. The doctrines they taught were so contrary to the desires of the flesh and so humbling to human pride that surely they would be laughed out of existence. Yet, before seventy years had passed, that story had gone out to the ends of the earth, and men in every nation had accepted this crucified Jesus as Savior and Lord! In this simple little phrase is the divine wonder of the expansion of the church . . . which on purely human grounds would have been impossible.

Because we believe, do we take for granted the fact that other people living in another time and other places also believed? Do we casually dismiss the fact that thousands upon thousands of our fellow believers have been tortured and martyred that we too might hear the gospel? Have we forgotten that we have a rich heritage that wraps around the world and weaves its thread into every nation of people? Are we not amazed?

Ask Isaac Watts how He feels about Jesus, and he will answer, "I am not ashamed to own my Lord."

Ask Newton what he thinks of the gospel, and hear him say, "Amazing grace, how sweet the sound."

Ask Cowper what he thinks, and he will say, "There is a fountain filled with blood."

"Charles Wesley, what do you think?" And he replies, "Jesus, lover of my soul."

"Fannie Crosby, what is Jesus to you?" She says, "Blessed assurance, Jesus is mine."

Beyond that . . . ask Solomon, and he will answer, "Lily of the valley."

"David, what do you think of Him?" And he says, "The Lord is my Shepherd."

What is He to John? "The Bright and Morning Star."

"Paul, what is He to you?" Paul quickly answers, "Christ is all in all."

Christ Jesus our Lord believed on in the world. What a glorious mystery!

Mystery #6: Glorification

"Taken up in glory . . ."

This, of course, refers to the ascension. The story of Jesus begins in heaven and ends in heaven. This Man who lived as a Servant to all, was labeled as a criminal, died the humiliating death of a Roman cross, rose with the nailprints still in His hands, wonder of wonders, He ended up in glory! Men say that Jesus is not God, but that's all right. He is in Glory! Men revile His gospel and mock His cross, but they cannot dim the luster of His crown for He is in Glory! They even try to slay His people, but He is in Glory waiting for His own!

Oh, dear friend, we dare not lose the awe and wonder of Jesus glorified! For day, one glorious day, we shall behold His coronation. Oh, picture the blessed event!

>From the farthest past, led by the prophets of old, they will come.

>From the early days of the gospel, led by the apostles, they will come.

>From centuries still ahead of us, led by heroes of the faith we know not of, they will come.

Like a mighty tree with autumn leaves piled all around, Jesus will stand with worshipers at His feet. And then, from the largest audience ever assembled in the history of the world, there will go up a shout: "Crown Him! Crown Him! Crown Him!" And the Father, who said long ago, "I will give Thee the heathen for Thine inheritance and the uttermost parts of the earth for Thy possession," shall set the crown upon that forehead still scarred with the marks of the crucifixion, and all the hosts of heaven will drop to their knees, crying, "Hail, King of earth! King of heaven! King of saints! King of angels! Thy kingdom is everlasting! Amen and Amen!"

Conclusion

And mystery of all mysteries . . . I will be there. Do I understand that? No! A thousand times, No! But I believe it as surely as I believe any of these six mysteries! Am I in awe? Oh, yes. For the only reason I will be present for the coronation ceremony will be because He did, by mystery and miracle, become flesh and, by mystery and miracle, pay my way.

Oh, we dare take none of this lightly. We are involved in the great, wondrous work of the ages. Just as, beholding the glare of the sun, men lose their power of vision, so if we raise our eyes to the brilliance of Jesus, we are blinded by the splendor of His unspeakable gift. If you have lost that sense of wonder and awe, I urge you to grasp it once again before the callousness becomes impenetrable. Everything we do as believers is to have the mark of God on it.

When Sir Christopher Wren was building St. Paul's Cathedral, he was making a tour of the work being done. He asked one of the workmen, "What are you doing over there?"

The man said, "I am cutting this stone to a certain size and shape."

He asked another man the same question, to which he replied, "I am earning my hourly wage."

Finally, he came to a third man and asked him what he was doing. The man paused for a moment, then straightened himself up, and said, "I am helping Sir Christopher Wren build St. Paul's Cathedral."

The first two stated simple, cold facts. The third man had a sense of awe and mission in what he did. To that, we as believers are called today.

> There's the wonder of springtime and harvest,
> The wonder of sunset I see,
> But the wonder of wonders that thrills my soul
> Is the wonder that God loves me!
>
> Oh, the wonder of it all,
> The wonder of it all . . .
> Just to think that God loves me!

2
THE CHALLENGE OF BIBLICAL INTERPRETATION: CREATION

James I. Packer

My three presentations have a common title, "The Challenge of Biblical Interpretation." I think that word *challenge* is not unfair. When I was here last year I presented to you my understanding of the inerrancy of Scripture, a revealed truth of God, as I believe I put it to you and illustrated in some detail that Holy Scripture is totally trustworthy, though it must be correctly interpreted. When, however, it is correctly interpreted, all that it teaches in both the indicative and the imperative moods as a total message from God is, in very truth, His word, His word which applies to us as truly as it was ever applied to any generation of folk. You may well come back to me now and say, "I would like to see you working out your concept of inerrancy in some of the more difficult questions of biblical interpretation." You may say to me, "I would like to see your definition of inerrancy tested in use. I would like to see you working on some of the hard subjects over which some biblical interpreters have felt themselves bound to give up inerrancy altogether, believing that the concept is impossible to maintain under this complexity." If I am unable to make a worthwhile effort at interpreting some of these difficult topics, what I have said in this very hall about the inerrancy of Scripture will lose something of its credibility. Whereas, if I can succeed in finding a way through some of these difficult areas in which Scripture is supposed to speak out of, shall I say, both sides of its mouth, I shall be adding some credibility to the formula that I have given you.

My assigned topics are among the most controversial in the world of biblical interpretation: creation, women, and eschatology. While willing to accept the challenge of this task, I ask you bear in mind four things. One, it is inevitable that you will not all agree with everything that I say, for these are three areas on which biblical inerrantists can and do disagree with each other, as well as those who are not prepared to believe that all that Scripture says is true. Second, remember that disagreement about interpretation on subjects of this sort does not necessarily indicate lack of agreement either on the total truthfulness of Scripture or on the method whereby those who believe in the total truthfulness of Scripture should set about discovering its meaning and its message. Belief in biblical inerrancy requires us to seek understanding of the total Scripture testimony on each subject that is internally coherent and that involves no assumption of error or contradiction, either factual or theological, in the sacred text. This is my understanding of a quest for canonical interpretation of the Word of God. Yet it is possible for folk who agree that this is what we are seeking still to come up with syntheses that differ in detail.

Third, all biblical interpretation is provisional. We must give the task our best, but as the church continues in history and fresh questions arise, ultimately I believe by the Spirit of God, who then leads us to see things that were not seen before as we work with these new questions. Old interpretations of Scripture are sometimes made to appear not indeed wrong, but inadequate, incomplete. Statements which perhaps were regarded as the whole truth, now are shown as being only part of the truth because there is more to be said. My three presentations will no doubt have that character; they shall represent my best effort but remain provisional. Fourth, please appreciate that the practice of interpretation of Scripture, like the confession of the inerrancy of Scripture is, so far as I am concerned, a nonpolitical business. I know that in the Southern Baptist Convention, there are political questions which bear directly on and are affected directly by the whole discussion of the inerrancy interpretation of Scripture. Please understand that I am seeking the truth and wisdom as best I can. I come to you from another tradition. I am an Episcopalian, not a Southern Baptist, and I shall simply share with you what I think I see without any thought, frankly, of political implications. I am interpreting Scripture, and I am trying to keep my eye on that task.

Concerning the task and method of biblical interpretation, there is this: The goal is to extract from Scripture, the Word of God written, the message that is there for us. The best simple way of describing the nature of Holy Scripture is to say, "This is God preaching." That formula seems to catch the dynamism of Holy Scripture along with its divine origin, and I value a phrase that does both those things together. When, therefore, I think of the Bible as the Word of God, I mean by that the message of God. I am thinking of more than simply its divine origin as a collection of some two million words; I am thinking of what it has to say to us. I echo very happily the words of Augustine's prayer, "What thy scripture says, thou dost say." I listen to Scripture to hear God preaching and instructing me in matters theological and practical, matters of belief and matters of behavior, matters of doctrine, matters of doxology, matters of devotion, matters of orthodoxy, like belief, and matters of orthopraxy (right living). When I speak of getting from the written text the message that is there for us, I am thinking both of our extracting it as truth by exegesis and exposition, exegesis that avoids eisegesis, reading into the text what isn't there, and exposition that avoids being imposition, pushing onto the text things that aren't there. I am thinking of exegesis and exposition as an academic discipline that depends on using one's mind to write. But I am also thinking of going beyond the conceptual framework of the message extracted from Scripture to the spiritual recognition of that message. In short, biblical interpretation is a task that makes extraordinary demands upon the mind and the heart. The task of exegesis is, thus, a spiritual discipline.

To practice this discipline successfully, we have to ask each passage three sets of questions. I call them the exegetical, hermeneutical, and practical questions. The exegetical question focuses on what was meant, what was the writer's message to his envisaged readership. To answer that question, we must practice a discipline which is called the grammatical historical method. We are seeking what we sometimes call the literal, the natural, the historical sense of the text, and in order to do that we must put ourselves in the shoes of the writer and his expected readers. We must be aware of the cultural milieu to which they both belonged. We must be aware of their specific situation and, to use a modern word, we must recognize the distance between them in their situation and us in ours. This is step one. This is the exegetical discipline.

Then we have to ask the hermeneutical question, which takes this form: What then does this message given long ago by a man of God concerning the worship and service of God mean as the word of God to us. We have to move from what it meant historically to what it means for us in the present. In addition, we have to ask another question: Is there anything in us that will act as an obstacle to our understanding what it means for us and how it applies to us? Are there any cultural prejudices operating in our lives as distorting spectacles, keeping us from seeing how this message applies to us in our own situation? In other words, have we any blind spots? That is a crucial hermeneutical question that has to be asked over and over again. The modern theologian Godimer has used an interesting image. Horizons, he says, must fuse in biblical interpretation. The Bible point of view must come over the horizon, that is to say the limits of our present outlook on things, and perhaps shatter those limits and reshape our thinking. This means that the Word of God coming over the horizon of our thinking into the center of our outlook must relativize us, relativize our prejudices, relativize our age, for God's Word is the absolute and we are more or less off center in relation to it. So it must be allowed to come into our minds and hearts to set us straight. This is the hermeneutical inquiry which used to be expressed, and validly, by the question, "How does it all apply?"

Third, we have to ask the practical question: What then must we do? How must this message for the Word of God change our ways, our thoughts our practice? What, in other words, must we start doing now that we have not been doing up to this point, and what must we stop doing now that we have been doing up to this point, both at the level thinking and behavior? Again, to put it in fundamental terms, how must this Word of God change us? What does obedience to it amount to in our thought and action today? The Holy Spirit is involved in all three inquiries. We shall be more conscious of this operation in the hermeneutical inquiry than in the historical exegetical inquiry. Nonetheless, the Holy Spirit must be with us in that also if we are to understand. We shall be most conscious of all, I suspect, of the Holy Spirit's activity at level three, when we are asking the practical question of what obedience to this word involves. But let us be clear, the Holy Spirit must be with us in all three stages of the inquiry. Otherwise, it will fail.

I have introduced the entire process of interpretation so that you might understand the method which I am following as we consider together several thorny problems of interpretation. This is the way that we are going to go as we look together at the theme of creation. What I am going to address is, I suppose, the tensest issue among evangelicals when the doctrine of creation is being explored from Scripture. I am going to look with you at the first two chapters of the Book of Genesis, and I am going to try to explore some of the problems of understanding those chapters, which are viewed so differently by so many different people.

What do I bring to the task? I bring to it first a theological concept of creation which I have learned not only from the first two chapters of Genesis but also from the Book of Job, the Psalms, Isaiah, and from many places in the New Testament. It is a concept which one theologian defined pretty much like this (I put it that way because I have amended his definition slightly): Creation is a free act or series of acts of the Triune God whereby in the beginning, according to His own will and for His own glory, He brought into being the entire universe without use of preexisting material and gave it an existence dependent on His will but distinct from His own. That is the biblical notion of creation spelled out in full theological form. It is that creation that is made explicit in Psalm 33:6,9. "By the word of the Lord the heavens were made and all the host of them by the breath of his mouth. He spoke and it was done. He commanded and they were created." Hebrews 11:3 speaks in the same terms. The language is nontechnical, but the meaning is clear: "By faith we understand that the worlds were framed by the word of God so that the things that are were not made of things which do appear." That is to say there was no preexisting material out of which God made the worlds. There is more to creation, in other words, than craftsmanship. Craftsmanship works on preexisting material; creation is a matter of God saying as in Genesis, chapter 1, "Let there be." And by His very word He calls forth that which He says should be, so that henceforth it exists. Creation is mystery, like all the acts of God in the final analysis are mystery. We don't know how God did it. We couldn't do it ourselves. We must, therefore, stand in awe of it. We don't know how creation can happen. All we know from Scripture is that it did happen. God spoke and it was done. It is a marvel, a matter for praise and adoration, one of the marvelous works of God. He created the world.

The second thing that I bring to my study of these chapters, and this I believe to be very important, is a theological concept of natural science as practiced today. What I have to say here is crucial to me; a great deal hangs on it. The natural sciences, grew up under the aegis of Scripture. They began to develop in the Christian West in the late sixteenth and seventeenth centuries. But the sciences neither ask nor answer the questions about the world which the Bible answers. The sciences study the regularities, the processes, the proportions, the correlations, the behavior patterns that operate within the created system, asking always how does it work? The sciences then only take notice of what used to be called second causes within the system, that is second causes within the order of creation. The sciences have no means of telling how the system started, nor have they any means of telling us how God stands related to it now that it is a going concern. If scientists seek on the basis of science to answer such questions, the proper response is to say, "Sir, as a scientist, none of your data tells you anything about any of this. You would be wiser to keep your mouth shut." Of course modern cosmologists are able to tell us with great confidence that the world cannot be more than ten to twenty billion years old. They may be right. I am sure I don't know. But even if they are right, that says nothing about where it all came from. Science, as such, cannot do so.

Scripture, by contrast with the sciences, deals always with the first cause, God Himself. The question that the Bible is answering always when it deals with the order of creation and speaks of specific created things is the question, "For what purpose is it there, working as it does?" What is the value and the significance of this part of the created order or indeed of creation as a whole? What is its significance, that is, for God and the glory of God and for man living under God. Different questions, you see, are being asked. Different methods of inquiry are being followed. The scientific method is go and look, guess and check. It is an empirical study. Biblical method is listen and learn, let God tell you. In Holy Scripture He does tell us, but what He tells us is not what the scientist seeks to know. What God tells us in the Word is what the significance of creation is for Him and for us who were made to live to Him and serve Him. The goals of scientific inquiry and of biblical study are also different. Science studies the way that the system works with a view to managing it and developing what we call a technology. Scripture, by contrast, tells about the created order with a view to leading us to worship the God who made it, admire His workmanship, and praise Him for what He has done, and lead us into a richer knowledge of God the Creator.

World views are brought to the sciences by the scientists. Christians bring a Christian understanding of this world as God's creation, and they made that the frame into which they fit their scientific knowledge. Atheists, deists, pantheists bring a different view of ultimate reality to their science. These views of God cannot be read out of science, but they do get read into science. These days the scientist is so venerated a member of our society that he is allowed to pontificate as a scientist about religion, and people suppose that it is his science which has taught him what he believes or disbelieves about God. It is not so. It is a confusion to suppose that it ever was so or ever could be so. I quote from a recent book which seems to me to be very right-minded of this point. Scripture is "ascientific, . . . It does not speak unscientifically in ways that modern science would judge to be mistaken. Nor does it speak anti-scientifically in the sense of rejecting what empirical study of the world would indicate." That is exactly right as I understand the matter. Scripture speaks about created things in non-technical, naive, observational language, the language of ordinary human experience which simply records what things look like and what impressions they make on the ordinary observer. Science has its technical language, but the Bible doesn't talk that technical language. Theology too has its technical language, and the Bible provides a foundation for the forming of that language, but as far as scientific language is concerned, the Bible doesn't take us forward at all. The Bible is not teaching science. This, I think, comes to expression very clearly when you compare the way in which Jesus in Scripture in the Sermon on the Mount in Matthew 5 spoke about the rain in the same way that we speak about the rain. We say, "It rains." And if we were asked to explain how it is that it rains, we would explain that there is evaporation and clouds are formed and then barometric pressure drops and other things happen to the clouds and the precipitation is delivered. Jesus did not talk that language. Jesus said, "God sends his rains on the just and on the unjust, on the evil and on the good." These are two quite different points of view. They are complimentary in relation to each other, but they don't overlap because Jesus is talking about God the first cause, God whose providence is the first cause of all that happens. We in our scientific culture talk about the natural mechanics that produce the precipitation. These are two different worlds of thought. Biblical and scientific accounts of natural order are complimentary, but not contradictory. They supplement each other, but they do not challenge each other because first and second causes do not overlap. I bring that view of natural science to my study of Genesis chapters 1 and 2, and its relevance will appear.

Finally, I bring to the study of these chapters theological rules for the exegesis of these texts and all other texts. You must attend to the writer's expressed meaning and not allegorize. You must attend to the writer's didactic nurturing purpose. Every Bible writer wrote what he did in order to do people good spiritually. One must be clear as to what effect, what impact, what spiritual fruit he was hoping that his words would have. Otherwise you have not fully understood his meaning. Third, you must attend to the writer's literary strategy, his choice of what is nowadays called *genre*. That is a French word that means the type of writing that you are doing. Poetry is one genre, and prose is another genre. Do we understand the difference, I wonder, between prose and poetry? In poetry what you are always doing, whether it is poetry that rhymes or poetry that doesn't, is trying to concentrate experience and perception in forms that will communicate your perception of things to the reader. Your imagination is involved very much; it is that kind of communication. Prose, by contrast, is connected, factual description intended to enable people to envisage what you saw and observed and to imagine themselves in particular scenes and visualize it. No imagination is used, or at least, as little as possible in prose. The ideal of prose is found in newspaper reports of things that happen, which are purely factual, purely descriptive, not imaginative at all. Between the poles, the extremes of prose such as we read in our newspapers and poetries such as Shakespeare, there are any number of intermediate positions. These are all literary genres, to use that interesting word. You have to be clear what sort of material it is that you are handling in the Bible in order to, know what you should do with it. How do you determine the genre of a particular piece? By reading it, of course. You read it, and you reread it, and you keep on rereading it until you can see what kind of material it is. You do not impose anything on the text.

There are two units of Scripture which we have to examine, and we will take them separately. There is Genesis 1:1—2:3. Then there is Genesis 2:4-25, which picks up another story and, in fact, goes on to the end of Genesis 3. It is chiefly concerned with the origin of evil in this created world. Taking the first section, we start asking some questions. Question 1: What is the purpose of this piece of writing? What job is it meant to do for us as readers? Certainly, it is solemn writing, even churchly writing, celebrating the fact of creation and the glory of creation. The repetition of formula in the first chapter of Genesis surely makes that plain. It is, in fact, the first part, the first unit in the first eleven chapters of Genesis which form a unit in themselves, a kind of prologue to the rest of the Pentatuch which is telling the story of how God contemplating the fall of the world chose a man, Abram, and made out of that man a nation, and redeemed that nation from captivity in Egypt and entered into covenant with them. Deuteronomy is really the climax of the Pentatuch, if I read the Pentatuch right. For there through the model of ancient vessel treaties as modern Old Testament expositors have now seen, God announces through Moses in great detail the abiding terms of this covenant relationship with his own people. The story of the covenant runs, then, from Genesis chapter 12 through the end of the Book of Deuteronomy, and Genesis chapters 1-11 are prologue to it. Genesis chapter 1 is the prologue to the prologue, the beginning of it all.

Looking again at the chapter, one asks, what was the writer's didactic purpose? To start with, the writer certainly meant to give knowledge of the Creator. What he is saying is not meet the creation, as if you have never seen the sun and the moon and the stars and the animals and human beings before, but meet the Creator. That is the burden of Genesis chapter 1: See what He did and from what He did see what sort of being He is! Furthermore, from Genesis chapter 1 it is plain that the author means to give us knowledge of ourselves, of ourselves as made in God's image, made then with greater dignity than the rest of the creatures, made, however, in dependence on the God who brought it all into being. We are only His image. We are not gods ourselves. He wants us to know that God commanded mankind His noblest creature to manage this world for Him, to replenish the earth and subdue it and be His vice-regent within it. Finally, it is plain from the story that the writer wants us to understand about the sabbath. God having made the world rested and sanctified the seventh day, our sabbath of rest also. These are the three didactic concerns which are here plain on the fact of the chapter.

There seems also to be a polemical concern. Writing back in the very early days of the human race this writer, and I shall call him Moses until better instructed, proclaimed the one God who made it all and thus excluded polytheism. In the ancient world most religions were polytheistic, that is, they involved faith in many gods between all of whom worship and loyalty had to be divided. We owe everything to the God who has an absolute claim on our lives. There is one God, and He is to be worshiped with all that we have. Polytheism is excluded, and magic, incidentally, is also excluded. In those far off days the magician, the medicine man, was preeminent. He was supposed to be able to create and destroy by his spells. Genesis 1 teaches us that no one creates except the Lord God. All the superstitious cults are ruled out by Genesis chapter 1, and this seems to be deliberate.

Finally, Genesis 1 has a nurturing purpose. Genesis chapter 1, the celebration of creation, is meant to call forth awe and adoration, an appreciation for the Creator and for the dignity that He has given to man and for the special significance of the sabbath of rest, and by calling forth appreciation for these things to promote praise to the God who has made Himself known as our Creator and has given us our day of rest for worship and for our good. With that it is clear that Genesis 1 is intended to direct all its readers to the cultural task which God gave our race: Replenish the earth and subdue it. But undertake that task within a proper rhythm of work and rest, six days work and one day's rest. That is one of the many things that human nature was designed for, a day of rest following six days of work. Experience has proved that that makes for health and wisdom. Experience has proved that by disregarding the rhythm of six days work and one day's rest, human beings lay up for themselves trouble, trouble with their own physical systems which get over strained. God knew what He was doing when He made the sabbath for man.

Now we have to ask another question, and this is the tricky one. What are we to make of the seven days, the six days of work and the one day of rest, the divine day of rest, following them? This question, in modern discussion, often gets linked with the scientific question about origins. There are four opinions, basically, about the seven days. This first is the literalist hypothesis which maintains that what we are reading about is twenty-four hour days by our clocks, that what we are being told in Genesis 1 is that the whole world came to be formed within what we would recognize as a working week. The hypothesis assumes that what we have in Genesis is descriptive prose.

The second view is that each of the days of the creation is an allegorical figure. What each of the references to the evening and the morning represent is a geological epoch, a very, very long period of time, hundreds of thousands of years probably. There has been much effort in the last hundred years by those who have understood the days this way to try and show that the order of things in Genesis 1 corresponds to the best scientific account that can be given of how specific items emerged and took their place in the order of the world. A witty Roman Catholic writer half a century ago described this method of understanding as an attempt to raise Moses' credit by giving him a B.S. Those who take this view assume that the purpose of Genesis 1 or part of the purpose of Genesis 1 was to give us scientific information about the stages by which things came to be.

Third is what is called the revelation day theory, which takes the six evenings and mornings as signifying that creation was revealed in a story with six installments, each installment being given to the inspired writer on a separate day. After the first installment had been given, the writer said there was evening and there was morning. That is a way of saying that God gave him the next bit of the story the next day. Fourth there is the so-called framework view, sometimes called the literary view of the six days. This view says that the six days, evening and morning, are part of a total poetical picture of the fact of creation, that is, a total pictorial presentation of the reality of God bringing the world into being. The fact is presented in the form of the story of a week's work.

Without going into the details of argument about these different views, let me tell you straightaway that in my judgement this fourth view is the only viable one. Why? Because light appears on the first day and God only makes the sun and the moon and the stars on the fourth day. That fact alone it seems to me shows that what we have here is not anything that can be called science. What we have here, rather, is a pattern. On the first day light and darkness were separated. On the second day the expanse of the sky was set between waters below and waters above it. On the third day land and sea were created. Here, you might say, are three milieus, three areas of space. Then on days four, five and six, they are populated. The sun, the moon, and the stars are created to rule the day and the night, to manage as you might say the light and the darkness. "Rule," of course, is poetry when you think about it. It is not science. As for the sky, the fifth day tells us how God created birds to fly in the sky, and as for the dry land, the sixth day tells us how the animals and finally man were set. The vegetation, of course, is day three. This is a beautiful pattern, but on the fact of it, it is not science. No, it is a patterned way of presenting the fact of creation. It seems to me that this way of understanding the chapter is entirely in line with other Scripture references to the fact of creation. I have given you the reason I take the choice that I do and believe it to be the choice that the writer of Genesis wanted me to take. On the face of it this seems to be, if I read it right, a celebratory presentation of the fact of creation for purposes of doxology and basic instruction made in the form of a picture of a week's work. There are many pictorial presentations of God at work in Scripture. This is one of them.

Turning our attention to Genesis 2:4-25 and portions of chapter 3, I want to pose questions and suggest some brief answers. Question 1: Is the story properly called myth? Lots of modern commentaries do call it myth. Is that a proper way to describe it? The first thing we have to do is define *myth* because the word is a nose of wax and different people mean very different things when they use it. I use it to signify a non-historical, non-scientific, note I do not say unhistorical and unscientific, imaginative story expressing personal experience with nature and with one's environment and expressing also, perhaps, one's sense of identity, destiny, and maybe duty in that environment. Is this story a story of that kind? I answer no. Adam and Eve are connected by genealogy with the rest of the race according to the Genesis story. That is Moses' way of showing that he means them to be understood as figures in space-time history. We should not understand their story as being non-historical, unhistorical, non-scientific, or the like. This is historical fact. So it is presented, and so a Bible believer will regard it. Further, in the New Testament neither the Lord Jesus nor Paul had any doubt about the historicity of Adam, and they refer to Adam and Eve on a number of occasions. Those who would categorize the story as myth have regularly said we should understand that Adam is Everyman. There is a sense in which that is true. The story of Genesis chapters 2 and 3 may well be held up as a mirror before us all. But I want us to understand that according to the mind of Moses, Adam is only Everyman because first Adam was Adam, our first father, head of the race. That is my answer to the question about myth. Myth is the wrong category. This is history. Different scholars have different ways of describing it. Some, like Barth, call it saga and a German word which is untranslatable, which means primal history of a special sort. Some call it epic. What they are all trying to say is that it is history that goes further back than any independent inquiry by any historian can go. These are matters on which we must either take God's word about things or remain ignorant. But certainly it is history, though presented in a particular way.

This leads to the next question: What sort of history is this? It is a rather unique sort of history. Much like the narrative one might hear from the witness stand in a courtroom, this is a story told and interpreted as its told, interpreted, in fact, by the way it's being told. It's history told by the use of didactic symbols that enable us to understand very well its meaning even though we can't always visualize what we would have seen if we'd been there to watch it happening. How do I know this? First, if you take it as newspaper prose, plain, unvarnished, unimaginative, descriptive narrative, you run into problems. Consider the geography of Eden. Where was it? Look at what is said about Eden in verses 10-14. "A river flowed out of Eden to water the garden and it divided and became four rivers." A big river becomes four, and then the names of the rivers are given. Two of them we recognize, the Tigris and the Euphrates. But the other two are called Pishon and Gihon; and what are they and where are they? Some guess that the Gihon is the Nile and the Pishon is Indus. Some guess that the Gihon is the Blue Nile and the Pishon is the White Nile. Different suggestions are made, but the point is that you cannot find that geographical feature of one great river that becomes four, two of which are Tigris and Euphrates. You cannot find that anywhere in the world, which leads me to suppose that this way of putting the matter is the writer's way of alerting us, the readers, to the fact that he is not telling us history in a way which enables us to track it down or locate it on a map or identify the place where it happened or describe by our own wit all the details of what happened. It is not that kind of material.

The generic name Adam and the generic name Eve seems to say the same. *Adam*, after all, means *mankind*. What about the biology of Adam's formation? I understand the theology of it perfectly well, and so do you, but what are we to make of God taking the rib out of man's side, and what are we to make of the snake who in due course receives a snake's curse? "Thus shalt thou eat and on thy belly shalt thou go all the days of your life." And what, for that matter are we to make of verse 7: "The Lord God formed man of dust from the ground, breathed into his nostrils the breath of life, and man became a living being." I think that what we are meant to do with all of these features is to understand them as symbols chosen in order to express the meaning and significance of things which we are not able to imagine physically because they are not being described in unimaginative prose. Other biblical writers seem to take many of the details of the story of Genesis 2 and 3 in the same way. The tree of life appears in Proverbs 3:18; wisdom is the tree of life there. The tree of life appears in Paradise in Revelation 2:7 and again 22:2, and the serpent is identified as Satan in Revelation 12:9; compare 2 Corinthians 11:3,14. The serpent who is unambiguously a serpent in Genesis 3 is interpreted as Satan by these New Testament passages.

What am I affirming about Genesis 2? The events were space-time events, though their location, date, and visual aspect are veiled from us by style. That's how the writer meant it to be. I am being, I believe, faithful to him in understanding what he wrote this way. The symbols given me in order to help me understand the significance of bits of the story include at least these: Eden, the Hebrew word for *delight*, picture the total happiness and fulfillment that the first man and woman enjoyed before they fell. The tree of life is a symbol of the enjoyment of God and all things in God that would have been mankind's still had man not fallen. The rib pictures the truth that the woman is a side—it does actually literally mean side in a number of metaphorical senses as well as the literal ones—of the man's personal being so that he recognizes in the woman the complement of himself. That is the deepest truth about the differentiation of the sexes still. The nakedness of Adam and Eve is a symbolic detail pointing to the fact that they had no cause for shame before the face of God. The snake is the perfect symbol for Satan, a symbol which makes the story immediately intelligible in all cultures. The human race dislikes snakes, and even where snake gods have been worshipped as in some polytheistic systems, they have been worshiped out of fear and dislike. God's walk in the garden of Eden pictures His felt presence coming close. God's curses on Adam and Eve symbolize all those experiences of painful frustration, including those that are specified in the text and others also, in a world that is now felt as hostile, frustrating, and painful. The clothes of skins which God made for Adam and Eve signify God's mercy, and perhaps there is a hint of atoning sacrifice because animals have to die before coats of skins can be made. That is an old interpretation, and I think there is something in it. In a similar fashion, I think that God's strangely expressed curse on the snake surely means more than that humans will have enmity with snakes. Surely there is a pointer to that final victory that the woman's seed will one day win, even though at great cost and pain to himself. This is my, briefly expressed, interpretation of Genesis 2, my own effort to understand what the writer was trying to communicate.

Finally, the hermeneutical question has to be asked. The hermeneutical question is this: What is there? Is there anything in our minds and culture which makes it hard for us to appreciate the narrative told in this way? I think there are three things in our culture that make it very hard for us to get in tune with this sort of exegesis. One barrier is our literary culture. Modern newspapers and works of fiction, written as they are, do not attune us to this kind of highly symbolic, imaginative writing, poetry in prose it is almost, and we find it hard to appreciate it when we are confronted with it. We want the prose of the Bible to be unimaginative narrative because that is what we are used to in our books and our newspapers. Second, our scientific mindset which is so much a part of our culture predisposes us to assume that any account of the natural order must be written in order to answer the scientists' questions about it, and that is wrong. But we think it, we assume it, and then we try to make it happen. And I think that sets us at cross purposes with the text itself and gets us into all kinds of trouble. Third, we are rightly committed in apologetics to countering evolutionism as a philosophy of life. Because evolutionism originates with a particular view about the origin of the species, we try to bring Genesis 1 and 2 into line to become ammunition for countering evolutionism. But what I have suggested to you is that this was no part of the purpose of Moses, and the two chapters do not really bear on the intricacies of the evolution debate one way or the other. If we could adjust our minds at these three points, then I believe we would hear the world of God in Genesis 1 and 2 ore clearly than we do.

The final question is the applicatory question: What, then, should we do, having learned these things from our two chapters? The one sentence answer is know God, know ourselves as God made us to be and as we have become, know what sin is, know what God's judgment is (I have moved into Genesis chapter 3, but then it is part of the story), understand these things, praise the Creator, praise Him for making the world, praise Him for our redemption, humble ourselves before Him as the God who has mercy on sinners, and learn to hate sin as a principle of life.

RESPONSE: Kenneth A. Mathews

Dr. Packer's paper is an excellent starting point for hermeneutical discussion. In his opening remarks, he described a proper biblical hermeneutic as consisting of three elements: (1) exegetical (2) hermeneutical and (3) practical. I agree that these three are necessary for developing an appropriate interpretive scheme. In particular, I applaud his emphasis on an objective hermeneutic, in which the text is believed to have deteminative meaning—a position advocated by E. D. Hirsch, Jr., and in a mitigating way by Paul Riceour. Professor Packer defined the exegetical step as one addressing historical, critical questions or, in other words, what the text originally meant. I concur, but would want to broaden the exegetical step to include the interpreter in the process. Readers also participate in determining the meaning of texts. I am not suggesting that the locus of meaning is in the interpreter and that as a result all readings are equally valid. Rather, I am voicing what has become increasingly apparent in current discussions of hermeneutical theory. There is no truly objective interpretation of a text. Interpreters, like their biblical texts, are conditioned by presuppositions and their historical-cultural context. Dr. Packer's paper is testimony to this since he acknowledged that he comes to the subject of creation with three theological assumptions: (1) a theological concept of creation (2) a theological concept of natural science, and (3) certain theological rules for the exegesis of texts. When, for example, he characterizes the context of Genesis as "churchly," this description reflects our Christian era of thinking. I do not find fault here; on the contrary, it is inevitable. We all bring to our exegesis a sense of Christian canon, a particular tradition of the church in which we work, and our spiritual life which is fed by the community of believers in which we live. Although I admit that my reading as an interpreter will be colored by my setting, I remain committed to an author-oriented hermeneutic as my highest priority. This does not mean that we can psychoanalyze the writer; we can know intention only by the evidence the author has deposited with us—that is, the text itself. Thus, text linguistics, narrative discourse strategies, genre criticism, and the like coupled with historical-critical concerns are essential to our enterprise.

For me, the proper hermeneutic approach to the creation account of Genesis requires us to read the text twice: (1) first, we must attempt to read it as the first audience understood it, and (2) second, we read it in its canonical shape as the Christian church has done so for two thousand years. These two foci have been integrated in Dr. Packer's exegesis. For instance, Professor Packer began his exegesis by setting the creation in an expanding canonical context; he extended the context of the creation account to the primordial history of Genesis 1—11 and then to its role within the whole pentateuchal story of God's convenantal commitment to Israel. When creation is read in this widening context, its meaning takes on a different shade than when it is read in isolation. This is a necessary and profitable effort, as long as we first concentrate on the immediate context. When I do approach the text from the perspective of canon, I read it along the historical plane; I attempt to discover how the creation account grew in its meaning through the canonical materials—from Pentateuch to Psalms to Prophets to the Gospels.

In the remainder of my response I would like to discuss how we should attempt to read the text as the first audience understood it, and in the process I will touch upon several matters Dr. Packer has called to our attention. To discover the ancient context, the interpreter must be acquainted with the competing world views of the time, that is, how ancient men and women understood the origins of life and how they viewed themselves as individuals in relation to the physical world and to society. I am not suggesting that contemporary interpreters should, or even can, completely avoid reading Genesis without the influence of today's concerns. I am pleading, however, that the interpreter must consciously refrain from imposing on the biblical account an extraneous authority, namely, the findings of science.

When I choose not to read the text in light of the present debate about origins, I do not mean that the account is *against* science in the sense that it is inaccurate or misleading. Rather, I am suggesting that we cannot stretch the sacred text to answer questions or give data for parameters of inquiry that Genesis never intended to answer. We must be careful not to secularize the text by reducing it to the status of a pawn in the hands of literalists, concordists, or evolutionists who have an agenda different from the ancient context. We do not honor the Holy Scriptures by giving them over to geologists to manipulate them as they please.

By reading Genesis through the eyeglasses of the "Genesis debate," we fail at three points: (1) We are anachronistic in our reading; (2) we err by expecting too much from the text; and (3) and most importantly, we risk missing the significance of the account altogether. The challenge for us as interpreters is to read the text and not to rewrite it.

I am reminded by John Barton in his volume *Reading the Old Testament* that the starting point for reading any text is to know the literary rules under which the composition was authored. Literature of all kinds have conventions or rules which enable the reader to derive meaning from a literary product. Let me illustrate this by an experience common to us all. In a few weeks I expect to receive correspondence fro the Internal Revenue Service. If I take from my mailbox a brown envelope and I see inside through its window a green card that bears my name, "Kenneth A. Mathews," I will sigh with relief knowing that I have been contacted by the U.S. Treasury Department and that I am receiving money back! On the other hand, I might receive a white, business #10 envelope with the return address of the IRS. It too has "Kenneth A. Mathews" visible but it is typed on the outside of the envelope. While both pieces of mail have to do with my financial health, just the packaging with my name alone will dictate how I am to read the correspondence contained. When I read the letter from the white envelope, I will find these opening two words "Dear Sir." Because I know the nature of such correspondence and the conventions of that kind, these two simple words tell me a great deal. I know, for instance, that the government is not asking me to attend a prayer breakfast! It doesn't say "Dear Ken" or even "Dear Bro. Mathews." When the IRS says "Dear," I know to understand it as anything other than a word of endearment, and when I read "Sir" I know that the IRS has not dubbed me a person of nobility. I can anticipate that the rest of the letter is requiring me to attend an audit. We all interpret our reading within certain forms of literary presentation; these are clues dictating how we should interpret the message communicated by the author.

I am describing, of course, the function of literary genre in interpretation. To be better readers of the text, we must know the literary genre which packages the message to be decoded. When we turn to Genesis, the first question we must raise concerns its literary rules. Do we read it as historical narrative in the same sense that we read the great histories of Kings and Chronicles? Is it descriptive poetry as we find it in Job and Psalms? Is it apocalyptic or symbolic like that of Daniel's beasts of chapter seven? The answer to these questions, I think, is no. The genre of Genesis is too complex to fall neatly into any one of these categories. Genesis is hymnic, but not a hymn. It has the marks of history-telling, but it is not simple historical narrative. It has features similar to some of the hymns we read in Psalms and its purpose is certainly doxological like the Psalms, but it is not a direct praise of God. Yet, at the same time it moves from problem to resolution with a chronological framework like that of historical prose. As a result, we must conclude that it partakes of both hymn and prose. It is written in colloquial language and, therefore, possesses figurative expression, but it clearly functions as a historical introduction to God's convenantal promises to Abraham. This is what the six-day arrangement achieves; it tells the reader that creation is tied to history and is not myth.

We need to be perfectly clear about what is meant by myth versus history. Myth, which is opposed to history, is a literary vehicle that is inextricably bound up with the way in which pagan men and women understood reality. These stories were not just fanciful tales and legends about the lives of gods and people in another world or in the primordial past. On the contrary, myths are intimately related to the physical world we know and say as much about the present as they do the past. This is because the events of the past were believed by the ancients to continue to be lived out in the present. The events of myth have no cessation. They are caught in the web of a cyclical pattern of nature and are relived through cultic ritual which is performed by temple and royal functionaries.

In order to have myth it was necessary to assume that the divine is immanent in nature. For the modern mind, the physical world is inanimate, but ancient peoples viewed the natural realm as living personality. Biblical religion, on the other hand, tells us that all physical phenomena are impersonal, but it also insists that God, who is above and independent of nature, sovereignly superintends the universe. Certainly, Genesis is non-mythical in its perception of reality; this is apparent to anyone who has read ancient Near Eastern mythological texts. The Genesis account of creation has no biography about God; it does not tell us of His origins because He is the preexistent, self-sufficient Lord. Genesis silences myth; biblical religion makes history and science possible. No longer is there a divine heaven and earth or a hostile world which serves as a playground for capricious deities, but rather a divine personal being.[1]

Now, in order to discover the competing world views commonly held by those who first read Genesis, we are informed by the cosmogonies of Israel's neighbors. Mary K. Wakeman in her book *God's Battle with the Monster: A Study in Biblical Imagery,* based on her Ph.D. dissertation at Brandeis University, gave an analysis of twelve myths coming from the great centers of ancient civilization. She concluded that the cosmogonies agreed on three essential points: (1) that there existed before the created cosmos, anti-creation forces or monsters who opposed a created order, (2) that a champion gladiator from among the gods emerged to defeat the repressive monsters and thereby enable life, and (3) that this champion deity was hailed by the pantheon of gods as King over the universe who ruled the newly-created order.[2] By way of illustration, let me briefly tell the best known of these myths, the Akkadian *Enuma Elish*. The myth begins by describing conditions before the existence of heaven and earth. There were two primordial watery masses named Apsu, the male waters, and Tiamat, the female counterpart. From the union of these inert, watery entities came a host of gods whose noisy activity annoyed and threatened their father Apsu. Apsu planned to destroy the troublesome gods, but he was lured to sleep by one of the deities who then killed him. Tiamat and her armies swore to avenge her husband's death by killing all her offspring. A young champion deity named Marduk came forward and agreed to fight Tiamat if the gods would recognize him as their king. After Marduk delivered the fatal blow to defeat Tiamat, he split her carcus into two parts; one portion became the sky and the other the earth. Eventually Marduk brought order and cosmos into being, and he reigned as sovereign over the gods and the universe.

This view of a cosmic battle initiating the world's origins was widely accepted, as we can see indicated by the number of different peoples who held to a version of it. What was common in their thinking of origins was that there were forces or circumstances which were hostile to life's enabling systems. For these ancient peoples this threatening situation corresponded to their present reality as they struggled against their physical environment.

The mythic imagery of these cosmic battles between anti-creation monsters and heroic gods provided the biblical writers a storehouse of poetic figures from which in the language of their day they could describe the one true God of Israel as Creator and Covenant Champion. Allusions are made to these monsters, such as Leviathan, Rahab, and the Tannin, translated "dragon" (KJV) There are many examples from Psalms, Job, and the Prophets which we can cite (e.g., Job 3; 26; Pss. 74; 104; Isa. 27), but for our purposes we will mention only one. Isaiah 51:9 says, "Awake, awake, put on strength, O arm of the Lord; awake, as in the ancient days, in the generations of old. Art thou not it that hath cut Rahab, and wounded the dragon [lit. Tannin]?" Who are these figures, Rahab and the dragon? From extra-biblical sources, we know that these were the anti-creation monsters of Canaanite myth which were defeated by Baal and his consort Anat. Of course, it is inconceivable that the biblical writers who were such ardent opponents of idolatry and fertility religions would have accepted the philosophy that nurtured polytheism. They did not adopt pagan theology nor did they simply demythologize the mythic notions of their neighbors; they chose to adapt the mythopoetic language of their neighbors to convey their own theological ends.

The creation account also alludes to ancient Near Eastern myths. These allusions served as a polemic against pagan cosmogonies; they corrected the folly of pagan thinking about the origins of the universe. The Genesis creation has significant points of contact with the popular beliefs of the ancient world; however, it becomes clear by the way in which they are presented, that they function as foils against which the truth about origins can be more clearly apprehended and the power of the event of creation can be more strongly felt. One scholar has stated the significance of this polemic when he said, "It asserts that God is outside the realm of nature, which is wholly subservient to Him. He has no myth; that is, there are no stories about any events in His life. Magic plays no part in the worship of Him."[3]

Not only does the biblical account use mythic language, the primeval history of Genesis 1—11 has a literary arrangement like the ancient cosmogonies. Very similar to the Genesis account of origins is an Akkadian text called the *Epic of Atrahasis,* dating at about 1600 BC, which tells of the origin of the gods, the universe, mankind, the rise of human civilization, and the coming of a flood which will destroy the human race. There may have been a common literary presentation for telling about origins. It is in the light of these ancient myths and Israel's tendency toward polemic that we can best appreciate how the first readers of Genesis understood it.

While the allusions are many in the creation account, permit me to note one to demonstrate how Genesis magnifies the Creator and at the same time corrects wrong-headed, foolish notions about the beginnings of the world.[4]

As we have seen already, the Sumero-Akkadian culture believed that there were primeval waters that gave rise to the gods and the universe. Genesis 1:2 also speaks of a watery deep and seas, but these are not monsters that threaten the God of Israel. They are no more than tranquil waters in God's presence; His spirit governs them from the outset and they remain timid under His control. In Genesis no god has its beginnings in the deep neither are the origins of life found there. There is no procreation, no cosmic egg which hatched to give heaven and earth, as the Egyptians thought, and no fertility of deities as the peoples of the Near East had come to think of their gods.

I will conclude with these final remarks. Since Genesis 1 and 2 are not described in language we would expect today, this question arises: Can we affirm anything about life's origins? I agree with Dr. Packer that the text, though couched in a non-technical description, reflects historical reality. The literary strategy of Genesis requires this: (1) The literary framework of six days requires the reader to see creation as historical as opposed to myth, and (2) the genealogies of Genesis require us to understand the man and woman as real individuals who also are tied to historical processes. Therefore, we can say, given its own method of description, that the creation account is true and accurate.

We can proceed then to affirm what the creation account affirms. The biblical account answers these questions: Who? What? and Why? The creation account answers the question Who? by telling us about the Creator first and foremost. Second, the creation account answers the question What? by telling us about the creation itself—about the character of the created order and His chief creation, human life. The creation account is teleological and answers the question Why? by telling us that God has created because "it is very good"; the beauty of the creation pleases God.

But the creation account does not answer the two questions we choose to have it answer, namely, How? (except, of course, that God commanded it) and when? Like the disciples who quizzed Jesus about the coming of the kingdom they wanted to know when it would come. But Jesus did not answer because the "when" of the coming of the kingdom was God's private concern and the disciples ought to be busy doing the work of the kingdom and not waiting for it. Even so, the first question for us is not the *when* of creation but the *who* of creation. As a result, what are we to do about it? We must busy ourselves in praise and obedience.

Notes

1. For a discussion of ancient thought and myth, see the collected essays of *The Intellectual Adventure of Ancient Man* (Chicago: University of Chicago, 1946); also, N. M. Sarna, *Understanding Genesis* (New York: Schocken, 1966).

2. For a summary discussion of Wakeman's findings and their bearing on our subject, see B. K. Waltke, *Creation and Chaos* (Portland: Western Conservative Baptist Seminary, 1974).

3. Sarna, p. 3.

4. There are many discussions treating Genesis as a polemic; consult in particular, A. Heidel, *The Babylonian Genesis* (Chicago: University of Chicago Press, 1954), and G. F. Hasel, "The Polemical Nature of the Genesis Cosmology," *EvQ* 46 (1974); pp. 81-102.

RESPONSE: John D. W. Watts

Welcome back to Ridgecrest, Dr. Packer. Your presentation of six rules for the interpretation of Scripture in a lecture last year made you a natural candidate to be invited for the conference this year.[1]

This response was written with only the outline of your lecture before me and may differ from what I would say to your full presentation.

As I understand your notes, the theses concerning Genesis 1 and 2 which you put forward are these:

that Genesis 1:1 to 2:3
1. should be read within the context of the Pentateuch.
2. has these purposes:
   a. didactic—knowledge of the creator, of our own creatureliness, and of the Sabbath.
   b. polemic—to exclude polytheism and establish God as sole owner of all; to exclude magic and teach the fixity of things.
   c. nurturing—to call forth awe, appreciation, etc.
3. that the seven days form a literary framework for the story and are to be interpreted in this way.

that Genesis 2:4-25 (3:24) is not a myth but is offered as historical narrative using didactic symbols.

But then you suggest three obstacles that make it hard for "modern Christians" to accept your theses. Do you mean by "modern Christians" conservative evangelicals like ourselves? I presume you do, and I recognize the application.

Do you also mean that these same obstacles inhibit your own thinking and work to a certain degree? You seem to be working your way out of them and to be pointing the way toward the freedom we need to be authentic interpreters of the Word. Evangelical exegesis and response to creation texts and to creation as a theological theme has been characterized by a defensive attitude for more than a century now. It is high time that the cycle of bondage be broken so that evangelical interpreters, exegetes and theologians alike, may rid ourselves of these obstacles and get on with our task. You have accurately described the obstacles and you have partially escaped their grasp, it seems to me. Others are also moving forward toward the freedom.

Your first obstacle: "Our literary culture does not attune us to writing of this kind." Again I assume that "our" refers to evangelical conservatives like ourselves. You evince a struggle here in your discussion of myth and historical narrative using didactic symbols. Yet some directions in current literary theory and practice may be moving toward setting us free at this point. The interest which a number of evangelical scholars have shown in this field can be very promising for the future. The renewed study of genre relating to ancient literature, including the Bible, has opened doors to greater understanding. Gordon Wenham's exciting new commentary on *Genesis 1—15* deals positively with the issue.[2] He shows the genre of primeval narrative to be parallel to others known in the Ancient Near East. The Genesis account agrees with a number of ideas in them, but differs profoundly in other ways. He shows how Genesis is "a fundamental challenge to the ideologies of civilized men and women" ancient and modern. Wenham urges us to read Genesis on its own terms rather than to use it to serve narrow polemic interests. In this I gather his concern parallels your own.

Others have made progress in understanding some of the issues to which Genesis speaks (and to which the creator/creation texts of the Bible speak). Bernard Anderson's *Creation versus Chaos*[3] with his followup article "Mythopoetic and Theological Dimensions of Biblical Creation Faith"[4] shows how our summary elimination of "myth" as a dimension of biblical literature makes it impossible for us to deal in depth with basic issues relating to these texts. Jon D. Levenson's *Creation and the Persistence of Evil* demonstrates the theological power and scope of thought, building on this base, as well as the contemporary relevance of the issues involved.[5]

Your second obstacle is: "Our scientific mindset predisposes us to assume that any account of the nature order must be written to answer our scientific questions about it." For whom are you speaking? If you are speaking for most contemporary conservative inerrantists, I can only agree. Your lengthy treatment of "a theological concept of natural science" suggests that this is still an issue for you. But it often seems that "our scientific questions" are basically still those of a half-century ago. Current scientists, especially physicists, no longer think and work in the way that is usually opposed. Sir Arthur Peacock in the Mendenhall Lectures at Depauw University, 1983[6] and in his Norton Lectures at The Southern Baptist Theological Seminary in 1986 discussed "the roles of model and metaphor in science and theology" and showed how changing views of reality in the scientific community open new opportunities for dialogue between science and reality. Quantum physics has totally changed the rules of the game in relating to science. But we have hardly noticed. However, *some* interpreters and theologians *have* noticed and are utilizing the opportunity to let theology and biblical interpretations do their work without the preoccupation with "scientific assumptions" which have been such obstacles to many of us.

Sir Arthur Peacock writes of the current relation of religion (and the Bible) and science:

> "There is a hierarchy of order in the natural world, . . . if God is the reality that Christians believe he is. . . . Since the theological enterprise refers to a higher level in the hierarchy of complexity, the interaction of nature, man, and God, . . . will have to listen to and adapt to, but not be subservient to, . . . new discoveries concerning the realities of the natural world" which science develops at less complex levels.

Similarly the sciences, which are *human* creative activities and have repercussions that are sometimes destructive of nature and society, will have to be more willing than in the past to see their models of reality as partial and applicable at restricted levels only in the multiform intricacies of the real and always to be related to the wider intimations of reality that are vouchsafed to mankind. It was to these intimations that two significant writers have turned in passages full of meaning for our times; one has followed that hard way of Christian faith through suffering and desolation, the other the path of science through the thicket of the natural. Both ways are needed.

First, then, the Christian, Aleksandr Solzhenitsyn's conclusion to that 1983 Templeton Prize address.

> "Material laws alone do not explain our life or give it direction. The laws of physics and physiology will never reveal the indisputable manner in which the Creator constantly, day in and day out, participates in the life of each of us, unfailingly granting us the energy of existence; when this assistance leaves us, we die. In the life of our entire planet, the Divine Spirit moves with no less force: this we must grasp in our dark and terrible hour."

And, finally, a voice "from below," from one following the path of the really natural to the naturally Real that gave it being—the words of Loren Eiseley, the American biologist:

> "It is not sufficient any longer to listen at the end of a wire to the rustlings of galaxies; it is not enough even to examine the great coil of DNA in which is coded the very alphabet of life. These are our extended perceptions. But beyond lies the great darkness of the ultimate Dreamer, who dreamed the light and the galaxies. Before act was, or substance existed, imagination grew in the dark. Man partakes of that ultimate wonder and creativeness. As we turn from the galaxies to the swarming cells of our own being, which toil for something, some entity beyond their grasp, let us remember man, the self-fabricator who came across an ice age to look into the mirrors and the magic of sci-

ence. Surely he did not come to see himself or his wild visage only. He came because he is at heart a listener and a searcher for some transcendent realm beyond himself. This he has worshiped by many names, even in the dismal caves of his beginning. Man, the self-fabricator, is so by reason of gifts he had no part in devising." (L. Eiseley, *The Star Thrower,* London: Wildwood House, 1978, 120-21.)[7]

Your third obstacle: "Our apologetic preoccupation with countering evolutionism prompts us to press the narrative into the service of young-earth, recent creationist speculations, on which they do not really bear." Your critique on this issue is welcome and timely. Your treatment seems totally free of it. This "preoccupation" which has lasted in various forms for three quarters of a century has many faults, not the least of which is that it prevents us from fully dealing with the theological implications of these wonderful chapters and this powerful theme of creation in ways that touch on current issues and needs. But while we are holding back, others, thank God, are pressing forward. Langdon Gilkey's insightful book, *Maker of Heaven and Earth* probes the doctrine which arises from these chapters.[8] Jurgen Moltmann's 1984-85 Gifford lectures present a modern treatment of topics related to creation with a welcome emphasis (I think biblical) on God as creator.[9] Zachary Hayes spoke of "a new reading of the sources" and new shapes for the doctrine of creation.[10] And, of course, there are others.

Your recognition of symbols as a key to interpretation in Genesis 2 opens the door to "in depth" interpretation. But you stop short of symbolic perception in the entire account. Moltmann seizes that opportunity in full. He writes: Theology

> will also take up and use symbols, which mould the unconscious and guide awareness in a way which is unknown to the conscious mind. Finally, there is an expectant and creative imagination in the spheres of the potential and the future which we have to call poetic. If we were to exclude this from a doctrine of creation, we could not talk about "the future of creation" at all. Theology always includes the imagination, fantasy for God and his kingdom. If we were to ban the images of the imagination from theology, we should be robbing it of its best possession, Eschatologically orientated theology is dependent on a messianic imagination of the future, and sets this imagination free.[11]

When this is done, the application of the passage's meaning may move beyond the generalities of "knowledge of God, of ourselves and of our world" to deal with the urgent issues of our day, such as ecology, dominion, the threat of disintegration under nuclear attack, or social disorder or natural catastrophe, and the goodness of creation and the "persistence of evil."

Your paper points the way and opens a door. It is up to the rest of us to press on toward the full meaning of this great doctrine and these wonderful chapters.

Notes

1. J. I. Packer, "Problem Areas Related to Biblical Inerrancy," *The Proceedings of The Conference on Biblical Inerrancy* (Nashville: Broadman Press, 1987), pp. 208-210.

2. Gordon Wenham, *Genesis 1—15*, Word Biblical Commentary (Waco: Word Books, 1987).

3. Bernard Anderson, *Creation versus Chaos* (New York: Association, 1967).

4. Bernard Anderson, "Mythopoetic and Theological Dimensions of Biblical Creation Faith," *Creation in the Old Testament,* ed. B. Anderson (Philadelphia: Fortress, 1984), pp. 1-24.

5. Jon D. Levenson, *Creation and the Persistence of Evil* (San Francisco: Harper & Row, 1988).

6. Arthur Peacock, *Intimations of Reality. Critical Realism in Science and Religion* (Notre Dame, Ind.: University of Notre Dame Press, 1984).

7. Ibid., pp. 51-53.

8. Langdon Gilkey, *Maker of Heaven and Earth* (Garden City, N.Y.: Anchor Books, Doubleday, 1959).

9. Jurgen Moltmann, *God in Creation* (San Francisco: Harper & Row, 1985).

10. Zachary Hayes, *What Are They Saying About Creation* (New York: Paulist, 1980).

11. Moltmann, p. 4.

3
HOPE
Jeremiah 32:1-12

Daniel Vestal

I left the Southern Baptist Convention last year with a grief and pain that almost rendered me in a state of mild depression. Our family had already planned our annual vacation, and I was never so glad to see a period of rest and renewal come as I was to see that time. As we embarked on that vacation, I sought a word from the Lord, a direction not for the Southern Baptist Convention, but for my own life. And I stand here today to say humbly, but sincerely, I heard that word. I rediscovered the prophet Jeremiah and found in him a model of integrity and faithfulness. This message was born out of that rediscovery.

> This is the word that came to Jeremiah from the Lord in the tenth year of Zedekiah king of Judah, which was the eighteenth year of Nebuchadnezzar. The army of the king of Babylon was then besieging Jerusalem, and Jeremiah the prophet was confined in the courtyard of the guard in the royal palace of Judah. Now Zedekiah king of Judah had imprisoned him there, saying, "Why do you prophesy as you do? You say, 'This is what the Lord says: I am about to hand this city over to the king of Babylon, and he will capture it. Zedekiah king of Judah will not escape out of the hands of the Babylonians but will certainly be handed over to the king of Babylon, and will speak with him face to face and see him with his own eyes. He will take Zedekiah to Babylon, where he will remain until I deal with him, declares the Lord. If you fight against the Babylonians, you will not succeed.'" Jeremiah said, "The word of the Lord came to me: Hanamel son of Shallum your uncle is going to come to you and say, 'Buy my field at Anathoth, because as nearest relative it is your right and duty to buy it.' Then just as the Lord had said, my cousin Hanamel came to me in the courtyard of the guard and said, 'Buy my field at Anathoth in the territory of Benjamin. Since it is your right to redeem it and possess it, buy it for yourself.' I knew that this was the word of the Lord, so I bought the field at Anathoth from my cousin Hanamel and weighed out for him seventeen shekels of sliver. I signed and sealed the deed, had it witnessed, and weighed out the silver on the scales. I took the deed of purchase—the sealed copy containing the terms and conditions, as well as the unsealed copy. And I gave this deed to Baruch son of Neriah, the son of Mahseiah, in the presence of my cousin Hanamel and of

the witnesses who had signed the deed and of all the Jews sitting in the courtyard of the guard."

Jeremiah was called to be a prophet while still a young man. He lived and prophesied under the last five kings of Judah (Josiah, Jehoahaz, Jehoakim, Jehoakin, Zedekiah, and even Gedaliah). He witnessed the collapse of Judah, the destruction of Jerusalem, and the Exile. He preached a message no one wanted to hear. He counselled kings, and they refused his counsel. He was forbidden to marry and participate in normal social functions, such as weddings and funerals. He heard God's call but struggled with God's ways. He spoke judgment on the nation, but he was a patriot.

As much as any Old Testament figure, he embodied and epitomized a man of personal and spiritual religion. He described sin as a matter of the heart, an inward infection, a spiritual disease. He predicted judgment as an inevitable spiritual consequence of sin. Everything about Jeremiah was a call to spiritual and personal religion and a rebuke to a religion which was hollow and empty.

Jeremiah's message was also a message of social religion, and that is the primary focus of today's text.

Social tragedy and catastrophe have a greater impact on us than personal tragedy. I may have cancer or a heart attack and suffer greatly. But, when a crisis occurs that uproots and disrupts whole families and neighborhoods and even cities and countries, then personal suffering is multiplied, creating a social upheaval that can border on anarchy.

There are those moments in history when such upheaval is catastrophic. I have become involved with the Vietnamese Baptists in this country. It is difficult for them to talk of leaving their homeland, seeing it overthrown and overtaken by the Communists—to the point that some of them cannot talk about it. It is difficult to listen as they talk of their families being separated and some of them living in abject poverty in Vietnam now under the Communists.

Most of us have not suffered through such social upheaval as that. But all of us have suffered and struggled through other disasters that were devastating in varying degrees and threatened the social fabric of our lives. A world war, a depression, a bank collapse are all social disasters that affect lives and change the way we live. And who knows what will happen in the future? The threat of nuclear war hangs over our heads like the sword of Damocles. Economic peril is always with us. The AIDS epidemic poses a great threat to our way of life. And who can foretell the future of institutions that make up elements of our society—home, schools, governments, and religious denominations? I don't need to tell you that a great part of the social context in which you and I minister—the SBC—is in a serious crisis. Some say it is the gravest crisis we have ever faced. What is to be our perspective and attitude?

First, in times of social crises, we must not give up. We must not quit. Jeremiah faced a social disaster of overwhelming proportions. The very fabric of Judah's existence was being altered—governmental rule, societal institutions, economic patterns, even family relations were being changed. The collapse of the monarchy, the capture and deportation of the leading citizens, the desecration and destruction of the Temple altered the very fabric of society. And yet Jeremiah refused up to give up hope.

The text that we've read is a symbolic and prophetic act. Jeremiah purchased the title to a piece of family property. It was a tangible demonstration of his faith and hope for the future restoration of his people. In what Jeremiah did God was speaking to him, to Judah, and to us. And the essential message from God is that in times of social upheaval we are to have hope. Our hope is in anticipation—an anticipation of a salvation and deliverance only the God of history can bring to pass.

Our hope is that God is the Lord of history. Just as He has judged sin in the past, He will judge sin in the future. Just as He has vindicated His people and purposes in the past, He will do so in the future. Just as He has been true to His Word in the past, He will do so in the future.

I find great help from Jeremiah because he did not run from the present or did not try to escape the consequences of the past. I don't know how many times I have wished I could have been a Southern Baptist at some time other than the present. I don't know how many times I have wanted to retreat to the way people say it used to be. But I cannot do that. I must not do that. I must not try to retreat at all, either into a real or an idealized past. I must not quit the present.

And the way I do that is by having hope for the future. Not a superficial, shallow hope, but a sure hope based on the character of God, the promises of His Word. This was Jeremiah's hope. He purchased that property at Anathoth because his confidence was in God's naked Word. He would not quit or try to retreat.

In whatever social disasters we face—we don't give up. We don't quit. We keep our eyes on the future that is in God's hand.

> This is my Father's world, O let me ne'er forget
> That though the wrong seems oft so strong,
>   God is the Ruler yet.
> This is my Father's world, The battle is not done;
> Jesus who died shall be satisfied,
>   And earth and heaven be one.

Second, in times of social disaster we must be busy about hope-filled tasks. Jeremiah was living during the reign of the last king of Judah—Zedekiah. It was the eighteenth year of Nebuchadnezzar (587). While Babylon was at the gates of Jerusalem, Jeremiah purchased a piece of property and got a title deed to it. He knew that he himself would never live on that property, but he made sure that those in the future would.

What would you do if by some divine revelation you knew that the SBC was, indeed, inevitably divided—and would in a generation dissolve? What would you do? What did Jeremiah do? He engaged in a hope-filled task. He acted with the future in mind and those who would live after him. He believed in a return and a remnant, but most of all he believed in God.

Martin Luther was once asked, "If you knew the end of the world would come tomorrow, what would you do?" He replied, "I'd go out and plant a tree." John Wesley was asked if he knew Christ would come tomorrow, what would he do, and he replied, "I'd preach this afternoon as planned, travel to my next point, pray, read Scripture, retire and wake up in glory."

In 1939 a young theologian-pastor, Detrich Bonhoffer, was in the U.S. for a lecture tour. He returned to Germany (under Nazi rule) and determined to resist the forces of evil. He knew what it would cost him. He was arrested at the age of thirty-seven and put in prison, only to be executed two years later. He watched not only his native country destroyed but also his own life swallowed up in a prison. What did he do in that prison? He did what Jeremiah did in buying a field. He wrote his famous *Letters and Papers From Prison* (a collection of writings that have had profound impact). He ministered to his fellow prisoners and guards. He prayed, studied, read and preached.

He filled his life with hope-filled tasks. Now I cannot tell you what hope-filled task will be appropriate for you. That must be communicated to you by God Himself. Jeremiah said, "The word of the Lord came to me saying, 'Hanamel, son of Shallum, your uncle is going to come to you saying, "Buy the field at Anathoth, and you're to do it"'" (v. 6).

In the intimacy of your communion with God and in your own conscience, you must know what your hope-filled task is to be. It may be to preach or to write or to teach or to invest in a discipleship relationship with one person. But you must discover it and do it.

The message of Jeremiah is that in times of social disaster we must keep our eyes on the future, a future secured by a sovereign God. We busy ourselves with tasks that show our confidence in that God.

4
HOW WE INTERPRET THE BIBLE: BIBLICAL INTERPRETATION AND LITERARY CRITICISM

Robert Jackson

How do we interpret the Bible? I want this morning to use literary criticism as a model for helping us understand how indeed we go about our task. Let us pray before we begin.

Lord God, we desire to be your faithful stewards. We desire to live under your word, to be informed by it, challenged, shaped, directed. Help us, Lord, that we might be better interpreters, understanding your word as you've given it to us. We pray in Jesus' name. Amen.

Twenty-five years ago, the relevant pronouncement for an evengelical theologian (or minister) to make concerned the necessity of combining evangelism with social concern, proclamation with demonstration, the message of regeneration with a cup of cold water. The debate over the last twenty-five years, therefore, has centered not over whether such questions of social justice should be on the church's agenda, they are, but rather on *how* evangelical involvement is to be expressed.

Now, in an analogous way, the most frequently repeated agenda among evangelical scholars today concerns the need for evangelicals for Christians to develop skills in biblical interpretation. That is why we are having this conference at Ridgecrest. A decade ago, Dick France, writing in *Femelios*, the English evangelical student publication, bemoaned the fact that we've taught and learned the answers rather than the method for finding them. Clark Pennock, who was here last year, similarly and repeatedly has argued that the area in which a maturing of our evangelical understanding is most urgently needed is the interface between inspiration and interpretation—the interface between last year's conference and this years. Surely, "Biblical authority is an empty notion unless we know how to determine what the Bible means," states Jim Packer. We who are evangelicals want Scripture to stand over us and judge us, not vice versa. The Bible is our soul and final authority. But for Scripture to function thusly, we must be able to read it properly. We must be able to interpret what it says.

But as soon as the subject of interpretation is raised, some become uncomfortable. Doesn't a commitment to interpretation end up supplanting God's Word with human opinion as the final authority. Where is that firm foundation of theology if we say the Bible must be interpreted? There seem as many interpretations as interpreters.

J. Barton Payne expressed this fear eloquently (if not wrongheadedly) in his early article in the *Evangelical Theological Society Bulletin* entitled "Hermeneutics as a Cloak for the Denial of Scripture." Harold Lindsell expressed a similar perspective in his book *God's Incomparable Word*. He wrote, "There is one weapon that Satan uses today. It is an enemy of the Bible which it persistently undermines—*The Historical Critical Method*." Francis Schaeffer provides a third example from popular evangelicalism of this approach. His pamphlet responded to the Lausanne Statement on Scripture. Their statement on Scripture was, "The Bible is without error in all that it affirms." Schaeffer, uncomfortable with that, commented on Genesis 3: "The historic fall is not an interpretation, it is a brute fact. There is no room for hermeneutics here."

Schaeffer, Lindsell, and Payne are representatives of those who are fearful of going behind the text to ask of the author's intention or historic context, for this seems too subjective. If Paul states that women should not speak, we should leave it at that. It is wrong to inquire how these words might have been understood in his day. Was he attempting to speak about fundamental distinctions between male and female. Or was he addressing a particular problem in his day? Did he mean to use creational patterns illustratively or foundationally? And so on.

Such questions deal with Scripture's human words, with the human context of Scripture, the author and his or her setting. While some remain suspicious of critical methodology and continue to read Scripture in a more literal manner (i.e., they try to take the words of the text at their face value), most evangelicals recognize the need for grounding their interpretation of the text in literary and historical study. This is A. W. Tozer's point in his straightforward article, "The Perils of Textualism." It is also Carl Henry's theme in his critique of Lindsell's book *The Battle For The Bible*. Carl Henry, perhaps the dean of evangelical theologians writes:

> Dr. Lindsell regards the historical-critical method as in itself an enemy of Orthodox Christian faith. He seems totally unaware that even evangelical seminaries of which he approves are committed to historical criticism. Surely, Dr. Lindsell does not want the seminaries to take an uncritical, unhistorical approach to the Bible.

What I have illustrated for you is one current debate within evangelicalism. It is a debate over Scripture's intentions and historical contexts, and it lies behind some of the controversy that you are facing today. Do we concentrate our interpretive energies on the text alone, irrespective of its original context? Or are we concerned more with the implied author's intention for that text? That is, do we stress in our interpretation the author and his or her intended meaning of the text, or do we go at the text itself and alone? Let me begin a schematic on the blackboard that will develop as I proceed.

AUTHOR————TEXT

One question we face is whether we concentrate on the author or authors or editors who brought together that document or on the words of the text alone, irrespective of their historical context.

There is a second major question currently debated among evangelicals. We can perhaps gain insight into it by considering the question of Old Testament interpretation. Do we read the Old Testament primarily in terms of its historical intention or in terms of our Christian faith? Do we accept the text in its original setting and context or do we read it in terms of an inner meaning centering in Jesus Christ Himself? Can we, that is, accept Bonhoeffer's Christological approach to the Psalms? Or Philip Keller's interpretation of Joshua in light of Jesus? One might think the answer straightforward until the same perspective is applied to a reading of the New Testament. Again, should Jesus' acceptance of women as equals in the Gospels be read into our interpretation of 1 Corinthians 14?

Some might believe that I have asked the wrong question, imposing an "either-or" alternative—either Scripture is read according to some larger world view or it's read in its original context. Can't one accept both approaches as valid? The answer is, of course, yes, as I will argue later. But the fact is we tend to interpret Scripture using one or another approach. Thus, some evangelicals, some Southern Baptists, in their reading Scripture emphasize neither a literal reading of the text, nor a historical reading of the text, but a spiritual reading of the text, while concentrating in the world view expressed in and through the document.

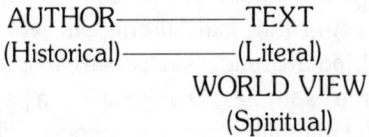

Dispensationalism has long used this approach and provides perhaps the most accessible evangelical example. Norman Geisler, for example, in his *A Popular Study of the Old Testament* (Geisler is, as you know, a philosopher of religion and, thus, it is not surprising that he opts for his interpretive approach, one based on Scripture's world view or philosophy) locates Scripture's inner plan in the presentation of Christ Himself. "There is no other way for a Christian to understand the Old Testament. (1) Christ is the theme of both testaments of the Bible, (2) Christ is the theme of each of the eight sections of scripture and (3) Christocentric themes and truths may be found in each of the sixty-six books of the Bible." If we come to the Bible with an overall picture of the person of Christ, Geisler thinks all the parts will fit more easily into place. Rather than stress either the biblical text or the author's intention, Geisler wants us to focus on Christ, the reality lying in and behind the text. You with me?

There is still a fourth contemporary evangelical option for biblical interpretation, one that has surfaced more recently and one that is creating much debate. In this approach, the focus is not on the text or the author of the text or the spiritual reality lying in and behind the text; it is on the reader of the text and his or her context.

```
        AUTHOR————————TEXT————————READER
       (Historical)————————(Literal)————————(Pragmatic)
                         WORLD VIEW
                         (Spiritual)
```

Some evangelicals believe that to emphasize the contemporary situation in one's biblical interpretation is wrongly to bring the Bible under the control of existentialism. R. C. Sproul, for example, in his excellent book *Knowing Scripture* (I am sure many of you have used it) argues for an "objective understanding of scripture" in which the Bible student reads "without mixing in his own prejudices." Walter Kaiser in his article "Legitimate Hermeneutics" is even more pointed. Following E. D. Hirsch, he distinguishes between meaning (going through the text to that single idea which was meant by the human author) and significance (the relationship between that single meaning and the reader). Hermeneutics, for Kaiser, has only to do with the first, with the meaning, the single intention. "To interpret we must in every case reproduce the sense the scriptural writer intended for his own words." Although segments of traditional evangelicalism in this way remain suspicious of interpretive strategies that would focus on the reader, a growing number of American evangelicals have sought to distinguish between the arbitrary and destructive subjectivism of some reader oriented criticism. And that faithful criticism which affirms the text's full authority while recognizing the reader's necessary role in the interpretive process. Let me give you three examples. One taken from psychology, one taken from anthropology, and the third taken from philosophy. Those involved with relational theology have perhaps led the way here for those of us who are evangelicals, leaning heavily on the insights of psychology and the human potential movements. The organization Faith at Work, for example, has published a steady stream of relational Bible studies. I suspect many of you have used them or the *Serendipity Bible* study sources of Lyman Coleman and so on. Karl Olsson, former Director of Leadership Training for Faith at Work, writes: "When accepted personally and relationally, the Bible, through the work of the Spirit, continually creates new relationships." Olsson continues:

> There are safer things than giving the Bible a personal, relational focus. Kierkegaard's story is not outdated. There is a room with two doors. Over

one there is a sign, "Heaven;" on the other a sign, "Lecture about Heaven." And people flock through the door to the lecture. It is safer to keep the Bible an object. If I do, I can worship it, attack it, or ignore it. But if I let the Bible become God's voice speaking to me and working in me, there is no escape, not even if I stick my fingers in my ears. I am on my way into the risk and beauty of salvation.

There is an obvious danger in such a relational approach to biblical interpretation. Shorn of its interpretive context, the biblical text is easily misused allegorically. Under the rubric of group "Bible" study, what often takes place is "Christian" sharing. There is, however, an obvious strength as well. Relational Bible study has recognized the need for the Bible to come alive as a living Word which is to be heard anew.

Drawing not from the field of psychology, but from other disciplines within the social sciences, particularly anthropology and linguistics, other evangelical, as well, have sought to spell out a reader-oriented theory of biblical interpretation. Missiologists have been particularly helpful here. You know that from your own interaction from your missionaries who have come back from other cultures who read that text with their own eyes and experiences and needs. Not only do missionaries do this but also evangelicals who live outside of the United States. Latin American evangelical C. Rene Padilla in his paper given at the Lausanne Consultation on Gospel and Culture argues that the "intuitive" approach common to older commentaries and common to contemporary popular preaching (what I have labeled lthe textual approach). He argues that the intuitive approach, in which Christians assume that "as long as the Bible is available in their own language, they have direct access to the meaning of the ancient text" is inadequate. So, too, is the "scientific" approach practiced by a large majority of biblical scholars today in which the need for understanding the original context is emphasized. Writes Padilla: "A serious problem of both methods is that they tend to be naive about the way contemporary social, economic, and political factors and other cultural forces affect the interpretive process." We don't read in a vacuum. Instead, Padilla argues for a "contextual" approach (a theory centering in the reader), one that appreciates "the role of today's world in conditioning the way contemporary readers are likely to 'hear' and understand the text." "The challenge of hermeneutics," states Padilla, "is to transpose the message from its original historical context into the context of present day readers so as to produce the same kind of impact on our lives as it did on the original hearers or readers."

To accomplish this task, Padilla proposes that interpretation be carried out within a "hermeneutical circle" or one could say spiral, in which interpreters and text (within its context) are mutually engaged. He says there must be a two-way conversation between the horizon of the historical situation and the horizon of the reader of the text.

> The contextual approach to the interpretation of Scripture involves a dialogue between the historical situation and Scripture, a dialogue in which the interpreters approach Scripture with a particular perspective (their world-and-life view) and approach their situation with a particular comprehension of the Word of God (their theology). . . .
>
> Hermeneutics thus has a "spiral structure" in which there is an ongoing circulation between the receptor culture and the biblical message, each enriching the understanding of the other.

It is this kind of model that he is hoping for. But as you ask questions of the text, the text confronts you, you move forward toward the truth.

Padilla's stress on two interpretive horizons becomes the theme of Anthony Thiselton's monumental work *The Two Horizons* (Eerdmans, 1980). Evaluating the contribution of philosophy to an understanding of the hermeneutical task, Thiselton examines in depth the thought of Heidegger, Bultmann, Gadamer, and Wittgenstein, particularly as it relates to the question of hermeneutic's two horizons. Thiselton's work offers a significant challenge to traditional evangelical interpretation from within. He is a warm evangelical. For rather than dismiss, for example, Bultmann's hermeneutical theory of preunderstanding as methodologically deficient, he instead argues that Bultmann's conclusions need not follow from his reader-oriented method. Thiselton's book is somewhat opaque. However, in an earlier popular essay written for the Second National Evangelical Anglican Congress in 1977, Thiselton provides the following guidelines for the interpreter:

1. Current debate shows the relevance of discussion on hermeneutics. Again, we are all in it together.
2. The task of understanding the Bible includes the study of its context. Here is the first horizon.
3. This may call for the use of specialists. Again the perspicuity of Scripture never meant that it was totally available to everybody regardless of their background or study. It, instead, meant that Scripture is available to all to bring faith and life as you come to it. But we always recognize the need of the scholar, the student, the pastor, the interpreter to dig into that text and help us understand it.
4. But the modern reader, as well as the ancient text, is also conditioned by his historical circumstance, and thus understanding will involve the horizon of the hearer as well. Here is the second horizon.
5. One should avoid premature "applications" of the text to one's present context.
6. But a fusion between the two horizons—those of the text's context and those of the modern reader—is ultimately necessary.
7. The reader's frame of reference both helps and hinders a right understanding of the text. We can hear often times our orientation as a way of

biasing us from understanding the text, but it can also move us into the text. I will give some examples in a minute.
8. Understanding is an ongoing process, an ongoing studying and listening.
9. Understanding, moreover, will issue not only in reflection, but in obedient response to God.
10. The Holy Spirit usually works through such hermeneutical procedures, not in independence of them.

What can be concluded from this survey? Can you follow this broad breaststroke overview? First, the typology that I have just offered suggests that evangelical biblical interpretation is remarkably similar to literary criticism more generally. Just as evangelicals have adopted multiple approaches, focusing primarily either on author, text, reader, or the spiritual reality, the world view lying in and through the text, so too in this history of literary criticism. Has there been a concentration on one or another of the elements of the literary circle? In fact, literary criticism has proven my model, given me my model, provided my typology.

Every adequate literary critical theory attempts to be comprehensive—to include all four aesthetic moments. Oh, there are some that have been reductive. Existentialists, for example, want to start just with the text and the reader and cut out the author. But in the history of criticism through the centuries all have attempted to include all of them. But each major theory tends to interpret one element as the key to understanding the significance and status of the others. Let me very quickly, because you are not here for a lecture in literary criticism, but to show you something of the scope here sketch how our understanding of the Bible correlates with how literary critics have read literature through the ages.

1. Mimetic Theories were given their classical expression by Plato and Aristotle. They focus on the "world" as revealed through the literary text. For Plato, the arts are imitations of those in eternal and unchanging ideas. For Aristotle, tragedy imitates unchanging human action. For both, it is a parallel universe (either hypothetical or real) which provides literature its source and subject matter. When you read the text, you are gaining access into that greater reality.

2. Objective Theories have in the twentieth-century been identified with "new critics" like R. P. Blackmur, Cleanth Brooks, who followed some of the spade work of T. S. Eliot. They thought approvingly of Archibald MacLeish's aphorism, "a poem should not mean/but be." A literary work from this perspective has its own autonomy apart from the author's otherwise stated intention and the reader's affectedness. How many times have you heard a literary author interviewed in which when asked, "What did you mean by this," the author says, "Read it"? Criticism should focus on analyzing the text and comparing its particular parts and complexities.

3. Expressive Theories are usually associated with the Romantics—with Shelley and Wordsworth. They concentrate on the way the writer invents, imagines, and judges. A literary work is valuable in mirroring, opening us up to, the mind of the poet. It is valuable in revealing the creative process in the writer.

4. Lastly, Pragmatic Theories center upon literature's ability to instruct and/or give pleasure to the reader. Literature's value, that is, lies in its ability to produce certain effects upon its audience, namely, to teach and delight. Leo Tolstoy had a pragmatic theory of literature, as did Philip Sidney.

Now all four types of literary criticism have their strengths, for each recognizes the significance and value of one of the aesthetic circle's four necessary moments (text, author, reader, world view), so that centering upon the shape of the world reflected in the text, centering upon the executive principle, centering upon the underlying prospective meaning allows the critic to wrestle with the question, "What universal truth is embodied in the text?" Or to put it in other terms, "How can we meet Jesus Christ through this passage?" A focus on the text itself allows the critic to ask, "What does it say?" A focus on the author allows us to say, "What does it mean?" A focus upon the reader allows us to say, "What does it mean to me?" Standard Bible study questions you all have used weekly. All four questions are both valid and helpful in the interpretive task.

Yet each critical approach also has its weaknesses, and if we are comfortable or more comfortable with one and less comfortable with another, we tend to forget about the weaknesses of our own and concentrate upon the weaknesses of a different approach. Mimetic theories have often failed to respect the autonomy of the work as a particular kind of action or attitude is read into the text based on the needs and interests of the critic. Here an example might be some Old Testament typological preaching or viewing the Song of Songs as being about Christ and His church. The result of such interpretive agendas is the loss of the unique perspective in a work to a system, or world view, extrinsic to it. Objective theories, though centering on the text, easily become merely formal or technical criticism. In our preaching they become teaching that doesn't get beyond giving the data to communicating the point and inspiring action. And we have all heard too many sermons, not our own, that are guilty of remaining at that textual level. The result is a substitution of the literature itself for that which the literature seeks to express. The result is a sterility. Expressive theories, those centering on the author, have tended to exalt the role of the writer, therefore, underestimating a given work's unique meaning and value. Is it Paul or his book to the Galatians that we study? Can we use Galatians 3:28 to explain all else that Paul says on women, for example? Expressive theories tend to move outside of the particular text to the larger authorial context and use that material to make a point. Finally, pragmatic theories have sometimes proven too subjective, revealing more about the critic than about the text. One's critical judgments have become biased by the end in view, and the literature has been turned into a tool of one's desired goal.

My point here is that each theory, each methodology, has its strength and its weakness. The value of adopting any particular strategy becomes dependent, therefore, not only on its inherent strength but also on its present persuasiveness and on the perceived likeliness of abuse in any given context.

Perhaps all that I have said sounds too abstract. Perhaps you are thinking, *Why not just go to the text and figure out what it says?* But is it what it "says," or should you be asking what it "means"? Or is it what it "means to me or to my congregation" that's crucial? Or is it what it "says about Jesus Christ" that should be my focus? I am sure that you wrestle, those of you who are preachers, with those questions every time you sit down to write your next sermon. My first simple point in this lecture is to help you see that all four questions are valid interpretive questions. Understood in terms of text, author, reader, and world view, there are questions you should take to any piece of literature, and particularly the Bible. Moreover, they are questions which have been taken by the best of literary interpreters through the ages.

Thus, it is historically inaccurate to say that a textual approach to the reading of Scripture, for example, is naive and reactive. Merely what Fundamentalists do. Merely the anti-intellectual response to German higher criticism. Men of letters such as T. S. Eliot have argued persuasively that a text like *Hamlet* should be read as a self-contained document independent of whether Shakespeare wrote it or not. After all, it is not Elizabethan England that we encounter, but Hamlet as the words of the text present him in their full interplay.

Similarly, one is historically inaccurate to judge contemporary reader-response theory as simply the latest example of modernity's attempt to relativize truth. It can be that, just as a textual approach can be a defensive reaction to modernity. But neither need be. Leo Tolstoy's "conversion" to free masonry caused him to re-evaluate the value of his writing in terms of how strongly any one of his literary works presented the theme of brotherhood in a convincing way. Tolstoy realized (perhaps as we today realize the power of movies to change and mold opinion) that a novel can be a subversive document. Thus, it must be judged not simply by what it expresses but also by what it accomplishes.

My first goal in this lecture, then, is to help you to see the historic range of interpretive options available to anyone who reads a literary text—and thus to anyone who reads the Bible, "God's-Word-as-human-words." My second goal is to help you to understand the value of using multiple approaches as you seek to faithfully interpret God's word.

There is a need for flexibility and openness as we approach a text so that the strengths of each critical perspective can be utilized and the possible weaknesses kept in check. Methodological diversity need not be deplored or countered. What one might underestimate or obscure using a particular approach, another might uncover. As literary scholar M. H. Abrams has argued in his book *The Mirror and the Lamp,* a Romantic writing, any carefully practiced critical theory can open the critic "to aspects of a work which other theories with different focus, different categories of discrimination have on principle overlooked, underestimated or obscured."

Let me skip a little in the interest of time. A helpful evangelical model or example of using multiple critical approaches is the Willowbank Report, the summary of the Lausanne Consultation on Gospel and Culture which was held in 1978, sponsored by the Graham organization. While arguing for a "contextual approach" in biblical interpretation (again Lausanne for the first time had a majority of nonwesterners), the Willowbank Report does not ignore the contributions of historical (or expressive theories centering on the author) and popular (that's their term for those objective literal theories). Historical interpretation

> takes with due seriousness the original historical and cultural context. It seeks also to discover what the text meant in its original language, and how it relates to the rest of Scripture. All this is an essential discipline because God spoke his word to a particular people in a particular context and time. So our understanding of God's message will grow when we probe deeply into these matters.

Popular interpretation (the text) is also helpful, reminding the interpreter that

> God intended his word for ordinary people; it is not to be regarded as the preserve of scholars; the central truths of salvation are plain for all to see; Scripture is "useful for teaching the truth, rebuking error, correcting faults, and giving instruction for right living."

Those concentrating on the text recognize the necessity of listening to God's Word and obeying it.

But understanding God's Word demands that one go further than popular or historical approaches allow. For the participants at the Willowbank Conference, "the cultural context of the contemporary readers as well as of the biblical text" must be taken seriously (again the two horizons). Moreover, "a dialogue must develop between the two." Thus, a contextual approach is proffered:

> Today's readers cannot come to the text in a personal vacuum, and should not try to. (This is what the respondent last night was saying.) Instead, they should come with an awareness of concerns stemming from their own cultural background, personal situation, and responsibility to others. These concerns will influence the questions which are put to the Scriptures. What is received back will not be the answers only, but more questions. As we address Scripture, Scripture addresses us. We find that our culturally condi-

tioned presuppositions are being challenged and our questions corrected. In fact, we are compelled to reformulate our previous questions and to ask fresh ones. So the living interaction proceeds.

Willowbank recognizes what evangelicals have recently experienced on such diverse issues as women in the church and home, the nature and function of the Holy Spirit, the relationship of Christianity to capitalism. Women, charismatics, and third-world Christians have all brought their particular perspectives to bear on the text in its context and the dialogue between the two cultures has enriched the church worldwide.

Let me take five or ten minutes and illustrate what I am thinking so you can have a reality check by looking at some particular examples. It is my hypothesis that all of us are more eclectic than we know. Yet, we are also perhaps unaware of this and thus do not carry out our interpretation with design and care so as to make the text God's-Word-in-human-words come alive for us today.

Let me just bracket for a minute and say I was at Southwestern Seminary several years ago, and one of their homiletics professors picked me up at the airport. We had a fascinating discussion about how everything that's learned at Southwestern seems to be forgotten once the student moves back into his or her preaching context, and how they go out into the churches and listen to preaching and it doesn't fit that historical contextual grid. I suspect it's because instinctually the preacher understands the need to link with the reader and thus does a poor job of combining or relating the multiple methodologies in order to get across savingly God's truth.

When you read Psalm 22:1, for example ("My God, my God, why hast thou forsaken me?"), do you focus on the psalmist's intention (on the author) or do you hear Jesus? When you read Psalm 51 ("Have mercy on me, O God, according to thy steadfast love," and so on), do you look at it as a psalm of lament with a predictable shape or pattern which begins with a direct address to God, and moves on to the lament, the petition, and the vow to praise God? Perhaps you do, but do you not also, and in a prior way, relate this psalm to David and the agony of his confession after Nathan had confronted him with his sin against Bathsheba, even though you remember that the titles and headings are later additions from the tradition and are not part of the canonical text.

When you read the fifth chapter of the Song of Songs which has a compelling song of yearning, of human longing for the beloved, do you seek to put that song in its historical context? Do you try to go back to the author? A few have. Or is there something universal about it that links it to your own experience, such that you begin to reflect on it in light of your own love-sickness? Or again, when you read Genesis 1, are not the clear, plain words of the text, Genesis 1:1, your focus? It states that in the beginning God created the world. For most of us, the words mean what they say and say what they mean. But I could not help but think, knowing that I was going to lecture this morning, as I heard the presentation on Genesis 1 of Gerhard Dirks. Perhaps some of you have heard his testimony. Perhaps he is dead now, I don't know. But in the late 60's I heard him give his testimony as the one who had invented the principle component for the memory cell used by all computers today. As an adult who came to this country with no faith, walking out in nature, he was overcome in awe and wonder at the creation he experienced, and saw and heard the creator which led him to Jesus Christ. When Gerhard Dirks reads Genesis 1, he reads it hermeneutically, to use Jim Packer's second category. And those hermeneutical perspectives are not negative questions that block him from hearing the text, but are invitations into the text. He can hear the awe and wonder of the God of creation seen in that Genesis 1:1 passage that most of us do not. We hear it as lecture.

What is my point? With Psalm 22, we tend to read it Christologically; with Psalm 51, historically. We read the Song of Songs personally. Genesis 1, textually (unless you are Gerhard Dirks and you are overwhelmed by the God of creation). Such variety is often lamented, as if evangelical interpreters of the Bible are "undressed" or naive in their approach. but one need not apologize for methodological diversity. It is what allows the Bible, God's-Word-as-human-words, to come alive for you and me today.

I was going to treat 1 Corinthians 14:33-40. You might want to do so. That's a nice text to test yourself as author-text-reader-world view. Women should keep silence in the church, that passage. Or again, you might look at Psalm 23. How are you to interpret this most familiar of all Psalms? How many of you memorized it as a child? I did. I learned the words even when I wasn't sure of their meaning. Perhaps you did. I stumbled over that last phrase, "Surely goodness and mercy." I didn't know who "Shirley" was, but if she wanted to follow me, that was okay.

When I have taught the Psalms, students have told their stories of memorizations; these are honest stories. One kid came up to me and said he had learned "thy rod and thy reel, they comfort me." Another young woman who had grown up in the city and had never experienced the country said that when she was a child, she had learned "he makes me to lie down in green pillow cases."

Psalm 23 is deservedly well-known, and it should be memorized by all, but how is it to be read? Do we seek to understand it according to ancient Near-Eastern customs? Or even modern Near-Eastern customs read back as a Philip Keller might? Do we hear in this Psalm a reference to Jesus, the good Shepherd? Do we read it mindful of the story of John Merick, the elephant man, who recited this psalm when all hope had been denied him, only for his simple biblical faith to prove his human salvation? I can never read Psalm 23 again without thinking of that film. Or does the psalm need no reference to its author's background, its reader's experience, its Christological completion, instead suggesting just a plain, straightforward textual reading of God's care and hospitality? Psalm 23 can be interpreted through its author's context, its reader's response. One of my friends had to read that Psalm, or was given the privilege of reading that psalm on his mother's deathbed, the last event that they shared together. He will never read that psalm again without that experience informing his understanding.

A "principled eclecticism" can facilitate evangelical biblical interpretation today. Here is, perhaps, the primary lesson that literary criticism offers the evangelical reader of the Bible. Given the real strengths and weaknesses of all four critical approaches to the reading of a text, and given the wider cultural changes that have traditionally portended the adoption of a new critical vantage point, one needs to know that each of these approaches tends to be associated with a given epoch or age ("classicism" with the mimetic theories, "neo-classicism" and the Renaissance to pragmatic theories, "Romanticism" to expressive theories, twentieth-century scientific-technological thought with objective theories). Given that interpreters should be leery of absolutizing their approaches.

God's Word is unchanging, not our approach to its interpretation. All critical strategies are "subjective." All methodologies have their weaknesses and are dependent on wider cultural forces. There is a certain tragic-comic quality to our present debate: tragic, for helpful insights and correctives are too often ignored; comic, for the irony of the present interpretive debate is all too present to those who observe us. Evangelicals need not be single-minded in their hermeneutical posture. What one overlooks, underestimates, obscures, using a particular interpretive strategy, another might uncover. It is the biblical text itself that should remain authoritative, not any particular approach to its reading.

5
INTERPRETING THE OLD TESTAMENT
Walter Kaiser

Lewis Carroll's *Through the Looking Glass* still provides the most down to earth description of the current dilemma in interpreting the Bible. The philosophical dialogue that forms the *locus classicus* of this debate goes as follows:

> ". . . There's glory for you!" [said Humpty Dumpty].
>
> "I don't know what you mean by 'glory,'" Alice said.
>
> Humpty Dumpty smiled contemptuously. "Of course you don't—till I tell you. I mean't 'there's a nice knock-down argument for you!'"
>
> "But 'glory' doesn't mean a 'nice knock-down argument,'" Alice objected.
>
> "When I use the word," Humpty Dumpty said, in a rather scornful tone, "it means just what I choose it to mean—neither more nor less."
>
> "The question is," said Alice, "whether you can make words mean so many different things."
>
> "The question is," said Humpty Dumpty, "which is to be master—that's all."
>
> Alice was too much puzzled to say anything, so after a minute Humpty Dumpty began again. "They've a temper, some of them—particularly verbs, they're the proudest—adjectives you can do anything with, but not verbs—however, I can manage the whole lot! Impenetrability! That's what I say!"
>
> "Would you tell me, please," said Alice, "what that means?"
>
> "Now you talk like a reasonable child," said Humpty Dumpty, looking very much pleased. "I meant by 'impenetrability' that we've had enough of that subject, and it would be just as well if you'd mention what you mean to do next, as I suppose you don't intend to stop here all the rest of your life."
>
> "That's a great deal to make one word mean," Alice said in a thoughtful tone.
>
> "When I make a word do a lot of work like that," said Humpty Dumpty, "I always pay it extra."[1]

As I read the modern debates on biblical hermeneutics, I often wonder if our laypeople do not feel as confused as Alice did when they too face our scholarly reenactments of Humpty Dumpty! Surely what Alice needed to counter Humpty Dumpty is exactly what we are desperately searching for in our day. The solution may be summarized in two basic principles.

The first principle is that the meaning of a literary work is determined by the author's intention. The principal thesis of E. D. Hirsch is still the most important contribution of the twentieth century (even though it has received almost unprecedented opposition from many different disciplines). Hirsch claimed that the meaning of a work was "determinate" and hence could not change. In opposition to "The Intentional Fallacy" that appeared in the *Swanee Review* in 1946[2] Hirsch advised:

> Verbal meaning is whatever someone has willed to convey by a particular sequence of linguistic signs and which can be conveyed (shared) by means of linguistic signs.[3]

What makes Lewis Carroll's work so amusing is his deliberate distortion of this whole principle. But the price Humpty Dumpty must pay is that poor Alice is lost and without any sense of what is being said. And that is the price modern exegetes on Scripture must pay if they are going to insist with our modern post-Kantian relativism that meaning is personal, subjective, and constantly changing—in other words, its "what speaks to me," "what turns me on," or "what I get out of a text"; not what an author meant by his or her use of the words.

All knowledge is reduced to the horizon of one's own personal prejudices and predilections. Such an interpretive solipsism has no escape. What was in the reader's mind, experience, and emotions prior to reading a text is what came out after the reading was over. The only way out of this modern maze is to accede to the principle that the meaning of a literary work is determined by the author's meaning.

Of course, one of our problems with *meaning* is that it can have at least five different senses: (1) meaning as a *referent*, identifies the person, object, or subject named; (2) meaning as *value*, "this means more to me than anything else"; (3) meaning as *entailment*, "this means war"; (4) meaning as *significance*, names a relationship between what the author meant and another situation, person, or idea; and (5) meaning as *intention*, which is the stable object of knowledge meant by the author in his or her use of a particular sign sequence in the text.[4] These various values must be separated if we are to make progress in our discussion. The most important distinction is the one between "meaning" and "significance." The former is that which is represented by the text and the latter only names a relationship to that meaning. Few distinctions in the interpretive process are as important and as helpful as this one is.

The second principle is "the principle of sharability." Succinctly stated, our concept of a literary work should impose no constraints on the interpretation of a work other than those imposed by the language in question.[5] By this principle Alice could have admonished Humpty Dumpty that assigning meanings to words is not a playground for opinions, fancies, or even private preferences. Unless Humpty Dumpty uses words in their shared meanings, i.e., those imposed by the language itself, communication itself will be jeopardized. Humpty Dumpty will, indeed, pay extra—no one will be able to understand him! Hirsch claims that an "indeterminate meaning is not sharable,"[6] i.e., it cannot signal a common sense for those who are speaking to each other. But it is still possible to share meanings, even when a particular word *in abstracto* may be ambiguous, if the author of that word places it in a literary context and according to the rules of usage. In fact, usage of words is precisely how we establish meanings for those words. People wrote and spoke long before they composed dictionaries and grammars. The same principles holds for interpreting the Bible.

Recently a new movement in hermeneutics has reversed the contention that the author's usage provides the only genuinely discriminating norm for determining what a text meant. What is variously called reader-response or reader-centered criticism and hermeneutics has now made the reader's own response the basis for interpreting what a literary work says.[7] "Meaning, for most of these writers, is always potential in terms of the text, but actual in relation to the reader. No meaning is already 'there' in a text, or at least 'there' in some objectivist sense, apart from a horizon of expectations brought to a text by the reader."[8]

However, we have already begun to see the results of the reader-response hermeneutic taken to its logical conclusion. It can be seen in the approach known as "deconstruction" as advocated by Jacques Derrida.[9] His conviction is that the more one attempts to find meaning in the text the more the text *deconstructs* itself into various other possible meanings. Thus, the, so called, "full meaning" of a text is created by the reader and is as polyvalent as the reader wishes to make it! Reader-response critics assert that there just is no single objective meaning available for any text. One must assume that that conclusion also applies to the assertions that the reader creates his or her own meanings and the assertion that objective meanings are unavailable! Surely we cannot allow the rules advocated by traditional hermeneutics to be temporarily reinstated until the thesis for this nihilistic position is asserted, only to revert to the alleged system advocated once the agreement has been made on traditionalist's grounds.

Some biblical scholars are legitimately worried that the legacies of the Enlightenment (i.e., the methodology of Rene Descartes's eliminating all preconceived notions as the basis for understanding and Francis Bacon's rigorous empirical examination of the physical, historical, and experiential data) might influence authorial intention advocates too much.[10] Such, it has been charged, has led to the wedding of authorial intention inerrantist with the school of Scottish Common Sense Realism. But this alliance, it has been charged by Hans-Georg Gadamer, established its "fundamental prejudice . . . . against prejudice itself, which deprives tradition of its power."[11]

But our case for authorial intention is not dependent on any of these alleged

Enlightenment influences. Instead, we have argued elsewhere, along with Moses Stuart,[12] that the principles of interpretation are as native and universal to the human race as is speech itself. The general principles of interpretation are not learned, invented, or discovered. They are part and parcel of the image of God in men and women. Given the gift of communication and speech, human beings began practicing the principles of hermeneutics the moment communication began with Adam in the Garden of Eden. Thus, interpretation is more a native art than it is a science. Only in a derived and secondary sense can it be described as a science. Therefore, we may say without prejudice that it precedes Descartes, Bacon, Common Sense Realism and Gadamer himself!

The issues before us may not be less serious than that of the Reformation itself. Unless we can effectively begin to resolve some of the problems introduced in this introduction, it is doubtful whether our generation will be able to speak with any degree of confidence on what God meant when He gave us His revelation.

An even greater irony could result: Our generation may have labored the hardest and longest to effect the most inclusive statement on the extent of divine inspiration of the Bible (i.e., a definition of its inerrancy) but may have thrown away any potential advantages of such a gain in the answers we gave to the hermeneutical questions set before us. There is still time to reverse this estimate of history—but barely! This missing part of the theological curriculum must be attended to at once, or we shall drown in our own solipsisms.

If it be objected, as it surely has been, that God's disclosure was not so much concerned with words as it was with ideas and concepts, we will appeal to the claims of the text itself, such as that great neglected text in bibliology, 1 Corinthians 2:6-16. There the apostle clearly affirmed that the Spirit of God "taught words" (v. 13), not in a mechanical or dictation view of inspiration, but in a way that brought all the free gifts of the author into a living assimilation of the truth.[13] Thus, the extent of the Spirit's help continues all the way up to the verbalizing process, thereby guaranteeing that the quality of the words is errorless when judged from the viewpoint of the human writer and what that writer was attempting to say.

Specific Issues in Old Testament Hermeneutics

Interpreting the Old Testament (hereafter OT) is not just one problem of many, it is the master problem of theology according to Emil G. Kraeling.[14] A. H. J. Gunneweg was even more insistent. In his judgment:

> It would be no exaggeration to understand the hermeneutical problem of the Old Testament as *the* problem of Christian theology, and not just one problem among others, seeing that all other questions of theology are affected in one way or another by its resolution.... No more fundamental question can

be posed in all theology; providing an answer for it defines the realm in which theology has to be done.[15]

Fortunately, the church has already successfully dealt with the inadequate solutions to this "master problem" of theology such as were set forth by the Marcionites, the Caninites, the Ebionites, the Gnostics, and now in their modern descendants. But even after all talk about the God of the OT not being the same as the God and Father of our Lord Jesus Christ has been put down, the feeling seems to persist that there just must be a difference between the two testaments.

A veritable tug of war has set in between the obviously temporal character of the OT and the high claims that both testaments attribute to the abiding nature of the OT. Surely the apostle Paul taught in 2 Timothy 3:15-17 that the Scripture of his day, which was nothing more or less than the entirety of the thirty-nine books of the OT, were indeed "profitable" for supplying to the church "teaching, reproof, correction, training in righteousness," "and making one wise for salvation through faith in Christ Jesus." That is some list.

Nevertheless, the questions still persist. Contemporary believers complain that they cannot see any connection between the document that focuses on Israel (=OT) and the one that focuses on the church (=NT). After all, shouldn't Christianity be viewed as a new beginning with a "New Covenant"? Isn't the subject of the OT too narrowly conceived—a special people, different from all the families on the earth? Are not the objects of faith in the OT and the method of salvation as utterly diverse as works is from faith? Are not the ethical injunctions, such as those that advocate the extermination of all Canaanites and Amalekites, on a lower moral plain than what we are accustomed to in the ethically superior teachings of the New Testament (hereafter NT)? And are not the expectations and hopes carried by the peoples of the two testaments as radically different as health, wealth, and material expectations in this life are from the spiritual coming of the kingdom of God in the NT?

There are enough questions to keep us busy for several monographs, let alone attempting to answer a few of them in the short scope of this essay. Nevertheless, these questions begin to illustrate how important the OT hermeneutical question really is. To these problems must also be added those that have come as a result of our modern investigations and the challenges contemporary scholarship has brought to those who would read the OT as a document of faith.

In order to address the most pressing issues raised in OT interpretation, the following seven questions will be treated:
1. Does the OT have a center or unifying theme and is that theme continuous with the NT in any way?
2. Did the OT writers consciously anticipate the Messiah and is a Christolog-

ical exegesis of the OT the only way to get at the abiding message of the NT?
3. Can the OT law, in its entirety or in its parts, give any normative instruction for the NT believer?
4. Are not the OT narratives, due to their temporal context and their particularity, purely descriptive in function rather than prescriptive for NT faith?
5. Does Genesis 1—11 reflect sets of ancient Near Eastern mythologies or normative teaching for the church today?
6. Does not the conditional and nationalistic aspects of the OT prophets make it impossible for believers to appropriate it for themselves since they live in other times and settings?
7. Have not the new critical methods of interpreting the OT negated any devotional or direct reading and interpreting of the OT?

This is hardly an exhaustive list, but it is representative of the types of hermeneutical problems Christians face when they open the pages of the OT and begin to ask how these texts apply to us, if at all.

The Issue of the Center and Unity of the OT

Modern scholars complain that pre-critical Bible study (i.e., that study which preceded source critical methods of reading Scripture) was "flat," "static," and unable to handle the diversity of viewpoints in the OT. Instead of searching for the unity within the OT, it became more popular to treat the diversity of concepts, themes, institutions, and literary forms.

To be sure, the OT certainly was not a static or flat book. And it did possess a great deal of diversity.[16] That was not the issue. The problem was that normally one expects a book to manifest a unity of perspective, aim, and theme. But this is precisely what modern scholars faulted the OT with not evidencing.

The charge was made so frequently that it became wearisome: "The Bible is full of contradictions." However, even that viewpoint needed to be qualified. What was meant by a "contradiction"? John Goldingay noted that some diversity did not involve mutual opposition.[17] For example, there were formal contradictions which involved not a difference in substance, but only a formal difference in words. Accordingly, 1 Samuel 15:11,29,35 states and denies that God changes His mind, but this only invites us to clarify the fact that the same word shows how God does not change in His nature, therefore, He changed in His response to individuals in order to maintain this consistency. There are also contextual contradictions in which varying contexts, reflecting a variety of circumstances, exhibit different statements which appear to contradict other statements made in another context. Thus Ezekiel 33:24 denies, but Isaiah 51:2 affirms, that God's dealings with Abraham might serve as a paradigm for the way God might deal with His people in or after the Exile.

If the OT has as much diversity as scholars are claiming, naturally the quest for any kind of theological unity would be mistaken. Some of the reasons advanced for the inappropriateness of searching for such theological coherence in the OT are:

1. This search incorrectly posits some type of metaphysical entity behind the OT texts,
2. It risks betraying the historical distinctiveness of OT witnesses that oppose each other,
3. It ignores the OT's own reticence for any quest of a systematic view,
4. It fails to take into account the primitive Oriental mind's tolerance for what Westerners call contradiction, and
5. It disregards the acceptance of divergent views on part of the collectors of Scripture.[18]

As Goldingay and others point out, however, this case for diversity and the case against unity is not as strong as it appears. The rebuttal to the diversity-only case is this:

1. The diversity argument assumes that historical exegesis is the sole valid interpretation of Scripture,
2. The search for unity is just as valid a search as is the one for diversity,[19]
3. The various books of the Bible became the one book, i.e., *ta Biblia* became *to Biblion,* in the life of the religious community, and
4. If Scripture is in some sense the Word of God, it would be natural to look for some such coherence on the assumption that the claim that God stands behind the revelation may indeed be vindicated by the evidence.[20]

Amid all the variety and multiplexity of the OT, there is both inductive and canonical precedence for locating a center and unity to the testament. That unity is more than simply affirming that God is the center of the OT as does Gerhard von Rad and Gerhard Hasel.[21] The problem with making God or Yahweh the center is that this statement has no predicate—God is or does what? But another affirmation lies close at hand to show that there was a fixed divine intention and plan for Israel and the Gentiles. That text is Genesis 12:2-3. Everything hangs on the passive form of the verb to bless in verse 3. And so crucial was this passive rendering of "bless" that Bertil Albrektson[22] acknowledged in his 1967 monograph that if the verb was passive and not reflexive (as he mistakenly concluded), then there was a clear plan in the OT in which God chose Abraham to be his instrument to reach all the nations of the earth. I believe that this text can supply the answer to our search for the OT *Mitte,* or center: it was the "Promise-plan" of God which was God's word that He would be or do what He pledged for Israel so that he could be and do the same for all the nations of the earth.[23] This theme was not only carried out in the rest of the OT, it continued and even became more explicit in the NT.[24]

The Issue of the Christological Interpretation of the OT

At the heart of the Promise-plan in the OT is the expectation of the Messiah. In spite of the fact that many remain skeptical of the fact that any doctrine of the Messiah appears in the OT, our Lord thought that such was the case and roundly scolded the two disciples on the road to Emmaus on that first Easter Sunday afternoon for not having understood that that expectation was taught in the OT (Luke 24:25-27,44-45).

It is not necessary to lapse into the so-called *Pesher* method of exegesis used in the Essene community of Qumran in order to derive an alleged secret messianic meaning not found in the surface meaning of the OT text. This is nothing less than a return to the subjective allegorization of some of the early Church fathers. Ultimately that is nothing less than eisegesis, an importation of meaning into the text. Such mystical or NT retrojections over the text are an open embarrassment to those of us who want to allow the OT text say what it wants to say first.

So large is the presence of the Messiah in the OT that the rabbis found Him or His times referred to in 456 OT passages.[25] While this list is overly inflated for any sober exegesis of the OT, it is sufficient to indicate the strength of the doctrine in the OT.

The Messiah was known by many names. He was: the "Seed" of Abraham, Isaac, Jacob, and David; the "Righteous Branch of the Lord;" "The Servant of the Lord;" "the Prophet" who would come; "The King" of the royal line of David;" and "the Stone" rejected by the builders which also became the "Chief Cornerstone."

But there is more. This "Son" to be born to David was no one less than God Himself as can be seen from his name in Isaiah 9:6 — "Almighty God, Father of Eternity, Prince of Peace, and Wonderful Counsellor." David Berger and Michael Wyschogrod attempted to avoid this surface meaning of the prophet Isaiah by suggesting that the sentence be translated "The mighty God, the eternal father, the prince of peace is *planning* a wonderful deed."[26] But the context demands that the name apply to the Son and not to the Father. Furthermore, the suggested translation cannot explain the absence of several linguistic features, such as the absence of the direct object sign, the use of the participle for "planning," "the One counselling," instead of the usual imperfect form of the verb "to be" and the like. On the contrary, this text asserts the full deity of the Son to be born in David's house.

Even the complaint by many Jewish and Christian scholars that the OT does not teach two separate comings for the Messiah is likewise deficient. No text speaks more directly to this charge than Zechariah 12:10 — "They will look on me, the one they have pierced, and they will mourn for him as one mourns for an only child, and grieve bitterly for him as one grieves for a first born son." Most interpreters will agree that the context for this saying is the Messianic times when peace is established on earth. But if that is so, how did the Messiah who will come in this time of peace get "pierced"? Who "pierced" him? And when did it happen? The only possible answer is that it happened during his first coming to earth!

Typical of the Jewish understanding of this verse is Gerald Sigal's attempt to disassocate "me" and "him" in verse 10. Sigal must make the unnatural supposition that the subject of the first verb, "will look," i.e., Israel, is different from the subject of the second verb, "pierced."[27] To interpolate "the nations" as the subject of the piercing is without any grammatical or textual justification.

To argue for two comings for Messiah in Zechariah 12:10 is not due to a Christian retrojection over the OT. In fact, when the NT writers cite an OT passage to support their Messianic claims for Jesus of Nazareth, they do not quote the OT in such a way as to add meanings that were not in the texts themselves. If the apostles had done such manipulating of the OT texts, it would be clear that that is precisely what the texts did not mean. Neither would it have reached the intended Jewish audience, for the obvious response would be right at hand—"I reject the associations you are making with this text for they cannot be adduced from what is said in the Tenak by any stretch of the imagination." On the other hand, Christians are to be blamed for not listening patiently and carefully to the OT Messianic texts.[28] Thus Peter in his preaching at Pentecost declared in Acts 2:29-33 that David foresaw and spoke of the resurrection of Jesus when he exclaimed in Psalm 16:10, "You will not let your Holy One [a term which taken on technical status much like 'Seed'] see decay." To argue for anything less is to resist the apostolic claim and to substitute our opinions for the apostle Peter's.

Once the legitimacy of the interpreting the Messiah in the OT is granted, does this mean that the only goal of OT exegesis is to make Christ the sum and substance of the meanings we derive from the OT? We think not. OT faith is Christocentric, but it is not Christoexclusivist. To only teach the Messianic promises, the Messianic times, and the gospel from the OT would be reductionistic and dishonoring to the full claims of the text. We must teach the "whole counsel of God" (Acts 20:27, KJV), for every omission only becomes the seedbed for the next generation's heresies.

The Issue of the Normativity of OT Law

Probably no single issue has raised a greater barrier for Christians using the OT than the problem of the OT Torah. Most blame the apostle Paul for this attitude. Did he not say that the law had a definite function for a specific period of time? ("Before this faith came, we were held prisoners by the law, locked up until faith should be revealed . . . But now that faith has come, we are no longer under the supervision of the law," Gal. 3:23-25). Therefore, it is incorrectly argued that "the law of Christ" (Gal. 6:2) has replaced the law of Moses.

Paul's attitude to the law is perhaps one of the most puzzling problems of all biblical study—apparently for the same reason that the OT is the master problem of theology. While one may collect passages that say that we are finished as Christians with the law in all its aspects (e.g., Rom. 7:1-10; Gal. 2:19; 2 Cor. 3:4-17; Eph. 2:14-16), we can cite just as many texts from Paul that show that the law is "holy, just, good, and spiritual" (Rom. 7:12-14). Faith did not abolish the law; instead, it established it (Rom. 3:31).

Even more spectacular is the discussion of Romans 9:30 to 10:13 where Paul contrasts the written law of Moses with invented oral traditions of the Jews of his day and concluded by affirming that his preaching and teaching was the same as what Moses had taught in Leviticus 18:5 and Deuteronomy 30:12-14. Indeed, much of our puzzlement over Paul's use of the law comes from our failure to recognize, as C. E. B. Cranfield has observed, that Paul had no separate word for what we today call "legalism," i.e., that system of works whereby we attempt to earn our own salvation.[29]

Since it is clear that Paul thought his teaching was in accord with the law and did not distort his call to faith in Christ, the hermeneutical problem is all the more sharpened. Do we take all of the law or only parts of it? And even if we only take some of it, how shall we apply the law to our contemporary questions which are so removed in time, culture, and complexity?

It was our Lord who taught in Matthew 23:23 that some parts of the law were "weightier" than others. Accordingly, even though we acknowledge that the law is one, some parts have priority over others. These, we will argue, are the moral aspects of the law based on the character of God.

Other parts of the law, we were warned even from their first announcement in the Torah, had a built-in obsolescence to them. This can be seen in the detailed list of instructions given from Exodus 25 through Leviticus on the Tabernacle and the services connected with it. Repeatedly Moses was told that what he was to make was only a "pattern" or a "model" (Hebrews say "shadow") of the real which appeared in heaven. Thus, all that legislation had a temporary lifespace. No longer are we bound to the precise forms of these laws even though they might exhibit principles which are still in effect.

But God is the Lord over all nations and not just over Israel. The standards of righteousness required of Israel were the same God expected from all citizens of all countries. If nations chose to disregard these laws of morality, God would "uproot" them (Jer. 12:16-17) by exercising his right as the Chief Potter (Jer. 18:7-10).

The heart of the OT law can be found in the Ten Commandments and in the Holiness Law ("Be holy as I, the Lord your God, am holy"). Only the commandment on the Sabbath is mixed, having ceremonial aspects (in that it spoke of the seventh day) along with moral aspects (in that God does have a right to a portion of our time in worship, service, and rest since He is Lord of time). The character and nature of God set the norm for what is moral, right, good, and pleasing to Him. The great measuring stick is that we are to "be . . . as" He is.

Four methods have been suggested for applying, teaching, and preaching from the law for our day. They are: (1) the method of analogy, (2) the method of middle axioms, (3) the method of general equity, and (4) the method of extracting precedents from earlier cases as a basis for making contemporary decisions.

The method of analogy is not helpful since it incorrectly assumes that there is some sort of expressed comparison between Israel's laws and the church. This is a basic hermeneutical blunder—equating, or likening, Israel to the church. True, as both Israel and the church are personally believing in the Man of Promise who is to come, our Lord Jesus Christ, they form one body. But these are insufficient grounds to say that since the part is related to another whole, then both parts are equal in their totality to each other!

Middle axioms have some benefit, but since they only provide us with a principle which is somewhere between a general abstraction and a specific concrete action, they end up being too abstract. What we need are practical applications which are rooted in particular texts of OT law.

To speak of the general equity of the law means that the law can apply to more cases than the one it particularly addresses. The reason for this expanding sphere of reference can be found in the fact that a general principle lies behind every particular law. Thus, the law against muzzling an ox in Deuteronomy 25:4 can have a legitimate application (not an allegorical interpretation) in 1 Corinthians 9:8-18 to paying church leaders their salaries. The equity of the text is this: giving, whether to tantalized oxen treading grain or people who are being taught the Word of God, engenders a spirit of gentleness and generosity in those who give. The primary concern of Deuteronomy 25 is for the growth of generosity in the owners of oxen, not for the oxen themselves in this case.[30]

It is worth noting that the interpretive framework for Deuteronomy 6—26 is nothing less than the Ten Commandments.[31] This section of Deuteronomy reflects in order each of the Ten Commandments. Behind all the specificity of this corpus of seemingly disparate laws shines the informing theology of the decalogue.

The most helpful method of extracting principles from biblical law for making practical applications to our modern needs is to build on the basis of the general equity of the text. This procedure will be much like the method we use in our courts today. A previous court decision will serve as a precedent for subsequent cases. From this precedent we may go on to build what we will call our "ladder of abstraction." Two ladders forming one peak may be pictured: one from its OT roots and another from our contemporary context. The interpreter may move from the lowest rung of the ancient specific cultural context up through the OT institution to the top rung of the abstract principle which lies behind all this specificity. The process may continue through the NT institution down to the lowest rung of the specific applications made of the same principle in our own day on the second ladder.[32] One more example might help. Luke T. Johnson has called to our attention the fact that the NT book of James might have as the heart of its message an exposition and application of a section from the Holiness Law in Leviticus 19:12-18.[33] Every verse except verse 14 of Leviticus 19 has a counterpart in the message of James. Surely this example can greatly strengthen our understandings of the uses of the law by the Christian.

The Issue of the Normativity of OT Narrative

Narratives occupy a large part of the OT text. They feature events, individuals, and situations which take place at special times, in special situations and to special people. The great issue of debate is this: How can texts which feature such obvious particularity have any normative or prescriptive applications for persons, situations, and institutions in totally removed circumstances such as we live in?

All too frequently, pastors and Bible teachers and readers have been guilty of substituting "thin moralizing" and imposing an allegorization over the narratives in order to gain a spiritual outcome from the study of these texts. Such extracting of "lessons," "examples," or "moral of the story" borders on spiritual fraud, for it has decided to get a "blessing" either "by hook or by crook"! In such situations, the point or truth that the teacher wishes to make has been decided on prior to investigating what the text itself has to say. The OT text becomes the length and shadow of some truth taught elsewhere, or worse still, the length and shadow of ourselves, our country, and our own culture.

These harangues against the poorest of our practices come easily enough. But what distinguishes such "moralizing, psychologizing, and spiritualizing" of the OT narratives from proper hermeneutical handling of this type of text?

Once again authorial intention in recording these episodes into the corpus of the text must function as the most important method for discovering how the narrative is to be understood. Thus, the incidents of Daniel's three friends being cast into the furnace in Daniel 3 and Daniel himself being thrown into the lion's den are not pieces of trivia in the midst of the more significant data, but function to demonstrate that God's kingdom and rule over the nations is able to triumph over the suffering and persecution experienced by His people.

Narrative is different from prose in that it prefers to say *indirectly* what prose prefers to assert directly. Therefore, the clues for the meaning of the text will be found in the immediate context, in the repetitions of themes or terms, and especially in the speeches or quotations from the central character. Rarely will the author intrude and supply his own value judgments or estimates. For example, it was the widow of Zarephath who occupied the "clean up hitter's" position in 1 Kings 17:24 and who made the whole point of the four episodes in the chapter, "Now I know that you are a man of God and that the word of the Lord from your mouth is the truth." That chapter was about discovering that the word of God was dependable—no matter what the setting in life might be.

Selection of detail and arrangement of the materials are two additional guides for determining meaning of narratives. Each episode must not be considered in isolation; instead, special care must be exercised to note how it was "woven" (from *texere*, "to weave," our word "text") into the relationships along side it. Sometimes the same event will be used in two or three different contexts to make separate teaching applications even though the principal point is the same. The most obvious example of this phenomenon is the varying order in the three Gospels of the temptation of our Lord.

In bridging this gap between the "now" and the "then" of the BC text, special care must be given not to confuse the descriptive material for what we would wish to teach prescriptively. Not everything the OT records is taught by the OT. Critics of inerrancy themselves frequently err in assuming that the careless confusion of description with prescription is thereby approved by this view. It is not. Even though the Bible says "there is no God," it does not teach it; only the fool would say that and at least he is smart enough to only say it in his heart! It is that same principle to which we would appeal to for narrative texts.

Many literary devices are available to the narrator: the *Leitwort* that explores the semanitic range of the root word, wordplay, synonymity, antonymity, recurrence of an image, quality or object that can function as a motif or theme and the like. The interpreter must be alert to the possible presence of any of these signals which the text can supply. We need be no more subtle than the ordinary listener who lived in the culture and understood the language when it was first communicated.[34]

The theological applications derived from narrative passages will often be those that are suggested by the analogy of antecedent Scripture. Often the incident under consideration will quote, allude or clearly refer to a preceding term, event, or theme. By so doing, the author will deliberately build his thought and intentions on the presumed backdrop and community consciousness of that earlier context and the truth taught there. Such a method of interpreting texts is much to be preferred over improperly employing the analogy of faith whereby a NT text is retrojected over the OT narrative and the passage leveled out eisegetically to say exactly what a similar NT text said.

Narratives are very special text forms; they have the ability to delight, charm, and winsomely to make their points. But they must be handled properly or they will be cheapened and eventually evaporate in the process, no matter how highly the text's inspiration is regarded!

The Issue of Mythology and Normativity in Genesis 1—11

Genesis 1—11 is, indeed, a challenge, no matter what hermeneutical system one espouses. But what is all too frequently left at the level of mere assertion by those who uncritically buy into modern descriptions of ancient parallels must be tested against the epigraphic evidence from antiquity.

Did the writer of Genesis 1—11 state in the symbols of his own day a naive or an accurate and useful cosmology? For example, did he not bother to correct the prevalent three-storied cosmology of the hard dome-like heavens, a flat earth, and a world under the earth? What is the literary character of these chapters, and what relationships do they bear to the rest of the revelation of God in Scripture?

The pre-exegetical commitment made by many contemporary scholars is that Israel is no exception to the general rule that a legendary age forms the idealistic background for her story and especially for all speculation on questions of origins.[35] Genesis 1—11 is consigned by definition and by fiat to a pre-literary and uncritical stage of society's development.

As early as 1895 Hermann Gunkel began to draw contrasts between history and Genesis 1—11. According to Gunkel, these were:

1. Genesis 1—11 originates in oral tradition while history is found in literate societies and in written documents of actual events.
2. Genesis 1—11 deals with personal and family stories while history concerns itself with the events of public interest.
3. Genesis 1—11 depends on the imagination of the raconteurs while history must be traced back to first-hand evidence.
4. Genesis 1—11 (and this is the "most significant" criterion) narrates the impossible (all streams on earth come from a single source, all animals in the ark, Ararat the highest mountain) whereas history narrates the possible.
5. Genesis 1—11 is poetic by nature and is intended to delight, inspire, and elevate while history is prose which seeks to inform.
6. Genesis 1—11 does not compare to the classical standard of Hebrew historiography found in the court history of David in 1 Samuel 9—20 which does not hesitate to tell the failures as well as the successes.[36]

Not too much has changed from Gunkel's day to the present advocates of a contrast between Genesis 1—11 and historical narrative. In his recent magisterial multivolume commentary on Genesis, Claus Westermann concurred: "It is no mere chance that there are so many parallels to Genesis 1—11 in the history of religions—more or less similar descriptions of creation, of the flood, as well as of other events . . . They range from tales, or primitive stories, through myth to mythical epic, as in Babylon . . ."[37]

It is impossible in the scope of this brief section to answer every charge that has been leveled against Genesis 1—11. Our interest is hermeneutical and not apologetical. However, the case for borrowing from these parallels does not appear to have been constructed on the basis of a control of the languages in which these alleged ancient Near Eastern parallels were written.

For example, the most basic reason given for asserting that Genesis 1 was dependent on the Babylonian myth of *Enuma Elish* was the fact that Hebrew *tehom*, "the deep" was linguistically related to the Babylonian goddess Tiamat.[38] However, this association is impossible even though it has been repeated almost nonstop for all of this century. If *tehom* were a loan word from Babylonian *ti'amat*, it would need to have a feminine (not its present masculine) ending and a gutteral letter *h* in the middle of the word *(tihamat)*. The fact that *tehom* occurs in fifteenth century BC Ugaritic with the meaning of "sea" or the like also does great damage to the theory of its alleged Babylonian origins.

Another point on which near unanimity has been reached by many modern scholars is the alleged pre-scientific diagram of the three storied universe.[39] A flat earth (Isa. 11:12; Rev. 20:8) supposedly is capped by a solid "firmament" (Gen. 1:7-8), outfitted with windows (Gen. 7:11; 8:12; 2 Kings 7:2) and supported by pillars (1 Sam. 2:8; Job 9:6) stretching up from Sheol and the "deep."

Every step of this diagram of a three storied universe depends more on the ingenuity of the modern scholar than it does on the so-called myth-making abilities of the original narrators. Nowhere does the OT state or imply that the heavens are solid or like a dome. This is a secondary idea, for *raqia'* is derived from the Latin Vulgate *firmamentum* and the Septuagint *stereoma*. The Hebrew word simply means an "expanse" with no connotations of its solidity or its vault-likeness whatsoever! Likewise, the reference to the "waters under the earth" merely means below the shore line, for that is where one goes fishing (Deut. 4:18). Of course, in some of the poetic passages there are metaphoric words used to describe the "foundations" of the earth, but these are no more unnatural than our current speech patterns by which we point to many of the same realities. Even the "windows" in heaven do not support the solid vault theory, since barley (2 Kings 7:2), trouble (Isa. 24:18), and blessings (Mal. 3:10) come through these same "windows"![40]

The style of Genesis 1—11 is more like narrative or historical prose than poetry, myth, or legend. The fundamental characteristics of biblical narrative are exhibited: the consecutive *waw* with the Hebrew form of the imperfect verb, the frequent use of the Hebrew direct object sign, the presence of the Hebrew relative *'asher,* and the use of the same organizing feature for the first eleven chapters of Genesis as for chapters 12—50, *viz.*, "the generations [or histories] of . . ." The few poetical texts in Genesis 1—11 can be easily identified by the presence of Hebrew parallelism, word pairs, and the like. Therefore, the text must be taken on its own terms as signaled by its own literary form.

Nor should the uniqueness of its subject matter be cause for our casting it into a pattern held by many Near Eastern mythological texts. Some of "the most telling parallel[s] happen . . . to be later than the Biblical account," advised W. G. Lambert[41] in his discussion of the Babylonian flood story, the *Gilgamesh Epic*.[42]

It is also impossible to show Babylonian influence by pointing, as so many English translations of Genesis 1:1-3 have done, to an alleged "When . . . then" construction. This proposal would make the first two verses dependent statements with the main verb coming in verse three. Certainly this grammatical feature can be illustrated elsewhere in the Hebrew Bible. But Genesis 1:1 is best taken as an independent statement pointing to an absolute beginning. This is indicated by the disjunctive accent used by the Massoretes (thereby showing their early understanding) under the word "In-the-beginning," the ancient versions with their indication that they understood the text as if it said "In *the* beginning," the position of the subject in verse 2, and the syntax of the three circumstantial clauses in verse 2 anticipating the main verb in verse 3. Genesis 1:1 argues for a wholly different point: an absolute beginning preceded by nothing other than God.[43]

Recently some new attempts have been made to propose a unitary reading for Genesis 1—11. Some are legitimately pointing out that many of the peculiarities of Genesis 1—11, which modern scholarship has interpreted as evidence for multiple authorship and disparate texts, are in fact present in other ancient texts.[44] In fact, the rest of the biblical text would fall apart were it not for these foundational concepts, settings, and the universal setting of Genesis 1—11. The gospel announced to Abraham in Genesis 12:2-3 is purposely extended to the mounting lists of genealogies and the table of seventy nations found in Genesis 10.

Genesis 1—11 must be taken on its own grounds rather than our imposing preconceived grids as shackles over the text in keeping with conventional scholarly wisdom of our day. A patient listening of the text, allowing for the uniqueness of its subject matter, will best proceed on much the same interpretive grounds as one would in interpreting narrative prose.

The Issue of the Conditional and Nationalistic Aspects of OT Prophecy

The OT prophets were God's messengers of salvation and judgment. More than mere fore-tellers, they were instead forth-tellers. Their great desire was to urge a moral revival, for the one word that epitomized the heart of their message was this: "turn" back to the Lord (Zech. 1:4).

But along with these messages urging national and personal revival were pointed words of deliverance and devastating destruction. So perfectly merged were many of these dual appendages to the prophet's call for repentance and a full turning back to God that contemporary scholars still debate whether the salvation or judgment message was the original word that accompanied the invitation. Once again, moderns have projected their own cultural biases and preferences over the text to the disadvantage of the BC speaker, much less God. A prophet, it was argued, could not represent both judgment and blessing; he had to be characterized by either one or the other.

But what has been lost by our generation of Bible readers, much less by the scholars, has been the key role that Leviticus 26 and Deuteronomy 28, with their presentation of alternative prospects depending on the response of the people, have played in the thinking and speaking of the prophets. There are literally hundreds of allusions and quotations from these two chapters in the major and minor prophets of the OT. And what is more important, these two chapters envisaged the prospect of either blessing (for obedience) or curses (for persistent national disobedience).

While Leviticus 26 and Deuteronomy 28 make clear the conditional nature of the alternatives that they pose, this conditional nature is by no means always plainly stated in Scripture, especially in the OT prophets. Thus, one must understand some unexpressed but underlying condition in many of the cases where judgment is threatened in no uncertain terms. This principle is set forth in plain terms in Jeremiah 18:7-10:

> If at any time I announce that a nation or kingdom is to [be] uprooted, torn down and destroyed, and if that nation I warned repents of its evil, then I will relent and not inflict on it the disaster I had planned. And if at another time I announce that a nation or kingdom is to be built up and planted, and if it does evil in my sight and does not obey me, then I will reconsider the good I had intended to do to it.

Acting on this principle, Jeremiah pled with the people—"reform your ways and your actions" (Jer. 7:3; 26:13). If the people would have repented, in one sense, then God would have repented, in another sense, and changed the judgment He had threatened.

It is this same message that we continue to announce today, for the word given to Jeremiah had already been principlized and applied to any nation, or any kingdom, in any culture, and at any time. Our word is the same as Ezekiel's message in 18:30—"Repent! Turn away from all your offenses: then sin will not be your downfall."

Accordingly, the actual fulfillment of almost all prophecy (except the covenant God made with the seasons in Gen. 8:22, the promise God gave to Abraham, Isaac, Jacob, and David, [for the gifts and calling of God are irrevocable, Rom. 11:29], the New Covenant, and the promise of the new heavens and the new earth) depends on the moral and spiritual condition of those on whose ears the prophecies fall. Even when the text does not explicitly state an "unless," "if," or "providing that," this conditional aspect must be understood. The best example of these conditional prophecies in the prophets is the narrative about Jonah. Jonah feared that God would *not* bring the threatened judgment he announced, for Jonah knew that the mercy of God was always available right up to the last of the threatened forty days prior to the certain destruction of Nineveh. And indeed, what Jonah feared turned out to be correct.

Again, the present-day interpreter must be careful not to be trapped in a false equation of Israel with modern America (or some other twentieth-century nation) and start preaching or teaching a civil religion. The prophets were conscious of the fact that they were ministering to an audience larger than Israel or Judah. Large sections of their books were set aside for this purpose with the words often being delivered by ambassadors to the capitols (Jer. 27:3, 51:61). In addition, the nations are promised the same restoration to their countries as Israel was offered if they will meet God's same standard of repentance and righteousness (Jer. 12:14-17). Yahweh does not have two separate scales of justice and righteousness, one for the Jews and the other for the Gentile nations. There is only one standard and his very character sets the norm for truth, justice, and equity over the whole face of the earth.

God loves the peoples of the earth so much that when they will not listen to His word, He will speak to them through a series of increasingly more disastrous episodes in the natural world, the world of economics, and the world of international politics. Few passages illustrate this series effect more graphically than the set in Amos 4:6-12. In spite of being faced with one disaster after another, the refrain for each was the mournful chorus, "yet you have not returned to me, declares the Lord." Since they had been hardened to the word, and now hardened to famine, drought, blight, mildew, locusts, plagues, war casualties, and the overthrow of some of their cities; Israel must "prepare to meet [her] God." The end of all patience had arrived and the fall of Samaria had come!

This connection between the sin of the nation and the effect it has on the natural world must not surprise us, for the informing theology of the antecedent Scripture of Genesis 3 should have prepared us to expect that when men and women get into trouble, the natural world also suffers along with us since that order of creation was made for humanity and not vice versa. This state of affairs will continue until in the coming redemption when we see Christ the whole creation, which groans and labors presently, will also find its release and redemption (Rom. 8:19-21).

But what of the fore-telling? The prophets did predict the future. Those who deny this must take an opposing position to our Lord and to His apostles. Did not Peter assert most clearly that David also was a "prophet" and that "he spoke of the resurrection of Christ" by "seeing what was ahead" when he affirmed in Psalm 16:8-11 that his *hasid*, "Holy One," would not see corruption

(Acts 2:29-31).[45] The prophets were aware of what they prophesied; it was only the "time and the circumstances of the time" (1 Pet. 1:10-12) that they did not know.[46] Indeed, it is incorrect to say that the prophets wrote better than they knew. How could revelation be better than itself? And if the answer be that there is a *sensus plenior,* a *pesher* meaning or some mysterious meaning which God meant, but which His prophets had no idea what He was saying, we will counter by noting that whatever else that meaning is, it is not Scripture. By its very nature Scripture is what is written in the grammar and syntax. But if these alleged surplus meanings are not found in the text, but are somehow written between the lines or found later on in the testament, then we declare that such meanings are not "Scripture," i.e. they are not written. And that is fatal for all such theories. On the other hand, if they are taught in the NT, then let us go to that passage for instruction on that point without importing the meaning in a backward flow of eisegesis over the OT.

Unfortunately, all too many read predictive prophecy in the OT as if they need only focus on the isolated word and the NT or fulfilling event. This turns the OT into a happy hunting ground for promise and fulfillment, concentrating only on the two ends of the spectrum with little attention to the original setting and no attention to the intervening times and actions of God that contributed to that same word-event continuum.

Such a distortion of prophecy often yielded a double sense to the predicted words, the BC word and the AD fulfillment. But this bifurcation runs counter to the single-meaning hermeneutic discussed in our introduction and it ultimately ends up forcing us to decide either to go wholly with the BC setting and application of the text or with its AD fulfillment. This is unnecessary.

Instead, we would propose that the OT predictions be handled by what Willis J. Beecher called a "generic prediction":[47]

> A generic prediction is one which regards an event as occurring in a series of parts, separated by intervals, and expresses itself in language that may apply indifferently to the nearest part, or to the remoter parts, or to the whole—in other words, a prediction which, in applying to the whole of a complex event, also applies to some of its parts.

Thus, there are three aspects to be embraced in our interpretation of the prophets: (1) the divine word, (2) the near fulfillments and the events in history whereby God continued to keep that word alive awaiting its final fulfillment, and (3) to climactic fulfillment in NT or apocalyptic times. If this perspective were to be outlined, it would appear somewhat like the sights on a gun barrel in which the closest sight could represent the first and nearest fulfillment of that word in the prophet's own day and context. The sight out at the end of the gun barrel would represent the climactic fulfillment. Only when the near and the climactic were lined up and shared in their common properties could the concept of their single meaning be grasped. Thus, the prophet Joel saw an immediate relief to the locust plague and the prediction of the Day of the Lord when God sent the immediate restoration of the land in Joel 2:19-27. But that same concept of the Day of the Lord was also lined up with the coming of the Holy Spirit at Pentecost and the return of our Lord at His second coming (Joel 2:28 to 3:21). The Day of the Lord was not a single twenty-four hour day; instead, it was the whole series of events when God acted in either judgment or salvation demonstrating that He was God over all things. Likewise, 1 John 2:18 warned that the "antichrist" was coming, but in fact, "even now many antichrists *have come*." In a similar manner, Elijah the prophet must come before that great and dreadful day of the Lord (Mal. 4:5). But Jesus both affirmed that Elijah had already come in his "spirit and power" in the person of John the Baptist, and that Elijah still must come in the future (Matt. 11:41; Luke 1:17; Matt. 17:11).[48]

Prophecy is both fore-telling and forth-telling, but the major emphasis falls on forth-telling. It remains totally relevant for the contemporary needs of the Church and must be shared if we, like the apostle Paul, are to "proclaim the whole counsel of God" to our generation (Acts 20:27).

The Issue of the Critical Methods of Interpreting the OT

It would be wrong to deny a legitimate place to a carefully defined critical investigation of the OT. Unfortunately, most critical methods advocated today have a heavy overlay of philosophical assumptions. No longer does criticism imply the investigation of issues, such as date, authorship, purpose, audience for which the book was intended, literary format, and the like. Instead, criticism carries the first definition of the *Oxford English Dictionary* meaning, "The action of criticizing, or passing judgment upon the qualities or merits of anything; faultfinding, censure." Actions suggested in this definition tend to set the critic above the text of Scripture. Is it any wonder that that same critic cannot stand under the Word of God and have that Word judge him or her?

One of the oldest of the critical methods was the "historical-critical" method. It "is not a uniform method but rather a set of assumptions thought to be operative in doing historical research."[49] These assumptions may be summarized as: (1) autonomy, the researcher can make up his or her own mind in light of the evidence, (2) analogy, the credibility of a past event is to be judged by its similarity to our present day experience, and (3) causality, each piece of evidence is part of a cause and effect series.[50]

The effect of the historical-critical method has been to set up a discrepancy between the portrayal of salvation-history found in the declarations of OT faith and the picture of history constructed by critical study. But a faith torn loose from its historical moorings is not a biblical faith. After all, we confess in the Apostles' Creed that "he suffered under Pontius Pilate, was crucified and buried. The third day he rose again." There certainly are historical roots to our faith. Mr. Lessing's "ditch" is bridged by the joining the facts of history with the values and significances set in the divine revelation of the word.

Ernst Troeltsch (1865-1923) systematized the historical-critical method with his three inseparable principles: criticism (our judgments about the past are not true or false, but possess either greater or lesser probability), analogy (our present experience is analogous with the past so that there are no occurrences outside this framework), and the principle of universal correlation (historical data are so interrelated and dependent that no change can occur in this historical nexus without a change in all that surrounds it).[51] Central to Troeltsch's historical-critical view was his principle of analogy. History, for him, had to be limited to our current range of experience and knowledge.

But Troeltsch was overly confident when he reduced all reality to our current range of experience and turned a *method* for investigating history into a *theory of reality*, according to Wolfhart Pannenberg.[52] Some events, Pannenberg warned, may burst our analogies and expose our own limitations when we set up our experience as the complete range of what is possible. Instead of insisting on this *negative* use of analogy (wherein an event is judged as doubtful since there are no other similar events which conform to our "critically informed beliefs about the world), Pannenberg suggests a *positive* use of analogy (wherein an event is judged to be *more likely* an historical event if it is known from other sources).

Pannenberg also stressed the original unity of historical facts and their meaning. The modern dichotomy between fact and meaning is itself an interpretation grounded in current historico-philosophical premises.[53] As Roland DeVaux argued in 1965 before the Society for Biblical Literature, "If the historical faith of Israel is not in a certain way founded in *history*, this faith is erroneous and cannot command my assent."[54] Yes, in some ways, "If Jericho be not razed, our faith is in vain."[55]

Recently George Ramsey has taken to task all who trust the reliability of the OT by saying that these evangelicals let the OT get off too easily: First they establish as probable that the past events and the claimed miracles did take place and were not fictitious; then they ask what happened in these OT events? But their answers are a foregone conclusion, moans Ramsey.

Is there an evangelical alternative model to the ones being proposed by theories dominated by negative criticism which has tended to degenerate into another faith system of its own? We believe there is. Nigel Cameron, using Stephen Toulmin's *The Uses of Argument*, has given us a whole new anatomy for using the various critical methods in ways that will help rather than detract.[56]

Instead of beginning with the phenomena of the OT (such as alleged historical improbabilities, insufficient evidence, modification of the materials, discrepancies between and within accounts, parallels with nonbiblical accounts, etc.),

Cameron proposes to start with the text of the OT and take it on its own terms. This procedure is much like our American system of jurisprudence: a person [or in this case, a text] is innocent until proven guilty. This would be followed with the biblical warrants for what the Bible says is true, viz., the views of Jesus on the text, the claims that the text makes for itself, and the testimony of the Church over the centuries.

It is only at this point that the qualifiers are introduced. Here is where compelling historical (or of other types) evidence to the contrary would now be introduced. It is not a question whether we will use the historical method, or any other critical method for that matter. It is only a question as to where it will appear. Will we introduce it as a warrant for reading the text as modern scholars do, or will we reserve it as a possible qualifier on the condition that it supplies a rebuttal to the data of the text and the warrants given in Jesus' view and the claims of the text?[57]

Here is where the battle for or against the Bible is being waged most fiercely. Again we assert that it is not a question as to whether we will use many of the critical methods. It is a question as to where they appear in our procedures. And it is also a question as to what we may expect from them?

Whether the method is Form Criticism, Redaction Criticism, Canon Criticism, Structuralism, or New Criticism, they cannot separately or collectively constitute one "valid" way of handling the text or help us arrive at some unique position from which to view the text authentically.[58] For example, the search to get behind the text is just as flawed as the attempt to rise above the grammatical, syntactical controls of the text and to achieve a brand new level of meaning which is uniquely my own.

Our conclusion circles back to where we began: The hermeneutics of the OT depend on our coming to terms with what the writer meant by what he had written in the text. Meaning cannot be vested in a text abstracted from its writer, in a narrative, a canon or an interpreter's own projections over the text; it must be attached to the author's own truth-intention as signaled by his use of his grammar, syntax, and vocabulary. Scripture was meant to be read and understood. Anything that helps that process ought to be welcomed. But if the method impedes understanding by requiring unnecessary and premature commitments as a price for modernity, we will resist these autocratic demands and insist that the methods serve the goals and not vice versa.

Scripture can be put into terms that Alice can understand. The church must not assume the autocratic posture of Humpty Dumpty—even if we always do pay extra when we make the words do a lot of work. Verbal meanings will always be connected with authorial truth-intentions or we will pay extra for refusing to agree—communication itself will cease. And there will be no word from God for a waiting generation.

Notes

1. This citation from Lewis Carroll has become a favorite as can be witnessed by its appearance in E. D. Hirsch, *The Aims of Interpretation* (Chicago: University of Chicago Press, 1976), pp. 51-52; Perry B. Yoder, *Toward Understanding the Bible* (Newton, Kansas: 1978), p. 1; James D. Strauss, "Hermeneutics, Intentionality, and Authoritative Scripture: Whose Meaning is Significant?" *A Journal For Christian Studies* 6 (1986-87):39-40.

2. W. K. Wimsatt and Monroe Beardsley, "The Intentional Fallacy," *Swanee Review,* 54 (1946). Reprinted in William K. Wimsatt, Jr., *The Verbal Icon: Studies in the Meaning of Poetry* (Lexington, Ken.: 1954), pp. 3-18; also reprinted in D. Newton-de-Molina, ed., *On Literary Intention* (Edinburgh: Edinburgh University Press, 1976), pp. 1-13. This view holds that a literary work is autonomous from its author and that it is a fallacy to look for what the author meant to say by his or her use of the words in the text.

3. E. D. Hirsch, Jr., *Validity in Interpretation* (New Haven: Yale University Press, 1967), p. 31.

4. These five "meanings" were offered by G. B. Caird, *The Language of the Bible* (Philadelphia: Westminster Press, 1980), pp. 37-40.

5. P. D. Juhl, *Interpretation: An Essay in the Philosophy of Literary Criticism* (Princeton: Princeton University Press, 1980), p. 18. Also see Newton-de-Molina.

6. Hirsch, *Validity in Interpretation,* p. 45.

7. Two sources for initiation into this critical movement, each with complete bibliography, are Jane P. Tomkins, ed., *Reader-Response Criticism* (Baltimore: Johns Hopkins Press, 1980) and Susan R. Suleiman and Inge Crosman, eds., *The Reader in the Text* (Princeton: Princeton University Press, 1980).

8. Anthony C. Thiselton, "Reader-Response Hermeneutics, Action Models, and the Parables of Jesus," in Roger Lundin, Anthony C. Thiselton, and Clarence Walhout, *The Responsibility of Hermeneutics* (Grand Rapids: Eerdmans, 1985), p. 94.

9. Jacques Derrida, *Dissemination,* trans. B. Johnson (Chicago: University of Chicago, 1981).

10. See, for example, Roger Lundin, "Our Hermeneutical Inheritance," in Lundin, Thiselton, and Walhout, pp. 4-23.

11. Hans-George Gadamer, *Truth and Method,* trans. Garrett Barden and John Cumming (New York: Crossroad, 1982), pp. 239-240.

12. Walter C. Kaiser, Jr., "Legitimate Hermeneutics" in Norman L. Geisler, ed., *Inerrancy* (Grand Rapids: Zondervan, 1979), pp. 117-147; also reprinted in Donald K. McKim, ed., *A Guide to Contemporary Hermeneutics: Major Trends in Biblical Interpretation* (Grand Rapids, Eerdmans, 1986), pp. 111-141. Also, Moses Stuart, "Remarks on Hahn's Definition of Interpretation. . . . ," *The Biblical Repository* 1 (1831):139-59; and *idem,* "Are the Same Principles of Interpretation to be Applied to the Scripture as to Other Books?" *The Biblical Repository* 2 (1832):124-137.

13. For further details, see Walter C. Kaiser, Jr., "A Neglected Text in Bibliology Discussions: 1 Corinthians 2:6-16," *Westminster Theological Journal* 43 (1981):301-319.

14. Emil G. Kraeling, *The Old Testament Since the Reformation* (New York: Harper, 1955), p. 8. My most recent attempt to treat this issue of the Old Testament as *the* Christian problem can be found in Walter C. Kaiser, Jr., *Toward Rediscovering the Old Testament* (Grand Rapids: Zondervan, 1987).

15. A. H. J. Gunneweg, *Understanding the Old Testament* (Philadelphia: Westminster, 1978), p. 2.

16. I have discussed the concept of "Progressive Revelation" in Walter C. Kaiser, Jr., *Toward Old Testament Ethics* (Grand Rapids: Zondervan, 1983), pp. 60-64. See also James I. Packer, "An Evangelical View of Progressive Revelation," in Kenneth S. Kantzer, ed., *Evangelical Roots: A Tribute to Wilbur Smith* (Nashville, Nelson, 1978), pp. 143-158.

17. John Goldingay, *Theological Diversity and the Authority of the Old Testament* (Grand Rapids: Eerdmans, 1987), pp. 15-25. While we concur with Goldingay's first two examples of contradiction, we cannot agree with his last two categories: substantial contradiction (which is not merely verbal or contextual, but conceptual and real), and fundamental contradiction (a basic disharmony on the ethical or religious level). If these latter two were true, which we deny, when could one expect to find theological coherence and religious authority in the OT? For my answers to many of these charges, see Walter C. Kaiser, Jr., *Hard Sayings of the Old Testament* (Downers Grove, Illinois: InterVarsity Press, [July] 1988).

18. See Goldingay, pp. 25-28 for this list of objections. Also see Paul Hanson, "The Theological Significance of Contradiction Within the Book of the Covenant," in George W. Coats and Burke O. Long, eds., *Canon and Authority: Essays in Old Testament Religion and Theology* (Philadelphia: Fortress Press, 1977), pp. 110-131.

19. M. T. O'Donovan, "The Possibility of a Biblical Ethic," *Theological Students Fellowship Bulletin* 67 (1973):15-23. Advised O'Donovan, The search for diversity is as much ". . . the result of [a] prior methodological decision as is the search for harmony, and cannot be defended on purely empirical grounds," (p. 19). See my fuller discussion of this issue in *Toward Old Testament Ethics*, pp. 24-29, and Walter C. Kaiser, Jr., "Ethics in the Bible," *Layman's Bible Dictionary* (Nashville: Holman, forthcoming).

20. Goldingay, pp. 25-26.

21. Gerhard Hasel, *Old Testament Theology: Basic Issues in the Current Debate*, rev. ed. (Grand Rapids, Eerdmans, 1975), p. 100. See his note 121 for the bibliography of others who hold this view.

22. Bertil Albrektson, *History and the Gods* (Lund: C. W. K. Gleerup Peno, 1967), pp. 68-77, especially p. 77.

23. Walter C. Kaiser, Jr., "The Identification of a Canonical Theological Center," in *Toward an Old Testament Theology* (Grand Rapids: Zondervan, 1978), pp. 20-40. See also Walter C. Kaiser, Jr., "Promise," *Layman's Bible Dictionary*. Also see Walter C. Kaiser, Jr., *Toward Rediscovering the Old Testament* (Grand Rapids: Zondervan, 1987), pp. 83-100.

24. Willis J. Beecher, *The Prophets and the Promise* (Grand Rapids: Baker, 1970), especially "The Promise-Doctrine as Taught in the New Testament," pp. 175-194.

25. Alfred Edersheim, *The Life and Times of Jesus the Messiah*, 2 vols. (Grand

Rapids, Eerdmans, 1953) 2:710-741. See also Kaiser, "The Old Testament as a Messianic Primer," in *Toward Rediscovering the Old Testament,* pp. 101-120.

26. David Berger and Michael Wyschogrod, *Jews and "Jewish Christianity"* (New York: Ktav, 1978), p. 36. A fine rebuttal can be found in E. J. Young, *The Book of Isaiah,* 3 vols. (Grand Rapids, Eerdmans, 1965) 1:332-333. See Kaiser, *Toward Rediscovering the Old Testament,* pp. 105-106.

27. Gerald Sigal, *The Jew and the Christian Missionary: A Jewish Response to Missionary Christianity* (New York: Ktav, 1981), pp. 80-82.

28. Walter C. Kaiser, Jr., *The Uses of the Old Testament in the New* (Chicago: Moody, 1985), pp. 17-57.

29. C. E. B. Cranfield, "St. Paul and the Law," *Scottish Journal of Theology* 17 (1964): 43-68.

30. Kaiser, "Applying the Principles of the Civil Law: Deuteronomy 25:4; 1 Corinthians 9:8-10," in *The Uses of the Old Testament in the New,* pp. 197-220; also Walter C. Kaiser, Jr., "A Case for a Single Biblical Ethic in Business," in the Baylor University series of volumes, *Foundational Questions to a Biblical View of Business* (Colorado Springs: Navigator Press, forthcoming).

31. Stephen A. Kaufman, "The Structure of the Deuteronomic Law," *MAARAV* 2 (1978-79):105-158; John H. Walton, "Deuteronomy: An Exposition of the Spirit of the Law," *Grace Theological Journal* 8 (1987):213-225; Kaiser, "The Law of Deuteronomy," in *Toward Old Testament Ethics,* pp. 127-137.

32. Kaiser, *Toward Rediscovering the Old Testament,* pp. 155-166; also ibid., "A Case for a Single Biblical Ethic in Business," pp. 1-24.

33. Luke T. Johnson, "The Use of Leviticus 19 in the Letter of James," *Journal of Biblical Literature* 101 (1982):391-401; Kaiser, "Applying the Principles of the Ceremonial Law: Leviticus 19 and James," in *The Uses of the Old Testament in the New,* pp. 221-224.

34. Robert Alter, *The Art of Biblical Narrative* (New York: Basic Books, 1981), pp. 3-22. Note the growing body of literature on this problem: Walter C. Kaiser, Jr., "The Use of Narrative in Expository Preaching," in *Toward an Exegetical Theology: Biblical Exegesis for Preaching and Teaching* (Grand Rapids: Baker, 1981), pp. 197-210; Sidney Greidanus, *Sola Scriptura: Problems and Principles in Preaching Historical Texts* (Toronto: Wedge, 1970); and Carl G. Kromminga, "Remember Lot's Wife: Preaching Old Testament Narrative Texts," *Calvin Theological Journal* 18 (1983): 33 ff.

35. This view is classically set forth by John Skinner, *A Critical and Exegetical Commentary on Genesis,* 2nd ed. (Edinburgh: T & T Clark, 1963), p. v.

36. Hermann Gunkel, *Das Buch Genesis,* (1922), pp. viii-xiv; also see John L. McKenzie, "The Literary Characteristics of Genesis 2-3," *Theological Studies* 15 (1954):541-572. See Walter C. Kaiser, Jr., "The Literary Form of Genesis 1-11," in *New Perspectives on the Old Testament,* ed. J. Barton Payne (Waco, Texas: Word, 1970), pp. 48-65.

37. Claus Westermann, *Genesis 1—11: A Commentary,* trans. John J. Scullion (Minneapolis: Augsburg, 1984), p. 4.

38. For representatives, see Bernhard W. Anderson, *Understanding the Old Testa-*

ment (Englewood Cliffs, N.J.: Prentice Hall, 1957), p. 385, note 11: "The Hebrew word for 'deep' *(tehom)* is equivalent to the Babylonian word for Tiamat; here we have a distant echo of the mythology of the ancient world;" Norman Gottwald, *A Light to the Nations* (New York: Harper, 1959), p. 457: "The Priestly term *tehom,* "the deep" is linguistically related to Babylonian Tiamat . . .;" and B. Davie Napier, *Song of the Vineyard* (New York: Harper, 1962), pp. 48-49.

39. T. H. Gaster, "Cosmogony," *The Interpreter's Dictionary of the Bible* (New York: Abingdon, 1962), 1:702; The same basic illustration is repeated in Sidney H. Hooke, *In the Beginning,* of *The Clarendon Bible* (Oxford: Clarendon, 1947) 6:20; Nahum M. Sarna, *Understanding Genesis* (New York: McGraw-Hill, 1966), p. 5, and many other volumes.

40. See for further support of our position, R. Laird Harris, "The Bible and Cosmology," *Bulletin of the Evangelical Theological Society* 5 (1962):11-17; ibid., "The Meaning of the Word Sheol as Shown by Parallels in Poetic Texts 4 (1961):129-135.

41. Wilfred G. Lambert, "A New Look at the Babylonian Background of Genesis," *Journal of Theological Studies,* New Series 16 (1965):292. Lambert made this comment in the context of noting that the Sumerian prototype of the flood story (1800 BC), nor any other, had any reference to the birds in Genesis 8:6-12! No copies earlier than 750 BC had this reference on Tablet XI, one of the most impressive parallels. Lambert, nevertheless, preferred to "hold that there is a certain dependence of the Hebrew writers on a Mesopotamian tradition"!

42. The Gilgamesh Epic is the name of the Babylonian flood story.

43. A good argument for these same points is made by Gerhard F. Hasel, "The Polemic Nature of Genesis Cosmology," *Evangelical Quarterly* 46 (1974):81-102; ibid., "Recent Translations of Gen 1:1," *The Bible Translator* 22 (1971):154-168; ibid., "The Significance of Cosmology in Genesis 1 in Relation to Ancient Near Eastern Parallels," *Andrews University Seminary Studies* 10 (1972):1-20.

44. Provisionally see Isaac M. Kikawada and Arthur Quinn, *Before Abraham Was: The Unity of Genesis 1–11* (Nashville: Abingdon, 1985). But note the critical review, P. Kyle McCarter, Jr., "A New Challenge to the Documentary Hypothesis," *Bible Review* 4 (1988):34-39.

45. Kaiser, "Foreseeing and Predicting the Resurrection: Psalm 16 and Acts 2:29-33," in *The Uses of the Old Testament in the New,* pp. 25-41. Note also ibid., "Respecting the Old Testament Context: Matthew's Use of Hosea and Jeremiah: Hosea 11:1 and Jeremiah 31:15," pp. 43-57.

46. Kaiser, *The Uses of the Old Testament in the New,* pp. 18-23.

47. Willis J. Beecher, *The Prophets and the Promise* (Grand Rapids: Baker, [1905] 1970), p. 130.

48. Kaiser, "Witnessing and Expecting the Arrival of Elijah: Malachi 4:4-5," *The Uses of the Old Testament in the New,* pp. 77-88; ibid., "Participating in and Expecting the Day of the Lord: Joel 2:28-32," pp. 89-100.

49 Archie L. Nations, "Historical Criticism and the Current Methodological Crisis," *Scottish Journal of Theology* 36 (1983):63.

50. For a good critic of this method, see George A. Kelly, *The New Biblical Theorists: Raymond E. Brown and Beyond* (Ann Arbor, Mich.: Servant, 1983), pp. 21 *ff.*

51. For bibliography and further discussion, see Kaiser, *Toward Rediscovering the Old Testament*, pp. 59-67.

52. Wolfhart Pannenberg, *Basic Questions in Theology* (Philadelphia: Fortress, 1970-71), 1:39-53.

53. Wolfhart Pannenberg, "The Revelation of God in Jesus Christ," *Theology as History* (New York: Harper and Row, 1967), p. 127 and Gerhard F. Hasel, *Old Testament Theology: Basic Issues in the Current Debate*, rev. ed. (Grand Rapids, Eerdmans, 1984), p. 101.

54. Roland DeVaux, "Method in the Study of Early Hebrew History," in *The Bible in Modern Scholarship*, ed. J. P. Hyatt (Nashville: Abingdon, 1965), p. 16.

55. This statement is put in the form of a question and answered negatively in George W. Ramsey, *The Quest of the Historical Israel* (Atlanta: Knox, 1981), pp. 107-124.

56. Nigel M. de S. Cameron, "Inspiration and Criticism: The Nineteenth-Century Crises," *Tyndale Bulletin* 35(1984):138; Stephen Toulmin, *The Uses of Argument* (Cambridge: Cambridge University, 1958).

57. For a fuller statement and defense of what we have outlined here, see Walter C. Kaiser, Jr., *Toward Rediscovering the OT*, pp. 59-79.

58. This view was set forth with unusual candor by John Barton, *Reading the Old Testament: Method in Biblical Study* (Philadelphia: Westminster, 1984), pp. 77-78.

6
THE MATCHLESS LOVE OF GOD
Jerry Vines

You probably don't need to turn in your Bible, but maybe you would like to turn in your Bible to my text for the message tonight: "For God so loved the world that He gave his only begotten Son that whosoever believeth in Him should not perish but have everlasting life."

In a magnificent sermon on this particular text, Dr. Bill Hull recounts that in 1878 archaeologists uncovered in the sands of Egypt a giant granite shaft. Immediately dubbed Cleopatra's needle, it was carried to London, England, and there erected. They determined that they would put a time vault in the base of the shaft and that in the vault they would place some memorabilia of that particular age. So, in the vault they put some coins and some currency of the time. They put a daily newspaper. They put some items of clothing. They included some toys that children used at that particular time. Photographs were added to give people an idea of what kind of world it was at that particular time. Then it was decided that a committee would select the greatest text in the Bible and include that text in the time vault. The committee met, and they all agreed. In 220 known languages and dialects of the time, they put John 3:16 into the vault.

I think all of us would agree that if not the greatest, this is one of the greatest texts in the all of the Bible. It has been called "the gospel in a nutshell." For here we find the mind of God, the emotion of God, and the will of God revealed in a single statement. There is enough gospel in this one verse of Scripture that if all the other verses in the Bible were lost and this one remained, enough would remain for anybody in the world to be saved who wants to be saved. So, it may, indeed, be the greatest text in all of the Bible. It has also been referred to as the inexhaustible text.

Henry Morehouse was a young preacher in England who began preaching at age sixteen and died at age thirty-three. You may remember that Morehouse was the one who influenced D. L. Moody to turn his preaching in the direction of the love of God. Here's the unusual thing about Morehouse: Morehouse never changed his text. His first sermon was on John 3:16, his last sermon was on John 3:16; and all of the sermons between had as their text, John 3:16. Oh, he preached a lot of different sermons, but he always used as his text,

John 3:16. There are many preachers in this building tonight. You and I could preach a long, long time. We would never exhaust the meaning that is found in this simple statement in the Word of God.

F. W. Borum, in his book on sermon texts that changed the lives of great figures in church history included at the conclusion of the book a chapter which he called everybody's text, and it was John 3:16. Here's a verse that is so simple that a little child can read it and be saved, yet so profound that scholars have never been able to plumb the depths of its meaning.

Of course, I have an impossible task. I have assigned to myself to describe the indescribable, to explain the inexplainable, and to try to exhaust the inexhaustible. Who can be adequate to deal adequately with the marvelous truth of God's love?

> Could we with ink the ocean fill?
> And, were the skies of parchment made?
> Were every man on earth, every stalk on earth a quill.
> And every man a scribe by trade.
> To ride the love of God above, would drain the ocean dry,
> nor could the scroll contain the whole though stretched from sky to sky.

So, for a little while tonight I want to talk to you about God's love as revealed in John 3:16. There are several statements I want to make about God's love from this verse.

Number one, God's love is incredible. I learned this from the opening phrase, "For God so loved the world." The word translated love there is the word *agape*. The Greeks used several words to describe and define love. One of those words was the word *eros* which would refer to a sensual love, erotic love. So odious is that word that it never finds its way into the sweet soil of Scripture. Another word is the word *philos,* which would refer to social love, affection, or friendship. That word was so corrupted that it was not included as it should have been, perhaps, in the New Testament Scriptures. But, the word that is found here is *agape,* the love of God, spiritual love, love to the highest degree.

God's love is incredible because of its origin. It is God who so loved the world. When that statement was first made in the New Testament world, it was an absolutely astounding and astonishing concept. It never occurred to them to think that God was a God of love. The gods of that time were gods who were capricious and vindictive and filled with judgment. But the Lord Jesus came, and He talked about a loving Father. The Bible says he that loveth not knoweth not God, for God is love. There are many wonderful manifestations of the character and attributes of God given in the Bible. But the first and fundamental truth of God is that God is love.

God's love is incredible also because of its incredible overflow. Notice in the text it says for God so loved the world. And the little adverb there could be translated "for God in this manner loved the world." Some prefer to put it "for God so greatly loved the world." Of course, that reminds us of the overflowing nature of God's love. The tense of the verb points us to eternity past. There was a time when you began to love your wife. There was a time when you began to love your children. There was never a time when God began to love you. Jeremiah 31:3 says that God has loved us with an everlasting love, and that word really means from vanishing point to vanishing point. The young people would put it this way, God's love is an out-of-sight love. That simply means before you were born. Before this world was founded, there was never a time in eternity past when God didn't love you. And, of course, it means there never will be a time when God will not love you. For you see, when you and I are gone and the stars fall from their sockets and when time is no more, there will never be a time when God does not love.

The love of God is not a trickling stream but an overflowing river. God's love is not a leaky faucet but a bottomless ocean. God's love is not a flickering candle. The love of God is a blazing sunrise. The love of God is abundant, overflowing love. It seems that the Apostle Paul was wrestling with a concept of the overwhelming nature of God's love, when in Ephesians, chapter 3, verses 18 and 19, he says that we may be able to comprehend with all saints the breadth and the depth and the length and the height and to know the love of Christ that passes all knowledge. God's love has dimensions to it. God's love is so wide, that it reaches out to all men everywhere. God's love is so long that there is no one beyond the reach of His reconciling arm. God's love is so deep that it reaches down to the uttermost sinner. God's love is so high that it takes that hell-deserving sinner and carries him all the way into heaven.

God's love is an incredible love because of its object. God so loved the world. God so loved the cosmos, not the cosmos of nature but the cosmos of sinful people, the cosmos of men, women, boys, and girls everywhere. This is a statement of the all inclusive nature of the love of God. This means that God loves all of the people of the world. God doesn't just love the American people. God loves all the people. God doesn't just love the white people. God loves all races of people. God doesn't just love good people, God loves all people. His love is amazing because of its object. Maybe that doesn't get to you, but let me move a little bit closer. It's one thing to say that God loves the world, let's move it a little closer. The Bible also says Christ loved the church and gave Himself for it. And, of course, we do know that He loves the redeemed. But maybe that doesn't grip your heart. Let's move it a little closer.

In Galatians, chapter 2, verse 20, Paul says, "I am crucified with Christ: nevertheless I live; yet not I, but Christ liveth in me: and the life which I now live in the flesh I live by the faith of the Son of God who loved me, and gave himself for me." Has it ever gripped your heart, friend, that God loves you?

I remember when I was a little boy in Sunday School, we used to sing a little song that went like this: "I am so glad that our Father in heaven tells of his love in the book he has given. Wonderful things in the Bible I see, this is the dearest that Jesus loves me."

I can't vouch for its truthfulness, but it does make good preaching. I heard about a great European theologian who had come over to America and was being interviewed by reporters. So one of the reporters asked him to share the most profound thought that ever gripped his mind. The theologian thought for a moment and then as tears welled up in his eyes he said, "Jesus loves me this I know for the Bible tells me so." If you and I really knew how much God loves us tonight, we'd never again be the same. God loves you so much it's as if you were the only person in all of the world.

Bill Hull shares an experience he had with a lady in his church. This particular lady had ten children. On an occasion he was talking with her about the large family she had, and he asked if sometimes because of the number of her children did she ever have a tendency to neglect a one of them. The mother said, "Oh, no, I never forget one of them, they're all precious to me." The love of God is like a mother's love. A mother's love operates not by the laws of division, one mother's heart divided ten ways, but it operates by the laws of multiplication, one mother's love multiplied ten times to include every child. God loves you totally and completely, and yet it does not diminish the love of God for every other creature on the face of the earth. Our hearts ought to be shouting as we contemplate the incredible nature of the love of God. God's love is incredible.

Now, secondly, I want to point out that God's love is not only incredible but also indisputable. You can't dispute the love of God. The second phrase says that He gave His only begotten Son. No man who understands the gift of God's Son, Jesus Christ, can ever question again the love of God. In Romans, chapter 5, verse 8, it says that God commendeth His love toward us in that while we were yet sinners, Christ died for us. And the word *commendeth* could be translated "exhibits" or "it proves His love toward us." The gift of God's Son puts beyond all question the indisputable nature of the love of God. The gift of God's Son was given definitely. There is something definite, affirmative, about the impact of the particular verb. Love is not merely an emotion, love is also a decision. We think so many times of love in terms of an emotion. I remember when I was a child we had a little poem about love and it went like this:

> Love is such a very funny thing
> it's shaped just like a lizard.
> It wraps its tail around your throat
> and goes right through your gizzard.

If you remember that old "puppy love," you remember how that was. But love's not just an emotion, love is a decision. Love always has to demonstrate itself. And love demonstrates its intensity by the degree to which it is willing to go.

I heard about a boy who wrote his girlfriend a love letter. He said, "Darling, I love you so much." He said, "I'd climb the highest mountain for you, darling." He said, "I'd swim the deepest river for you. I'd go through hail and snow just for you," and P.S., "If it doesn't rain on Friday night I'm coming over to see you."

God's love is a definite love in that God demonstrated, manifested His love toward us in that He sent His Son to be the propitiation for our sins. It's as if the Father surveyed the heavens and the universes, looking for one worthy to come. He looked at the seraphim and the cherubim, and they were not worthy. He looked at the angels and the archangels, and they would not do. Then His gaze fell upon the Son, and the Son was willing to come.

Have you ever thought how it must have been when Jesus left heaven. I can almost hear the angels as they said to Him, "Don't go down there, Jesus. They'll misunderstand and mistreat you. Don't go there, Jesus." On down He came, and as He came by Jupiter, maybe Jupiter shouted to its creator, "Don't go down there, Jesus. They'll lie on you, Jesus; they'll make fun of you; they'll mock you, Jesus." On down, down He came, down past the sun. And, the sun said, "Please don't go down there, Jesus. They'll drive nails in your hand. They'll ram a spear in your side." But down, down, down, down He came to this godless globe, to be born in a manger, to live in a little hick town, to die on a cross for our sins. Out of the ivory palaces into a world of woe, only His great eternal love made our Savior go. God gave His Son definitely.

God gave His Son uniquely. God so loved the world that He gave His only begotten Son. You recognize of course the word, *monogene*. I leave the full impact and the full meaning of that word to the scholars, but I would say that I would not be incorrect if I said that the word could be translated, "God gave His unique Son." God gave His only one of its kind Son. Though virgin birth may not be explicitly stated in the verse, it is certainly not excluded. The gift of God's Son was given in an absolutely unique way. There was a must about the incarnation of Christ. There was a must about the way Jesus Christ was born. There was mystery attached to it. The Bible says without controversy, great is the mystery of God manifested in the flesh.

When I was a pastor in Mobile, Alabama, I had a gynecologist in my church who at that time had delivered over 16,000 babies, more babies than the population of the little town I came from. I used to talk to him. I'd say, "Dr. Mitchell, please explain the meaning of birth to me." He'd give those long words, and I'd sit there like I understood everything he was saying. When he was over he would look at me and I'd look at him. We were aware of the fact that when you talk about birth you are in the realm of mystery. There is a mystery attached to the incarnation of Jesus Christ that defies the ability of man to understand or to explain. Dr. R. G. Lee put it this way: When Jesus was born, He was the only one ever born who had a heavenly father and no heavenly mother, who had an earthly mother and no earthly father. He's the only one ever born who was older than His mother and as old as His Father. Only Lee could put it that way.

Oh, yes, there is a must about it. I believe that there was a divine necessity attached to the virgin birth of Jesus Christ. You see the virgin birth is inseparately linked to two other essentials, to His subsitutionary atonement and to His sinless life. When Christ was conceived in the womb of the virgin Mary, the spirit of God short-circuited the sin cycle so that Christ was conceived without taint of human sin. God's son was uniquely born.

God gave His Son sacrificially. Some prefer to read it this way, "God gave up His Son." That's the way Moffett translates it. I do know in Romans 8, the Bible says, "He that spared not his own son but delivered him up for us all." You see, God not only gave His Son to the world, God gave His Son for the world. And all of Calvary is in that. God so loved the world that He gave up His Son, and, oh, what He gave Him up to. He gave Him up to the scourging as they ripped the back of the Lord Jesus Christ, and the blood fell from His back. After they had beaten Him within half an inch of His life, they took the Lord Jesus Christ and they dragged Him outside the city of Jerusalem to Golgatha, and there, amid the screaming and the spitting and the filth and the gore, they drove the bruised and bloody body of Jesus Christ to a cross, and they lifted that cross between heaven and hell, and dropped it into a hole prepared. Every movement sent pain running up and down His nervous system. His muscles pulled and His bones disjointed, and His lungs heaved, and His heart beat desperately. You and I will never understand what Jesus went through at Calvary's cross. None of the ransomed ever knew how deep were the waters crossed nor how dark was the night that the Lord passed through, ere He found his sheep that was lost. God *commended* His love. The term literally means "to put together." What it means is God put it all together at Calvary. God proved for all time and eternity His love for a fallen race when He gave up His Son to die. I don't ever want to get cold and callous to the cross. I want to stay so near the cross of Christ that it moves me, that it moves me to think of the gift of God's Son, our Savior, the Lord Jesus.

God's love is not only incredible, God's love is not only indisputable, but it is indispensable. You just can't live without it. The love of God is the only power that reaches humanity: God so loved the world that He gave His only begotten Son that whosoever believeth in Him. I'm glad He said, "Whosoever believeth in Him." I'm glad He didn't say that if Jerry Vines believeth in Him; it could be a case of mistaken identity. When I lived in Rome, Georgia, there was another man named Jerry Vines who lived in Rome. The reason I know that is that I got his bad bills. In fact, I got a letter from the water department one time that threatened to cut off my water if I did not pay my bill. That was fine with me because I was living on well water. They could cut off anything they wanted. It was a case of mistaken identity. But so there'll be no question about God's ability to reach to all men everywhere, the Bible says God so loved the world He gave His only begotten Son that who-so-ever. Go tell that old man tottering on his cane to a Christless eternity "whosoever." Tell that young person just beginning his career "whosoever." Go tell that businessman filling his pockets while his heart goes empty "whosoever." Go tell that single mother trying desperately to bring up those little ones without the aid of a father and a husband, go tell her "whosoever." If the world just knew that God loved them, I have a feeling you'd break the heart of many a one of them.

Recall the story of a shy rather unattractive little girl in a children's home who was something of a problem. The fact of the matter was they really were looking for an excuse to move her on to another home. One day they saw her steal across from the grounds of the home. They saw her climb up a tree and deposit some paper in one of the branches of the tree. When she climbed down and ran away, they rushed to the tree to see if they could find what it was that she put there. They climbed up the tree, got the paper, opened up the note, and it said, "To anybody who finds this, I love you." That's where you and I enter the picture. God is putting it in a book to say to anybody who finds this, "I love you." Our job is to go out there and tell people about it. God's love is indispensable. It's the only power that reaches humanity.

God's love is the only power that rescues from hell. "Should not perish." Look very closely at that little word "perish" and you will see worms crawling in that term. If you'll listen very carefully, you'll hear weeping and the gnashing of teeth in that worm. If you'll listen very carefully, you'll hear the screams of the doomed and the damned in that word. And I remind you that these words were evidently spoken by the lovely Lord Jesus, who had the tenderest heart that ever beat in a human breast. I have no problem with the doctrine of hell. The doctrine that gives me a problem is heaven. I can understand how there can be a hell for sinners like me to go to. What breaks me . . . what defies my understanding is how there can be a heaven for sinners like me to go to. Hell is God's insane asylum for the spiritually deranged. Hell is God's garbage dump of the universe, and Jesus said "should not perish"—do we really believe it? Do you really believe that people who die without Jesus Christ go to hell?

I have a dear preacher friend named Jess Henry. Some of you probably know Jess. I love him like a, well I can almost say like a great-grandfather; he's 80 years old. He has a unique background. A graduate of Georgia Tech, and having attended Southern Seminary, he is the only man I know who can give the lexical definition of all of the over 5,000 words in the Greek New Testament. He has been an evangelist all through the years. In fact, he has been known through his ministry as "Hell fire and damnation Henry." That's been a tag he's borne all through his ministry. I saw the hurt on his face one day as a smart-aleck preacher came up and said, "Well if it isn't 'old hell fire and damnation Henry.'" When the preacher left, with tears in his eyes, he looked at me and said, "You see Jerry," he said, "I don't only just believe there is a hell, I don't want anybody to go there."

You and I have to decide when we sit in our studies and look around at the finery of our churches whether Jesus meant what He said He meant when He said whosoever believeth in Him should not perish. It's the only power that rescues from hell.

Notice, "but have everlasting life." If you will look closely at that phrase, you will see gates of pearl and streets of gold. If you'll listen carefully to that phrase, you'll hear the anthems of angels and the shouts and songs of the saints. What a contrast. From hell to heaven in one brief statement. From the gory place to the glory place, from hell to heaven in one breath. But that's what the love of God can do. God's love is the only power that can redeem to a wonderful place called heaven. You see, man according to Old Testament Scripture is in a horrible pit of miry clay. He is sinking down in the depths of his sin. Mr. Pleasure comes by and looks at man in the pit and says, "Enjoy yourself." Mr. Morality comes along, looks in the pit at the sinner, and he says, "Improve yourself." Mr. Philosophy comes along, looks at the sinful man in the pit, and he says, "Understand thyself." Mr. Psychology comes along, and he says, "Know thyself." Mr. Religion comes along, and he says, "Save thyself." Then Jesus comes along, and he jumps down in the pit, and he lifts us out of the mire and the clay. "From sinking sand he lifted me; with tender hand he lifted me; from shades of night to planes of light; oh, praise his name; he lifted me."

It'll take heaven to unveil all of the meaning of the love of God. Not too far from here there used to be an old preacher and Bible teacher in one of our Baptist colleges named Charles Howard. I don't know if he's still alive. I used to hear Charles Howard preach, and I would cry for a week after he would preach. I remember him telling about a raw-boned farmer he married to a young lady there in his rural church community. Old Farmer John used tobacco. He was a poor man just getting started, and he was not able to buy his wife a wedding ring. She said, "John, I know you can't afford to buy me a wedding ring, but the truth of the matter is what I have always wanted is a string of real pearls. And John, if you ever get up any money and want to get me something, I'd like a string of real pearls."

Old John gave up his tobacco. He took his tobacco pouch, put it in the lower drawer, and every time he wanted some tobacco, he'd just put the money for it in the drawer. The years went by, and John became better off as a farmer. His wife became an invalid. He treated her with all the tenderness and the affection of a little child. On a wedding anniversary, Dr. Howard was invited to come and celebrate the anniversary supper. They had a lovely, country meal. After it was over, John picked up his wife, carried her into the living room to her favorite chair, and sat her down. He said, "Now close your eyes, don't peek." John went over to the lower shelf, pulled it out, reached in, got that tobacco pouch, opened it up and out of it he pulled a string of real pearls.

He went over to where she was and said, "Now don't open your eyes." And he latched that string of pearls around her neck, came around in front of her, and stood there beaming with pride and said, "All right, Sugar, open your eyes." When she did, her eyes fell on those pearls. And she said, "Oh, John, are they real?" He said, "You had better believe it." And she said, "Oh, John, they are so beautiful and so lovely. John, why did you do it?" That big raw-boned farmer fell on his knees and buried his face in her lap and he said, "Just because I love you."

Friends, one of these days we are going to leave this world, either by death or rapture. We are going to go home to heaven, and we'll see those gates of pearl, and we'll walk down those streets of gold, and we'll hear the anthems of the angels and the shouts of the redeemed of God. There in the presence of the Father perhaps you and I will say, "Father, you've done all of this, you've saved me, you've kept me out of hell, you've given me this wonderful eternity with you. Oh, Father, tell me why did you do it." Could it be that the Father will say, "Just because I love you"?

7
THE CHALLENGE OF BIBLICAL INTERPRETATION: WOMEN
James I. Packer

The subject under consideration is "The Challenge of Biblical Interpretation: Women." I start with a hermeneutical consideration. I start with one or two words about the situational background of this study, the background that is mine and the background that is yours because it is the background of our culture. The place and role of women in the church and community is a matter of intense discussion at this present time. Why should this be? The discussion as far as we are concerned has two distinct roots, two distinct sources, one of them secular and one properly Christian and churchly.

Take the secular one first. It is the question raised and pressed by so many women of securing freedom and justice and equality for women in the modern world. This is a question which the modern world raised for itself, but it presses now upon the church. Why does it arise? There are a number of reasons. Homemaking for most women is no longer a full-time job because of the mechanical aids that are available, and therefore life in the home leaves her with energy to spare. Luther's formula that a woman's life should be a matter of children, church, and kitchen (*Kinder, Kirche,* and *Kucher,* isn't it?), is unappealing to many women in the modern West. They become lonely, their homes contain no extended family for fellowship, they have no servants, there isn't a community within the house itself, and homemaking is not felt as a complete vocation. Further, the world welcomes women who leave the home and join the work force. The world has been doing that ever since the two world wars when women did such a significant job filling posts which men had left to go to the forces. Single women are expected to take their place in the work force. Married women are welcomed back into the work force just as soon as they like to come. But it is not the custom in our culture to pay the women always as well as the men are paid, and this is an irritant to career women and also to some mothers who have returned to work in hopes of hoisting the family income to a manageable level.

There is the further fact that we must acknowledge: Women have been hurt. They have been hurt in the world, where again and again they have been treated as second-class citizens to such an extent that a lady like Dorothy Sayers on one occasion wrote a very blunt essay "Are Women Human?" Women have been hurt in the home as well. There have been frustrating marriages. There have been abusive, neglectful, and domineering husbands, and there have been many abler, stronger, wiser wives who have felt that society was on the side of the husband who abused them and who have found that they are on the horns of a dilemma in the home. In any case they are unsatisfied, whether they accept or whether they challenge the inadequate leadership of the man to whom they are married. Out of all this has come the so-called women's movement, women's lib, the crusade for freedom and equality and justice, as it is announces itself. At the heart of it are hurt women, as I see it anyway, whose very energy in the cause arises out of the bad experience that they have had. So far as I can discern the purpose, it is to upstage men. To my mind, it is rivalry of a kind that is neither creative nor fulfilling. The church, as we know very well, is alternately attacked as a bastion of patriarchy and male dominance and appealed to to help change this situation out of compassion for women in trouble. That is the question which the world hashes over in relation to the position of women.

Alongside of that for us in the Christian church, there is a parallel question that needs to be distinguished quite sharply from the first one: How are we to secure the full use of women's gifts in ministry among the people of God. The New Testament proclaims that to every Christian, grace for service, gifts for service, are given by the Lord from His throne through the Holy Spirit. But the discussion of how to find and harness women's gifts in ministry unfortunately gets snarled up and skewed by being confused with the world's call for compassion, which has often, I think, created a bad conscience among Christian people because they have been prevailed on to believe that it is their fault. Then in the Christian church the folk at extremes rise up, take over the discussion, and lead it into fields of exploration which are not always very fruitful. There the liberal response is to call for the church to follow the world, to embrace the world's wisdom and the world's fashionable thoughts. Go that way and reshape your Christianity to make it fit in with, what you and I might call, the world's prejudices. Follow the world, climb on the secular bandwagon; that is the deepest motivation of liberal ethics. It is, of course, undiscerning and worldly in spirit. In practice, it is disastrous. I do not recommend any line of thought and action which would take that form. Following the world in this matter is not the way to go.

Then, at the other extreme there is the conservative reaction, which is no more than a reaction. Sometimes reactions are healthy. But they are not healthy if they remain reactions and do not issue in any constructive alternative. Here I am thinking of the reaction which would say all this talk about changing the woman's position in world and church is utterly misguided. Keep women in their traditional place. When folk say that, what they usually turn out to mean is what everybody else usually means when they talk about maintaining tradition on any point at all: keeping things the way they were about a hundred years ago. There was a good deal in the relation of the sexes a hundred years ago which, in my judgment, was manipulative and would better not be kept. In any case, I think it clear that mere negative reaction is never an adequate response to any problem among the people of God.

But the entire situation is one of real confusion. Much of the difficulty stems from a confusion of the world's question with the church's question. This results in a skewed discussion in which well meaning Christian people come to believe that the intra-church concern from women has to do with freedom, justice, and equality for women. I believe that to be a grave mistake. As a result of thinking in those terms, there are many bodies of opinion in the world church which say, "Well, surely the answer is to make able women into clergy persons and thus get them equal status with men and let them act as substitute men. That will fulfill their aspirations. That is what they want." My response is to say first that though it may be what some of them want, it is not, I believe, and here I speak as a Bible reader and a would-be theologian, what the Bible encourages women to want. Maybe they do want it, but should they? The question hangs in the air? Second, it is unlikely that this course of action will be a good solution to the problem despite all of the experience that's garnered sometimes from mission resources about how, in emergency situations, women have done a man's job as pastors of young congregations and so forth. This is so for several reasons.

First of all, to make a woman a clergy person is to give her status, but the question is about ministry. Second, just as in the family the ministry of mother and the ministry of father are two quite distinct sorts of ministry, though they belong together, so it is likely to be here. The clergy man's role and the clergy person's role has been defined as a man's job. It's been defined in terms of a male preacher/pastor/presbyter who teaches and rules, and I don't believe that we honor the order of creation if we simply draft women to be substitute men. That is not what God ever meant us to do. Third, only a few able women as compared with the number of troubled women will qualify for the clergy person's role, so you will have in the situation a very demeaning sort of tokenism which the women themselves are bound to feel. Just as in the early days of integration, the token Blacks felt it in American society. Fourth, I observe that the clergy man's role as defined in terms of the male presbyters which the New Testament knows, that role of ruling and teaching, is a role which many honest Bible students in the church believe to be improper for women. They believe, in fact, that the Bible actually forbids the role to women, and, therefore, if you push ahead with a policy of making women into presbyters, it is provocative and divisive in the body of Christ. Some churches, of course, have pushed ahead no matter what. My own Anglican communion is divided. There are women presbyters in the Anglican Church of Canada and in the Episcopal

Church in the States. There are no women clergy in the Church of England and very strong resistance to making any. The question is divisive; it creates strains and tensions. I do not think, frankly, that that is a wise way for the church to go, and I personally hope to see the day when enthusiasm for this course of action reduces to vanishing point.

At this point, I want to outline the hermeneutical factors that affect my study of the texts which have to do with the subject. To do so is only fair since these convictions will be reflected in my exposition. They are five in number.

One, I sympathize with women who have been hurt by men, and frankly I am ashamed for my sex. I am ashamed that some Christian men, even, have contributed to that misery and distress. The inhumanity of man to woman as I have met it over the years appalls me.

Second, I am opposed to everything that robs women of their dignity, the dignity that God gave them when He made them. So I am opposed to things like pornography, prostitution, and domestic dictatorship. I am opposed to everything else in home and society that falls short of love in the *agape* sense, love on the part of men toward women as the second sex. This is the attitude which should be found in all men toward all women.

Third, the concern for the future of the Western family ought to be animating us all. The family is dissolving away, and the grace of God in the family is suffering as a result. I think that the Western family calls for fresh investment of ourselves, and that's a word not only to fathers but to mothers also.

Fourth, I feel and wish to express strong zeal for every member ministry in the body of Christ, and that means every woman ministry as well as every man ministry in the body of Christ. So I accept the question about the ministry of women as a question which God is pressing on us these days.

Fifth, as I told you, I have a total lack of enthusiasm for women presbyters. I don't find myself able to say from Scripture that making women presbyters is explicitly forbidden, although I do think it plain that a woman in the order of God would not be sole pastor of a congregation; it is inappropriate certainly to give her that role. Whenever you do make a woman a presbyter, I think you show something less than respect for the created order of Genesis 2, of which I shall be speaking in a moment. I do not believe that this course of action is beneficial on the whole to women themselves, and I do believe that the answer to the real and pressing question about women's ministry lies elsewhere.

As I turn to the Scriptures, there are two interpretive guidelines to note. We are servants of Jesus Christ, and we had better say to ourselves explicitly that in this quest we are seeking the mind of Christ regarding women and their place in ministry in the church. Christ honored women as friends and disciples in the same way that He took men as friends and disciples. That is a clue. The mind of Christ, when we find it, will take the form of an interpretive scheme that does justice to all the Scripture, all the Scripture teaching about women, including

Scripture testimony to the way that Jesus regarded women in His only life. For Christ did own the Old Testament as the word of God and He did guarantee the New Testament to us as faithful witness to and interpretation of Himself. He guaranteed that by His promise of the Spirit. Now He rules us by the Bible as a whole. I think it not too much to say, and in preaching and teaching I constantly do say, our Lord Jesus tells us in effect if you want to be my faithful disciple, you must become the faithful disciple of this Book, this Book as a whole, in its totality, in the fullness of its teaching. Certainly, that is how it must be when our concern is with the woman question. We are New Testament believers; we live in the power of Christ's redemption. By bringing in the reality of redemption and establishing His kingdom, Jesus contextualized the Old Testament teaching which now has to be reapplied in the new situation, the kingdom situation as we may call it. That is one of the things we have to do in our interpreting of the word. Yet, I think we shall see it is quite wrong to suppose that the order of redemption in any way cancels out the roder of creation or that the biblical thinking about women's ministry runs counter to the Old Testament pattern reaffirmed in the New Testament of male primacy. Here, therefore, I want to warn against another false trail which some evangelicals have followed: the attempt to pour the biblical material into a feminist pattern of interpretation which does seem to dismiss the creation pattern of male primacy. Paul Jowett in his book *Man as Male and Female* tried to explore that route. Feminists like Ruether and Fiorenza have gone further. They take feminine experience, that is the experience of modern Western woman, as an epistomological principle to which they relativize the Bible. They thus drive a wedge between Jesus and the Old Testament, and it seems to me misinterpret much of the biblical teaching on our subject. That is not the route to go.

Second remember that we seek spiritual understanding, understanding, that is, from the Holy Spirit. This understanding will be reached by the route which Godimer has called fusing of the horizons, the correcting and amplifying and deepening and enriching of our thoughts by what comes over our horizon out of the word of God. We may find that we have prejudices that need to be exposed and corrected, for after all we are children of our culture and have in our minds, inevitably, stereotypes of male and female roles, which may or may not be biblical. We shall have to test them and see, and this I believe to be a theological truth which we need to bear in mind in this investigation in a very direct way. None of us fully knows ourselves. Therefore, none of us fully knows our own sexual identity at any point at all. None of us fully knows what it means to be either a man or a woman. None of us fully knows any of the dimensions of our own human existence. One day we shall know as we are known. One day these things will be clearer to us than they are now. But since at present we do not as a matter of fact fully understand our own sexual identities, we ought to put our hand on our mouth when we find ourselves tempted, having read something in the Bible that doesn't immediately appeal to us to say, "Well, that chap didn't understand about women, or didn't understand about men." That is to get the matter exactly backward. It is we who don't understand what it means to be men and women, and as for the rest of the law of God so in this area of relationships, we only find out the truth about our natures as we obey the world of God implicitly. I think that is a profound point of wide application with a very specific application here.

All that being clear, I move now to survey the biblical material. I am going to explore, sketchily, three matters: one, the co-equal responsibilities of women and men before God on which we shall find that the Scripture is clear; two, the cooperative relations of women with men in society about which we shall also find that the Bible has things to say; and three, the contributing roles of women alongside men in the home and the church.

As to the first of those topics, the co-equal responsibilities of women and men before God, the inferiority of women, essential or consequent, has in the past been affirmed quite often in the church. Aquinas, for instance, in the thirteen century affirmed the essential inferiority of women. Listen to this, "As regards the individual nature, woman is defective and misbegotten, for the active force in the male seed tends to the production of a perfect likeness in the masculine sex, while the production of women comes from a defect in the active force or from some material indisposition or even from some external influence such as a south wind." In the early third century, Tertullian affirmed what I call the consequent inferiority of women. He affirmed it like this: "God's sentence hangs still over all your sex and his punishment weighs down upon you. You are the devil's gateway. You are she who first violated the forbidden tree and broke the law of God. It was you who coaxed your way around him whom the devil had not the force to attack," etc. You are Eve and you are a rotter; that is what Tertullian is saying to women.

The Bible does not speak in those terms. Scripture affirms the equality of the sexes in creation and in redemption. Let me cite what seem to me to be the clearest passages. Genesis 1:26-28 reads, "God said, let us make man in our image after our likeness. God created man in his own image. In the image of God he created him, male and female he created them and God blessed them and God said to them, be fruitful and multiply and fill the earth and subdue it and have dominion." This is the story of the making of *Adam, mankind;* the two sexes are there, and there is no suggestion that the second sex is in any way inferior to the first. Both are made in the image of God, which speaks both of man's dependence because we are only God's image and of man's dignity because we are his image, and no other creature is made in the image of God. If we ask what constitutes the image of God, the answer must be gathered exegetically from the way that God has been presented to us in the earlier verses of Genesis, chapter 1, prior to the making of man in God's image. If you reread Genesis, chapter 1, the thoughts that emerge are of rationality, of relationality. God sets Himself in relation, you see, with the man and the women; part of the image of God is that we are made for relationships. Finally, righteousness in the broadest sense is part of the image, the righteousness that values and does good, which is seen in God making the world and finding it good as He makes it. We, men and women together, are made in the image of God for tasks of procreation and dominion in God's world. The creation mandate, "replenish the world and subdue it," is a shared privilege and a shared responsibility. Man and woman are together then in the tasks that they have been given.

Moving on, we need to examine chapter 2 and the narrative which runs from verses 18-23, a narrative that speaks of the way in which woman was made out of the rib, the side, of man. According to the picture, she was made to be man's helper, a help meet for him, as the old King James Version put it, a helper who really could help him because as a helper she really could be in personal fellowship with him in a way that the animals could not. She is a colleague, in other words. The male is there first according to the story, the primacy is his, and the initiative is going to be his. The woman is going to be his colleague and helper in the task that already God has set him to do. When the woman is brought to him, he says, "This at last is bone of my bones and flesh of my flesh." This is the complement and completion of me. She shall be called woman because she was taken out of man. She and I belong together. Surely Karl Barth is right in saying that what you have here is the doctrine of how the sexes perceive each other. This is not the doctrine of marriage yet. You don't meet the reality of marriage until verses 24-25. This is the two sexes each perceiving the other as having in it that which completes what the individual, male or female, is at present. This is mysterious, but it is also glorious. It is part of the enrichment of life that God gave us. It is part of his good gift to the human race. We call it sexuality. To some it's a bad word, but in truth it ought not to be a bad word. It has become a bad word, of course, because of the abuses which have taken place in the realm of sexuality over the years of this twentieth century. But really it is part of the glory of creation and ought to be seen as such.

Now we turn to the New Testament. This is the place where the famous text in Galatians 3:28 belongs, where Paul, speaking of the new creation and the order of redemption declare, "as many of you as were baptized into Christ have put on Christ, there is neither Jew nor Greek, there is neither slave nor free, there is neither male nor female, for you are all one man in Christ Jesus." Surely the thought there is not that distinctions established by creation and providence are to be treated as if they don't exist. The thought there is only this: That in the Christian fellowship, the Christian family, the Christian community, in which we all are vitally united to Christ and on the same level both as sinners and hopeless in ourselves and as children of God and heirs of supreme glory, we should treat each other as equals in Christ and determine our behavior toward each other by the fact that we are equals in Christ. Even if in human terms one of us is Jewish, one of us is Greek, one of us is slave, one of us is a free man, one of us is a man, one of us is a woman, in Christ we are all on a level and in love and fellowship should treat each other so. That is the point surely that is being made there. Paul doesn't develop it. He simply says this is how it is in the new creation, and this is what you have to live out. But as we shall shortly see, this does not in Paul's thinking cut across any of the elements in the creation pattern which he reaffirms in the Christian context.

That leads me into my next concern: the cooperative relations of women with men in community. Here we shall look at two subjects which I separate for study, although in fact they belong together and overlap. We shall talk first about the cooperative relations of men with women in marriage and second about the general question of male headship.

Take the marriage relation first. What is the Bible doctrine here? The basic doctrine of marriage is taught in Genesis 2:24-25: "A man leaves his father and mother and cleaves to his wife and they become one flesh," so says the writer. The author puts the word *therefore* at the beginning of the statement. Wherefore the therefore, we ask? The reason is that the woman whom a man takes to himself, the woman who lets him take her to himself in this way, is a person in whom he sees very vividly and precisely the completion of what he is, the complement of what he is. And therefore, he wants togetherness with her as long as life shall last. He doesn't refuse ever to make contact with his father and mother again, but the primary relation now is his relation to his wife. He leaves father and mother in terms of primary affection in order to cleave to his wife in terms of primary affection. They become one flesh in the total commitment of a personal covenant plus a physical relationship. You can see something of the glory and the beauty of this in the exuberance of the Song of Solomon, which Karl Barth described as the second charter of humanity, having already said these verses in Genesis chapter 2 are the first charter of humanity.

I am among those old shellbacks who believe it is right to read the Song of Solomon in terms of Christ and the church. This is so because the Lord from His throne clearly so read it and wanted the Laodician Christians so to read it, Revelation 3:20, "Behold, I stand at the door and knock. If any man hear my voice and open the door, I will come into him, sup with him, and he with me." That is Jesus picking up and applying to His own relation to His people the picture of Song of Solomon, chapter 5. Where the Lord leads, I intend to follow. At the same time it only could be the testament of love between the Lord and His people and the Lord's responsive people and their Savior by first being a rather torrid love song about him and her, Solomon and the Shunamite. It had to be the one in order to be the other. Certainly, this is the biblical ideal of marriage. It is to be exuberant, joyous, and wholehearted.

The Bible warns strongly in both testaments against physical sexual relationships outside the personal covenant of marriage. Read Proverbs 5, Proverbs 6, Proverbs 7, and 1 Corinthians 6. Such relations are destructive, says the Book of God. But on the basis of the total commitment, the personal covenant, the marriage bond, then the physical relationship is, as Roman Catholic theologians would say, transvalued and becomes one of the most precious things in life. So says the Scripture and so experience proves.

In Ephesians 5:22-33 Paul picked up the theme of marriage and layed down or set up ideal standards in terms of the noblest model, Christ and His church. It seems to have been natural for Paul to bring these two things together. The parallel is tremendously significant. The husband is to love his wife as Christ loves the church. He is to cherish her as Christ cherishes the church. He is to love her as he loves his own body. She respect him and prove herself a loyal helper, responding to his needs as the church must in its obedience to Christ. This is mutual subjection, says Paul. You remember, at least if you know the Greek, that the section that begins in verse 22 on wives and husbands is preceded by a participial phrase, "submitting your selves one to another out of reverence for Christ." It is plain that what Paul has to say about wives and husbands and then in chapter 6's opening verses about children and parents and about slaves and masters also spells out the concept of mutual submission, each being at the other's service according to the pattern that God has established in His providence, for this is the way we live in the body of Christ where we are all one man in Christ Jesus. I repeat and underline *mutual submission*. This is a key thought. Submission means that you put yourself at the other person's service to act toward him or her in love with a purpose of making that person great in the way that God reveals that He means that other person to be great. There is an irreversible shape to the mutual submission of husband and wife. It is given already by the order of creation and it is reaffirmed by the parallel of Christ and His church. The roles of Christ and church are not reversible, and in the same way the roles of husband and wife are not reversible. But it is love both ways. That is the point. The husband, playing Christ's role, takes the initiative in love. The wife, playing the church's role, makes the response in love. Love in both parties is the purpose of making the other great. And this is mutual submission in the body of Christ.

Peter picks up some of this in 1 Peter 3, the first seven verses, where he exhorts wives as to their attitude toward their husbands. Then in verse 7, he exhorts husbands as to how they are to live with their wives. He, like Paul, picks up the thought of submission. It is there in chapter 3, verse 1, but it is the sort of submission that is an expression of love. Peter as he talks about it comes to the point of saying explicitly that it is part of the wife's calling to act sweet, even when her husband acts sour. Then he says immediately to the husbands, verse 7, "you are to live considerately with your wives, bestowing honor on the woman as the weaker sex." You must care for her even though you sometimes feel that she is relatively feeble, weak in certain respects. That is not to stop you loving, cherishing, living considerately. Of course, the way of the fallen world is to lose interest with people who seem weak. You get to despise them and distance yourself from them and cease to bother about them. That is not to be the way in Christian marriage. Husbands take note. There is nothing in 1 Peter, incidentally, or Paul in Ephesians 5 to suggest anything that one could call martial passivity on the part of the wife. Here perhaps it is worth referring to the perfect wife of Proverbs 31, who is very far from being a passive person. She is, in fact, a homemaker and a guardian of the home's prosperity in a very significant and striking way. There is really nothing in Scripture to rule out the thought of women taking major responsibility as wives and mothers in the family circle.

Moving now to consider the issue of headship, in 1 Corinthians 11:3 and also in Ephesians 5:23, it is said that headship is a relation that operates between men and women. In 1 Corinthians 11, it is said thus, "I want you to understand that the head of every man is Christ, that the head of the woman is the man, and the head of Christ is God." Then in Ephesians 5:23 it says, "The husband is the head of the wife as Christ is the head of the church, his body of which he himself is the Savior." What does that relation of headship signify? This, as a matter of fact, is a matter still of controversy among philologists. Against the background of continuing debate, I am going to suppose that both the thoughts which are being canvassed are part of the truth, that one of the things that headship means is origin, and that the second thing that headship means is primacy, the sort of primacy that God the Father has in relation to Christ the Son and the sort of primacy that Christ has in relation to each male believer. In another context Paul could have said that same primacy operates between Christ and every woman believer, but that is not part of his argument here.

The result is that what we should be thinking of when we read that the husband is the head of the wife as Christ is the head of the church is that the responsibility for initiative rests on the man, that the pattern both of creation and of redemption is that the responsibility of leadership should be carried by the man. The woman should acknowledge that this is the way God meant it to be and fulfill her role in responsive cooperation and support. I believe that those are truths about human nature as God created it. If that is the right way to view the matter, we have given full weight to the thought of headship without saying anything about what is sometimes called hierarchy, what is sometimes called patriarchy, or what is sometimes called male dominion. Indeed, I do not think that the Bible requires us to think in those terms at all. *Co-operation* is the central biblical theme as between the sexes in general and as between husband and wife in particular.

Thus I understand headship, and understanding it so I now move on to what I have to say about my third and last subject: the contributing roles of women in home and church. In the home it is said specifically that the wife is to be a hardworking homemaker. Again I invoke Proverbs 31, also 1 Timothy 5:14 where Paul says, "I would that the younger widows marry their children, rule their households, and give the enemy no occasion to revile us." And again Titus 2:4-5, Paul says quite specifically, "Train the younger women to love their husbands and children, to be sensible, chaste, domestic, kind and submissive to their husbands that the word of God may not be discredited." In both those last texts, Paul is concerned that the way Christians live should project the thought of the dignity, worthwhileness, and excellence of the Christian way of living before the watching world. Paul is concerned that the way Christians live together in their families should excite admiration from the world rather than contempt, lest the word of God be evil spoken of.

What now about the church? Start with 1 Corinthians. While a difficult letter to exegete because Paul is discussing situations that he hasn't fully described and answering question that he doesn't fully elucidate, but it seems tolerably clear that in 1 Corinthians 7:3-16, Paul is saying, apparently as one of the traditions that he left the Corinthians, that a woman may lead in prayer and prophesy. You have this explicitly in verse 5, provided that she is covered in such a way (the precise nature of the covering is disputed) as to show the angels that she knows her place in the order of creation. By leading in prayer and uttering words of prophesy, she is not seeking to upstage men or usurp their role. Whatever else it means, it clearly means that. In 1 Timothy 2:8 Paul shows that his preference is for the men to be leading in prayer in church meetings. He says, "I will then that the men lift up holy hands in prayer to God." Clearly he is talking about public prayer, leading the congregation. So you would say that it is permission rather than ideal legislation on Paul's part when he says that the Corinthians may do it. He says that it is not wrong and it may be done, provided that it is done in a way that makes plain that the women doing it know their place in the created order.

In light of that, consider 1 Corinthians 14:33-35 where Paul says, "As in all the churches of the saints, the women should keep silence in the churches." They are not permitted to speak. They should be subordinate even as the law says. If there is anything they desire to know, let them ask their husbands at home for it's shameful for a woman to speak in church. Two plausible exegeses are offered. One is that Paul is trying to stop an abuse in Corinth, the abuse namely of women interrupting worship when something was said that they didn't understand. If so, that is the point of let them ask their husbands at home. It has often been said, and there is warrant for saying it, that inevitably the good news of freedom and equality in the family of God for women and men, would have turned the heads of some women and encouraged them, against the background of their very defective education which was the pattern in the ancient world, to throw their weight about. The suggestion is that this is just one instance of that, and Paul is writing to the Corinthians to quell that and make sure that it does not happen in the way that it has been happening. He tells the Corinthians that in all the churches of the saints he has this problem and makes the same rule. But it is a rule about interruption and not a rule about leading in prayer and prophesying because he has already made clear that that is permitted in chapter 11.

The alternative exegesis which is quite popular these days is to suppose that from the middle of verse 33 Paul quotes something that somebody in Corinth is saying very strongly, and that he quotes these words as something which he wants to refute because he understands them as cutting across the permission that he has just given for a woman to lead in prayer and prophesy provided she is covered. That, then, would be the point of his indignant exclamation in verse 36, "What, did the word originate with you, or are you the only ones it's reached?" Do you really think you have a right to make rules like this? And he sweeps the rule aside. Personally, I think that the first exegesis has much more to be said for it than the second, but the second has a lot of support these days, and either is fine. In neither case can one do as has sometimes been done and cite 1 Corinthians 14 as cancelling what was said in 1 Corinthians 11. Rational men don't write letters that way, and Paul was a rational man.

In 1 Timothy 2:12 he specifies that a woman may not teach. Again, more than one exegesis is possible when you get down to details, but the theological principle which is stated is that Eve was deceived in a way that Adam was not. Therefore, for a woman to teach is to increase the likelihood of deception in the church and Paul, as a rule of prudence presumably, does not allow a woman to teach at all. A clarifying comment is needed. In a situation where printing and literacy have come as they have in North America in 1988 all of us have our own Bibles, the activity of teaching doesn't involve the "take it from me" in the way that teaching did when Paul wrote these words in 1 Timothy against a background in which no one had a canonical New Testament because it did not yet exist. In those days teaching involved a very careful judgment not to go beyond what the apostles had been heard to teach and what was clear in the Old Testament, which Paul gave to those Gentile churches as their Bible. Teaching, in other words, is a different exercise today from what it was in Paul's day. I think it is an open question whether in our day Paul would have forbidden a woman to teach from the Bible. It is an open question whether he would have regarded what happened to Eve in the Garden of Eden as sufficient reason for forbidding a woman to teach from the Bible. When you teach from the Bible, in any situation at all, what you are saying to people is, "Look, I am trying to tell you what it says. I speak as to wise men and women. You have your Bibles. You follow along. You judge what I say." No claim to personal authority with regard to the substance of the message is being made at all. It seems to me that this significant difference between teaching then and teaching now does, in fact, mean that the prohibition on women preaching and teaching need not apply. We need not regard the apostle as having forbidden it if in our church situations it is thought good to do it. That is where I think the argument leads. And certainly, we should get out of our minds the thought that in our preaching from the Bible we are claiming any personal authority at all. We are seeking to be channels of the spiritual authority of Christ our Lord through the Spirit, but that is a different thing. For substance, it must always comes from the Bible and no other source.

Finally, consider 1 Timothy 3:11, "The women, likewise, must be serious, no slanders, but temperate, faithful in all things." Those words come in the middle of a paragraph, verses 8-13 of 1 Timothy 3 which are dealing with the office of the deacon. The only natural way to understand verse 11 is in terms of women deacons. Since the deacon's role, according to the New Testament, is to lead the church in practical care for the needy, I see every appropriateness and no inappropriateness whatever in asking women to take charge of that particular sphere of the church's service.

By way of conclusion, I continue to think that women's ministry in the church, whatever the specific role, will ordinarily be maternal rather than paternal in style, motherly rather than fatherly. Therefore, I think that it will always be best done informally in homes with informal groups. Whereas for the male pastors ministry will be best done often in front of large groups, that will not ordinarily be the way with the woman's best ministry. In our churches we have hardly begun to think out how to shape and model women's ministry in this informal, maternal style, simply because we have been distracted so long by the ordination question, which as you see I regard as an irrelevance. Meantime, thank God, countless Godly women have simply got on with the job. Look again at your churches and you will see, they have done it. Long may they continue to do it while we men scratch our heads trying to work all these things out.

RESPONSE: John Hewett

I wish to express my gratitude to Professor Packer for the reverence with which he approaches this library of documents we call the Bible; for his irenic and inclusive spirit in going about the difficult work of "rightly dividing the word of truth"; for his unwillingness to allow hermeneutics to function as a political exercise; for his reminder that affirmations of biblical inerrancy do not remove our need to do the hard work of asking "what it meant" and "what it means"; and for his humble declaration that all our interpretations are provisional and incomplete (we are on our way to the kingdom, but we have not yet fully arrived in power and glory).

Agreement is the provisional anticipation of the day when everything we bind or loose here will be bound or loosed in heaven. We will not all agree in our interpretations of these significant issues. We do already agree that we love the God and Father of our Lord Jesus Christ, who has called us out of darkness into his marvelous light. So we gather here as one family.

I also wish to thank Dr. Vines for his sermon on the love of God. The story he told about the professor is entirely accurate. The professor was Karl Barth, who came to America in the fifties and was met at the dock by the press. He was asked to summarize the truth contained in his massive *Church Dogmatics* in a few words. He replied, "Jesus loves me, this I know, for the Bible tells me so."

This is the same Karl Barth who was required by the Gestapo to begin his theological lectures with the "Heil Hitler." On his first morning in class after the order had been handed down, the slight, bespectacled man walked into his packed classroom, arms laden with books. He quietly put down his things, turned to the soldiers present, clicked his heels, thrust out his right arm, and exclaimed: "Heil Jesu!" Shortly thereafter he was shown to the Swiss border, where he waited out the war years as an expatriate.

In common allegiance to that same Lord Jesus Christ, let me offer "a" Christian biblical response to Dr. Packer's interpretation, with the grateful acceptance of another Christian biblical response to be offered in a few moments by my brother from Texas, Jimmy Draper.

First, some abiding convictions which shape my response. I confess to a built-in uneasiness whenever men gather to determine the proper role of women. It smacks of a lesser kind of theology "from above," in the sense that a male-dominated church has historically handed down its proscriptions to Christian women without benefit of their unique gifts in biblical interpretation. We should not be surprised when Christian women are also uneasy about this pattern. I would urge each of us to be sensitive to that sincere concern. My part on this program could better be served by having a woman respond, in my judgment.

Let me also affirm my belief in the active, dynamic power of the Holy Spirit of God at work in the church today, working in and through the body of Christ known as the church. It took a sheet let down from heaven to help Simon Peter get over his traditional prejudices (and he had solid textual reasons for feeling the way he did!). It took the persevering witness of our black brothers and sisters and the agonies of an uncivil war within our American family to help us learn not to call "half a person" those whom God had called "all Mine," and this when our Southern Baptist forebears a century ago were preaching and teaching the doctrine of the orders of creation to reinforce the first-century divisions of slave and free! As we struggle to rightly divide this library of sacred documents, we search for the timeless amid the timebound. We are guided in that search by the Spirit of God. I believe that once more the Spirit is powerfully at work, reversing the curse of Genesis 3:16, bringing the prophecy of my favorite Hebrew seer to pass:

> Be glad, O sons of Zion,
>   and rejoice in the Lord, your God;
> for he has given the early rain for your vindication,
>   he has poured down for you abundant rain,
>   the early and the latter rain, as before.
>
> The threshing floors shall be full of grain,
>   the vats shall overflow with wine and oil.
> I will restore to you the years
>   which the swarming locust has eaten,
> the hopper, the destroyer, and the cutter,
>   my great army, which I sent among you.
>
> You shall eat in plenty and be satisfied,
>   and praise the name of the Lord your God,
>   who has dealt wondrously with you.
>
> And my people shall never again be put to shame.
> You shall know that I am in the midst of Israel,

> And that I, the Lord, am your God
>   and there is none else.
> And my people shall never again be put to shame.
>
> And it shall come to pass afterward,
>   that I will pour out my spirit on all flesh;
> your sons and your daughters shall prophesy,
>   your old men shall dream dreams,
>   and your young men shall see visions.
>
> Even upon the menservants and maidservants
>   in those days, I will pour out my spirit
>   (Joel 2.23-29, RSV).

It seems good to me to feel the fresh winds of the Spirit blowing through the modern church, helping us overcome the hardness of our hearts which keeps us woodenly tied to those trees which impede our view of the forest (cf. Matt. 19:7-9).

I also want to affirm my deep gratitude to God for the godly women who were not silent in the First Baptist Church of Palatka, Florida, who taught me that "Jesus wanted me for a Sunbeam, to shine for Him each day," and who instilled in me a love for the Scriptures. Without their efforts to keep the church alive, I wouldn't be standing here tonight. Indeed, few of us would. I heard recently about a pastor who preached a Mother's Day sermon and invited all the women who worked outside the home to come forward at the invitation, repent, and quit their jobs so they could return home where they belonged. The next morning when he got to the office it was empty! He called his secretary and asked, "Why aren't you here?" She replied: "I'm home, praise God, where I belong!" My church would shut down pretty quickly if that happened.

Now, since the hour is late and I want to be redemptive to you tired and weary fellow-travelers, let me move on to some specific responses to Dr. Packer's statement. And, if you think what he did was "sketchy," watch this!

Though I agree with Packer's assertion that we are working tonight with what he has called the "churchly" taproot to the issue of women and Scripture, I feel compelled to offer another view of the secular taproot in the sake of honesty. I have not found it to be a movement characterized by a "stridency and passion to upstage men," nor have I encountered a "somewhat sick motivation which is neither creative or fulfilling." Indeed, the imagery of rivalry, in my judgment, is far from the center of the movement for women's liberation. In truth, the concerns of the women's movement were raised by men as well as women, as part of the larger struggle for truly human liberation. Does not the Scripture itself teach us that we were not created for isolation, but mutuality? Can't we hear the legitimately concerned voices of men and women who see injustice and want to make a difference? What sets my wife free sets me free. I thank God for those outside the church who saw something out of balance and moved to correct it.

Now to the churchly taproot. If the issue is, as Dr. Packer has argued, ministry, and not status, then there is room enough here tonight for massive repentance on the part of men in ministry. The same issue of tokenism applies to every good layman who was talked into the ministry by a misguided church leader who thought that commitment to Christ was evidence of a call to preach. I also find it strange for Southern Baptists, especially in this anniversary year for WMU, to hear of women doing men's jobs "in emergencies" as an "unfruitful policy." Lottie Moon went to China because no men were willing to go! Every time Southern Baptists do something powerful in the name of missions we name the cause after a woman. I don't think status is the issue at all.

I must also respond to Dr. Packer's assertion that "clergy roles are already defined in male patterns." By whom? What about Priscilla? She was co-pastor with Aquila of the church which met in their home, and she instructed Apollos, the silver-tongued preacher, in theology because his doctrine was weak. It is true that Jesus chose only males as the twelve. But they were also Jews! Should only male Jews serve as clergy today? And if so, what of circumcision? He also sent them out with a cloak and staff as itinerant preachers. Is that a timeless ministry pattern? Again, we strive for the timeless amid the time-bound, as "right dividers" of the Word.

I agree with Dr. Packer about the ordination of women presbyters. To quote Kenneth Kantzer, "to refuse ordination of women is to maintain that God does not call women to the ministry." The fact is, the Scripture says precious little about ordination, and offers scant justification for elevating the role of pastor above other churchly positions. If we're going to ordain deacons, we ought also to ordain the people who teach this Book every Sunday and who sing to the glory of God in worship.

My own position on the issue of the relationship of men to women is that which Harvie Conn has labeled "centrism." The egalitarian pattern is affirmed, but not to the point of androgyny. The roles are clearly different. Men are not women, nor should they try to be. Women are not men, nor should they want to be. The ideal is not patriarchy or matriarchy, but what Henlee Barnette calls "co-archy." The ideal is mutual subordination, as Dr. Packer clearly affirms. This is in harmony with the Genesis accounts of creation. If Eve is less than Adam because she was made from him, what must we conclude about Adam, who was made from dust? They were both made in God's image: "male and female he created them, and he blessed them and named them Adam when they were created" (Gen. 5:2).

Now our time is short. Let me hurry along to a few specific points raised by Dr. Packer and I am through.

He clearly eschews the notion of female inferiority. Did you hear the quotation from Tertullian?

> You are the devil's gateway; you are she who first violated the forbidden tree and broke the law of God.

Have you heard any language like that lately?

I cannot accept as so facile his interpretation of Galatians 3:28 as having a strictly horizontal reference. This is Paul's Magna Charta, in which he offers the vision of God's new community, a "God's-eye view" of kingdom people. Here is the place where Paul rises above the time-bound cultural limits of first-century Jewish-Christianity and sees beyond the horizon. We see it as well in the Corinthian correspondence: "Nevertheless, in the Lord woman is not independent of man nor man of woman; for as woman was made from man, so man is now born of woman. And all things are from God" (1 Cor. 11:11-12).

In response to Dr. Packer's hierarchical view of male-female relationships, I must ask: How is the male to be subject to the female out of reverence for Christ? He rightly affirms the truth of Ephesians 5:21 as the schema for this section (the Haustafel), but takes it no further. And again, what is the status of the unmarried woman? Is she to be subordinate to her father as long as she is single? Can you have subordination in spiritual things and still so neatly argue against female inferiority?

Dr. Packer, an inerrantist, has agreed that women may serve as deacons and ought not be prohibited from preaching and teaching. Did you hear that? This is not a liberal speaking. This is a man firmly committed to the inerrancy of this text. And I, who would not properly be classified an inerrantist, am in substantial agreement with him in many areas.

In response to his interpretation of 1 Timothy 2:12, I would add that Eve's deception was probably tied to her lack of information rather than some built-in weakness of women. Adam held a primacy of information. He had been around longer than she. When given the chance, he ate, too. Male teachers, beware!

Finally, let me thank Dr. Packer for his open invitation to dialogue on these and other issues. As he has concluded in his written outline, "Paul's rules remain rules of apostolic prudence rather than deliverance of apostolic doctrine. . . There is some room to rethink these rules of prudence in a different cultural situation from that in which they were given." Let us not make these tests of fellowship! Our fellowship is far too precious for that. For we are all headed toward the kingdom.

In conclusion, let me offer my own paraphrase of Romans 16:1, aptly interpreted this evening by Dr. Packer:

I commend to you our sisters, servants of the Southern Baptist churches, that you may receive them in the Lord as befits the saints, and help them in whatever they may require from you, for they have been helpers of many and of myself as well.

RESPONSE: James T. Draper, Jr.

This conference on biblical interpretation, with its wide representation from the various schools of thought within our Convention, holds the potential of becoming a significant and historic gathering. It just might turn out to be a turning point in our continuing attempt to define and deal with the problems which plague us. In order for this to be the case there are certain things which must happen.

(1) We must avoid the temptation to use the conference simply as a public relations event, in which we attempt to gloss over our genuine differences and portray a superficial consensus which may not really exist at this time.

(2) We must also avoid making this conference trivial by spending our time just reviewing the commonly held principles of hermeneutics. It would be difficult to find anyone on these grounds this week who would not affirm the desirability of contextual integration, the appropriate recognition of figures of speech, the priority of the original languages, the importance of progressive revelation, etc. Our problems do not lie in this area.

(3) Neither will it be particularly helpful to rehearse the historic 1949 dialogue between Alfred Ayer and Frederick Copleston concerning the validity and significance of religious language. However interesting and instructive such a discussion might be, it would also avoid our real problem.

(4) We must make this a genuine conference, that is, a time when we actually confer *with* each other, not simply a time when we read papers *at* each other, and then retreat into our groups to decide "who won." We need to seize every available moment to talk seriously and candidly with one another. We need to ask tough questions and, thus, discover fundamental commonalities and diversities. Then we need to seek possible solutions. If we do not do this, we are basically wasting our time.

(5) We must dispense with the myths and caricatures which conceal the real problem. Specifically, we must move beyond the widely reported scenario which largely attributes our present difficulty to a group of inadequately edu-

cated, power-hungry "fundamentalists," who have no sense of Southern Baptist history and tradition, no real grasp of the complexities and sophistication of modern biblical criticism, and no inclinations toward tolerance, diversity or cooperation, that these are people who would, if given the opportunity, transform our universities and seminaries into crude Bible trade schools, teaching the King James Bible as illuminated by the notes in the Scofield Reference Edition, and who would demand a convention-wide rigid conformity to their own excessively literal and painfully simplistic interpretations of Scripture.

This is all myth! Those in the Southern Baptist Convention with whom I am acquainted who are concerned about doctrinal integrity are not ignorant, unlearned, mean-spirited, politically motivated or uncooperative. They are godly men and women who are genuinely and sincerely concerned that the Convention they love not follow the twentieth-century theological defections which have reduced most of the once-great Christian denominations to mere shadows of what they once were.

Southern Baptists have been able to maintain their doctrinal integrity longer than any other major denomination in this century. However, the same pressures which have all but destroyed the other groups as witnesses to the historic Christian faith are now making some inroads among Southern Baptists.

What, then, is the central dilemma in our current controversy? I believe that it centers in the question of how much diversity in biblical "interpretation" can we accommodate, while still retaining our historic identity as Southern Baptists and being able to continue to cooperate together.

I know of no one in the Southern Baptist Convention who is seeking lock-step conformity in every area of biblical interpretation. Southern Baptists, and Bible-believing Christians in general, have long differed on many things. What is the nature of the millennium? Will Jesus Christ return before or after the Great Tribulation? Will there be a millennium at all? Does man consist of two parts: body and soul, or does he consist of three parts: body, soul, and spirit? Does man inherit his soul by natural generation, as he does his body, or does God create it immediately? Is God's elective purpose for man conditional or unconditional? Should women be ordained to pastoral positions? And the list goes on.

Most of us would agree that absolute dogmatism in these areas is inappropriate and that they should not become barriers to fellowship and cooperative efforts.

But what do we do when someone's interpretation of the Bible begins to strike at the very heart of the Christian faith? Baptists historically have emphasized soul-competency and the right of individual Baptists to interpret the Bible as guided by the Holy Spirit—without the arbitrary authority of a pope or the imposing of an ecclesiastical creed. This liberty was given to Baptist leaders as well as Baptist in general.

But, it is crucially important for us to understand that such interpretational autonomy was always assumed to be within the parameters of the historic Christian faith. Beyond those parameters, autonomous interpretations become *denials of the faith,* regardless of the hermeneutical terminology employed.

Let's become very practical and specific. Do we really want atheists and agnostics teaching theology in our schools? I certainly don't, and I doubt that anyone on these grounds this week wants that. I know that rank-and-file Southern Baptists won't knowingly support anything of that nature.

I am not saying that we have atheists and agnostics teaching theology in our schools. I am saying that if we can all agree that we must not appoint atheists and agnostics to Southern Baptist faculties of theology, then we are making progress because we have agreed to the principle that there must be some *minimum* theological parameters within which we operate. Even if the atheist or agnostic should suggest that he is not denying the Bible, but simply interpreting the "God-talk" in symbolic terms, we would have to conclude that his "interpretation" is unacceptable to Southern Baptists because it actually constitutes a denial of theism. We will have, thus, agreed that we cannot accommodate *all* diversity in interpretation.

But let's move ahead logically. Is a theistic position in itself sufficient to constitute our minimum parameters? Are not Unitarians theists? Are not Mormons and Jehovah's Witnesses theists? Are not Muslims theists? Do we want *them* teaching theology in our schools?

I suggest that the answer again must be *no.* Incidentally, if anyone here suggests that the answer should be *yes,* I would like to know how you plan to sell that idea to Southern Baptists! Must we not, then, narrow our parameters further?

We certainly need to affirm a *trinitarian* God, not a Unitarian God. Does that not, in turn, demand an affirmation of the deity of Jesus Christ? Do we want theological professors who call themselves Christians but deny that Jesus is God? And, if the *person* of Jesus Christ is crucial for our parameters, is not *his work* equally crucial? Did He really die for our sins in a penal, substitutionary sense? Did He really rise physically, bodily from the grave on the third day?

We are not dealing with far-out, unlikely, theoretical situations. Some of the most prominent and widely-honored churchmen of this century—names such as Paul Tillich, Rudolf Bultmann, and Reinhold Niebuhr—would not fall within these more stringent parameters.

Would all Southern Baptists fall within them? We really don't know. Remember that we are talking about biblical *interpretation.* Harry Emerson Fosdick, America's most famous liberal preacher, routinely claimed to be "reinterpreting" the Bible for modern man. He claimed that the Bible does not really teach the deity, pre-existence, incarnation, atonement, bodily resurrection, bodily ascension, or literal second coming of Jesus. He claimed that it may *seem* to the unsophisticated that the Bible teaches all of these things, but these are all meaningful *symbols* of God's majesty, love, concern, and ultimate triumph in the affairs of man. Does soul-competency and the priesthood of the believer qualify a Fosdick to teach in our schools?

Where do we draw the line? Just where are the parameters to be established? We have agreed, I think, that we cannot endorse *total* theological diversity. That produces anarchy and would erase any continuity with our Baptist heritage. We are also agreed, I think, that we don't want to make the parameters so narrow as to rule out legitimate diversity in non-essential areas.

Several years ago, I wrote a book entitled *Authority: The Critical Issue for Southern Baptists*. I suggested in that book that we must come together and agree on an irreducible minimum theology which we would then require of those who teach in our schools or who work in strategic positions in our agencies.

I suggested that the irreducible minimum might be (1) the deity and humanity of Jesus Christ, i.e. the hypostatic union; (2) the penal, substitutionary atonement of Christ as a necessity for fallen, depraved man; (3) the literal bodily resurrection, ascension, and return of Christ; and (4) justification by God's grace through faith alone.

I was surprised and puzzled by the cries of "creedalism" which arose. That's not creedalism—that's Christianity!

Now, let's take the next logical step. What I am suggesting is that we want our teachers, administrators, etc., to be *saved* persons. Certainly we would all expect that. We want them to be genuinely regenerate Christians. Must we not, then, set our parameters at the perimeter of the Christian faith? We expect our teachers, et al, to affirm *everything* essential for Christian salvation. We may also wish to require belief in specific *Baptist* doctrines, such as believer's baptism by immersion even though we recognize that it is certainly possible for a person who believes in infant baptism or sprinkling or pouring to be saved.

But, some may ask, "Do we not have something like that already in the Baptist Faith and Message statement and in the doctrinal abstracts in use in many of our schools?"

Perhaps, but the statements are frequently subjected to "loophole" interpretations, unforeseen by the original drafters. Who could have imagined, for example, that "truth without any mixture of error" would one day be taken by some to mean that the Bible contains both truth and error, but that they are not mixed?

Who could have imagined that Christ's death which "made provision for the redemption of men from sin" (BF&M) would one day be cited as not requiring a belief in substitutionary atonement?

A student in one of our seminaries asked a senior professor some time ago, "What will you do if one day you should be required to sign a statement of belief in biblical inerrancy in order to retain your position?" With a smile, and without hesitation, he answered, "I'll sign it—and then reinterpret the terms!"

It is unlikely, then, that doctrinal statements currently in place will resolve our problems by themselves. What we must do, and perhaps we might make a significant beginning this week, is to sit down together and talk *seriously* about theology.

What *precisely* is the *gospel?* Is man really lost without Christ? What are the consequences? Is there to be eternal punishment for the lost? Will all eventually be saved? What *exactly* did Christ accomplish on the cross? Did He really bear our sins? In what sense?

What *exactly* must one believe to be saved? What does *"Jesus is Lord"* really mean—*specifically?* What is Scripture? Not what does it say, but what is the nature of Scripture?

Take the atonement of Christ, for example. There are two basic understandings of the atonement of Christ. One is called the subjective view of the atonement, and other is called the objective view of the atonement.

The subjective view, essentially, says that the death of Christ paid for nothing. It was not penal. It was not substitutionary. It was simply a demonstration of God's love for man, which love then should prompt man to repentance.

And it is his repentance which saves him. The objective view of the atonement believes that Jesus Christ actually paid a price on the cross. He actually bore our sins and suffered the penal wrath of God upon those sins, and thus our salvation was bought and paid for by his blood. I believe that these two views are essentially irreconcilable.

Obviously, I hold to the objective view, and I believe that it can be clearly demonstrated that Southern Baptists historically have held to the objective view. But it appears from the writings and statements of some in our Convention that the subjective view is gaining some acceptance. We must decide whether both views are acceptable, whether both views bring salvation to the believing sinner, and whether both views can thus be accommodated within the historic gospel of Jesus Christ.

I do not believe that they can both be accommodated. Candidly, I believe that the subjective view of the atonement falls into the category of "another gospel," as Paul uses that terminology in Galatians 1. If that be true then it is a false gospel. It is not acceptable to God and thus cannot be acceptable to Christians. "How can two walk together except they be agreed?"

Only when we have worked our way through these basic questions can we determine just how diverse our "interpretations" actually are and whether or not it will be possible to accommodate all of them within the parameters of the historic Christian faith and the historic distinctives of the people called Southern Baptists.

I am more than ready to join hands with *all* Southern Baptists for the proclamation of the Gospel—*if* we can all agree as to what the gospel is. I pray that we can agree, but I'm not certain that we do. We need to find out. The controversy will not go away until we do.

For many of us it is a deep matter of conscience. Until we honestly and forthrightly deal with matters like these we will not put the tension aside and move on together. We have refused as yet to discuss the real issues. We have fanned the flames of emotion with broad sweeping accusations and generalizations. I say "we" for all of us have been guilty to some extent!

Let us create a forum where we can get at these issues and find out where we are and map a strategy for moving on together.

Some may still insist, "but the problem is purely political." I ask you, "How do you know?" Thus far there has been no opportunity to discuss the theological issues. We have simply talked *at* each other and *about* each other. We have yet to talk *with* each other.

I desperately hope that our dialogue will determine that most, if not all, Southern Baptist leaders do embrace essentially the same gospel and do affirm the same verities of the historic Christian faith. If this proves to be true, then I want to be in the forefront of the movement to bring us back together, to put aside our minor differences, and to move ahead in the proclamation of the gospel.

If, however, our dialogue should prove otherwise, then in good conscience we cannot continue to pretend that our differences are superficial when they could possibly be very real. We hear a lot today about the "bickering," "infighting," etc. We are then told that we as Christians need to put all of this aside and come together in Christ. I agree with that assessment 100 percent—assuming that our differences are, indeed, minor and inconsequential and thus unworthy of our continued attention. We must, however, determine that this is the case, and that the differences are not real and threatening to the integrity of our faith. The controversy will not go away until we make this investigation and come to some conclusions.

James Stalker once said, "Excessive aversion to controversy may be an indication that a church has no keen sense of possessing truth which is of any great worth, and that it has lost appreciation for the infinite difference in value between truth and error."

I wish we could just shake hands and forget the controversy and move on together. However, conscience will not allow it, until we have dealt with these issues with integrity. Only then can we find a basis for continued cooperation.

I believe the majority of Southern Baptists will fall into the parameters of historic Southern Baptist doctrinal integrity. But we will never know until we honestly face these serious theological questions.

Please hear my heart. Don't write this off as the rantings of a radical mind. I love this convention. I want to join hands with all Southern Baptists who will go on in the historic position so typical of our past. I do not desire everyone to think or interpret Scripture just like I do.

However, we Southern Baptists have always believed some things, not just anything. We must identify again who we are, what we believe and how we can move forward together.

8
LORD, STIR US AGAIN
2 Timothy 1:6-14

Ken Hemphill

Words like *bold, exciting, challenging* seem to be the passwords of our generation. Architects and clothiers alike tell us that their new designs, often those we don't appreciate, are *bold* new creations. Every season we have fabrics boasting *bold* new patterns or *bold* new colors. We even have a new and improved *Bold* detergent!

Christians are not to be excluded in this quest for descriptive words. In Southern Baptist life since the inception of *BOLD* Mission Thrust in 1976, the word *bold* has become an integral part of our denominational vocabulary. Out of this we have developed *bold* witnessing, *bold* giving, *bold* training, and *bold* church planting.

I'm not objecting to the terminology. I simply wonder if we have substituted a *bold* new vocabulary for *bold* action? Have we gone about giving or witnessing or training in a manner that is qualitatively different than in the past? Can you give testimony to growing *boldness* in your spiritual activities? If our own statistics tell us anything, our claims to *boldness* in the areas of training, Sunday School growth, or witnessing seem to be rather hollow. In the midst of Cecil Ray's book *Cooperation*, there is a chart showing the decadel growth of our convention that I find troubling. To cite only one statistic from that chart: Sunday School enrollment from 1940-1960 grew from 3,590,374 to 7,382,550. Those are statistics of unprecedented—and we might say *BOLD*—growth. But more troublesome are the twenty years from 1961-1980 in which Southern Baptists virtually marched in place; growing in Sunday School to only 7,433,405. By the way, updating these statistics to 1987 gives us little cause for rampant enthusiasm with Sunday School enrollment growing only to 7,957,106. Most would agree that such statistics give us due cause for concern. What has happened? What has caused this stagnation?

There are those who say it reflects Convention controversy; others maintain that it is a natural cycle of institutional growth and decline. Some say we have lost sight of the fundamentals like evangelism and Sunday School growth. It may even be that it has been a combination of these factors and others. I'm not sure we'll ever determine the why. In any case our common focus and concern now must be echoed in the prayer, "Lord, stir us again!" "Kindle afresh in us, Lord, the gift of God that is within us!"

You perhaps have recognized already the familiar and stirring words from the aging warrior, the apostle Paul, to young Timothy. Timothy was one of the young persons faced with the task of carrying the torch of the advancing church for a new generation. Paul knew Timothy well. Timothy had accompanied him on his second and third missionary journeys. Paul had been confident to send him on special assignments, knowing he would represent the gospel well.

There is some indication from texts like 1 Corinthians 16:10-11 that Timothy felt more comfortable working side by side with Paul than being sent out alone. "Now if Timothy comes, see that he is with you without cause to be afraid; he is doing the Lord's work, as I also am. Let no one therefore despise him. But send him on his way in peace, so that he may come to me." Of course, when we consider the volatile Corinthian community, and their estimation of Paul himself, Timothy may have had due cause to be frightened.

If we take these letters to Timothy as personal words of encouragement from the apostle to the young pastor of the church at Ephesus, we can understand their significance for Timothy and their relevance to today. Second Timothy, unlike 1 Timothy, shows little concern for ecclesiastical arrangements but concentrates on Timothy and the task which is being committed to him. A task which is at once challenging and frightening. This is a word of encouragement to all us Timothys who are called to a task beyond our natural temperament and ability.

Kindle Afresh the Gift *(vv. 6-7)*

Timothy had accepted heavy responsibility in the overseeing of the church at Ephesus. False teachers were commonplace in Procounsular Asia. Many commentators feel that Timothy had a naturally timid disposition and perhaps felt himself unsuited for the task before him and overwhelmed by the awesome responsibility.

Paul's first words of encouragement call Timothy to remember the gift of God in him—that he has not been given a spirit of timidity but one of power, love and discipline. In these words of comfort there are also words of challenge. Paul exhorts him "to stir up his smoldering embers into a living flame" or "to keep the flame at white heat." Either translation is acceptable. The good news of this challenge is that there is still the spark of life. There is no suggestion that Timothy had lost the fire. You can't rekindle a fire that has been extinguished. The good news for our Convention and for us is the presence of these glowing embers in our life.

There has been much debate about what gift Paul was referring to in this text since the Greek word for *gift* is *charisma,* which in many other references has a somewhat technical meaning as a reference to a particular gift for ministry. In earlier gift passages, such as 1 Corinthians and Romans 12, we have no indication that *charismata,* even for leadership, were communicated by the laying on of hands, which probably refers to some sort of commissioning or ordination service.

I think it is likely that *charisma* here has a somewhat less technical meaning and refers generally to the total empowering for the task of the ministry. Paul used *charisma* in a similar fashion in 1 Corinthians 7:7 in reference to the power enabling one to live a celibate life-style. Here Paul was referring not to a specific gift for ministry, but to the supernatural empowering of the Holy Spirit, equipping Timothy for the task of ministry. Thus Paul defined this gift in verse 7 as a spirit of power, love and discipline. We all need, from time to time, to be reminded that God's calling on our life is also accompanied by a promised sufficiency for every good work.

Paul in reminding Timothy of God's sufficiency, called upon him to keep the fire burning at full flame. We all know how easy it is for the flame to get doused. Controversy, personal problems or physical problems, stress, fatigue can all serve to turn down the wick on our spiritual fervor.

I am most fortunate to pastor one of the greatest congregations God ever entrusted to anyone's care. We have had rapid and demanding growth and the spirit of cooperation has been phenomenal. We have rarely had any questions or hesitancy about any matter brought before the congregation. Recently we were informed by our fire safety committee that by overcrowding the sanctuary for special events we were creating a potential safety hazard. We prayerfully and carefully researched the options. We decided that for multiple concert events, such as Easter or Christmas, tickets were the only sure means of control. Many of us on the church council struggled with the decision, but finally concluded it was the best method. The church overwhelmingly supported it, but it was somewhat controversial and troubling to some. I understood the feelings and wanted everyone to be happy and to do what was best for the whole. I answered all personal letters and objections. I thought I was handling everything fine and did not actually realize how it was affecting me until I snapped back at a staff member who wanted to convey one last response concerning the tickets to me. "I don't want to hear anything else," I snapped. It was then that I realized that my focus on this minor concern had actually sapped my energy and dampened my zeal for ministry. It is all too easy to lose our focus and our zeal.

What do we do when we recognize our zeal has been dampened? How do we stir it up? I think the keys for the stirring are in this text.

First, we must remember the past. Notice that Paul began his challenge to rekindle with the words, "I remind you." The emphasis on the past began with verse 5 where Paul called Timothy back to his roots. "For I am mindful of the sincere faith within you, which first dwelt in your grandmother Lois and your mother Eunice."

My dad is a pastor in North Carolina. My great-great-grandfather and great-grandfathers were also ministers. I am coming more and more to recognize the profound impact of my heritage on my own life. Paul, thus, called Timothy to remember his great heritage. Notice too that he called him to remember his commissioning or ordination. This symbolic act of the laying on of hands in which God makes His presence powerfully real serves as a constant reminder of our high calling. Every Christian minister, ordained and unordained, needs at times to be called to remember the greatness of his calling.

Second, the words "kindle afresh" may suggest that there are times we need to move the coals around, that is to say reorder our priorities. We partially heat our home with a wood stove. I fill it up at night and close the draft down to preserve the fuel during the night. In the morning all that remains are a few glowing embers. By reordering the embers, placing the burning ones against each other, opening the draft and adding new fuel, I can rekindle the fire.

Spiritually we often need to stir up the coals. Practically you may need to get around other folk who are on fire for the Lord. I'm always amazed at how negative, critical people tend to get around other negative, critical people. How depressed people seek out other depressed people. Man, when your fire is low get around somebody who's got some heat. The only way I know to spiritually open the draft is on my knees. I need the fresh word of the Holy Spirit to rekindle me. Do you remember that which made you white hot—that deep and personal devotional life? You were in the Word and on your knees and the wind of God's Spirit blew fresh upon you!

Third, recognize God's provision. The fresh fuel is always available. Look at God's provision in verse 7. "God has not given us a spirit of timidity, but of power and love and discipline." God has provided abundant resources. Perhaps Timothy did suffer from natural timidity, boldness was not easy for him, but he had not been called to minister in his own strength. Notice the three-fold listing of God's provision: power, love and discipline. His power overcomes natural deficiencies of personality or temperament. But power alone can be destructive so he balances it with love. The discipline is the key to keeping the spiritual flame white hot.

Fulfill Your Calling *(vv. 8-11)*

In light of this unique calling and God's sufficient empowering, Timothy was challenged to fulfill his calling. Paul exhorts him not to be ashamed of the Christian message. Timothy had been called to preach Christ crucified, foolishness to the world. He was to proclaim a faith that could cause social ostracism, suffering or even imprisonment and death.

Things have not changed all that much. When we stand for Christian convictions that run contrary to the world's standards, be they convictions on the family, divorce, abortion, race relations, or any number of topics, we face hostility. Let's be honest, the social stigma sometimes attached with a stand for convictions often causes us to remain silent. Personal pride and the fear of embarrassment are often large factors in our avoiding witnessing opportunities.

I have lived in the context of the church so long that I am often sheltered from the kidding and prodding that goes on related to the Christian life-style. This is particularly true in schools today. One evening at the dinner table we were carrying on a typical family discussion about the day at school. My oldest daughter (I have three) was in the fourth grade at the time. One evening as she was telling us about her day, she kept mentioning various daddies who had visited her class that day. One child's dad, she informed me, was an insurance salesman, another a doctor, and on down the line she went. Finally I asked the question that I later wished I could retract: "Babe, why didn't you invite me?"

After a bashful moment of squirming she replied: "Well Dad, you're just a preacher." Painful isn't it? I thank God for moments like that when He reminds us that other than our gifts and our calling we are just regular folk. As we discussed her reason for not inviting me, it became apparent that already she was facing some harassment for her faith and for her dad's faith. At that moment I could identify with those great words of challenge: "Do not be ashamed of the testimony of our Lord or of me His prisoner."

Verses 9 and 10 give substance to Paul's words of encouragement. Many commentators believe they were part of an early Christian hymn or confession of faith. This would certainly be most appropriate. Notice the integral relationship between salvation and vocation. He has saved us and called us. We are not just rescued from a life of sin and condemnation; we also are called with a holy calling.

Every word echoes the high calling and empowering of the Christian. God has done for us in salvation what we could not do for ourselves. He has done so out of the sheer majesty of His love, not because of any merit on our part. We readily give testimony to the sovereign gracious work of God in our salvation experience, but frequently forget its parallel in our vocation.

Listen to these majestic and sobering words concerning our calling which was: "According to His own purpose and grace which was granted us in Christ Jesus from all eternity. But now has been revealed by the appearing of our Savior Christ Jesus, who abolished death and brought life and immortality to light through the Gospel."

The thought of God's eternal purpose of grace is so beyond our comprehension that we can only begin to comprehend it in the incarnation of our Savior Jesus Christ. In Him the horror and specter of death is removed and life itself is illuminated. Both life and immortality have been flooded with light by the revelation of God in Christ.

Notice it is the magnificence of the Gospel itself that puts our calling into its proper perspective. Paul, in an almost breathless wonder, connects his own ministry to the gospel: "for which I was appointed a preacher and an apostle and a teacher." We can detect this same boyish wonder in verses like 2 Corinthians 4:1: "Therefore, since we have this ministry, as we received mercy, we do not lose heart." Or Ephesians 1:7-8: "Of which I was made a minister according to the gift of God's grace which was given to me according to the working of His power. To me, the very least of the saints, this grace was given, to preach to the Gentiles the unfathomable riches of Christ." Or in the first chapter of Colossians, where Paul, after describing the incomparable Christ, reflects on the gospel "which was proclaimed in all creation under heaven, and of which I, Paul, was made a minister" (1:23). And again in 1:25, "Of this church I was made a minister according to the stewardship from God bestowed on me for your benefit that I might fully carry out the preaching of the word of God."

It is the magnificence of the gospel itself which calls us to live boldly and burn brightly for the gospel.

Given the context of his calling, Paul's suffering brings no shame, only glory and greater resolve to stand with conviction! The most beautiful phrase in all of Scripture may be these words, "For I know whom." It is not I know "what" or "where," but I know "whom." Paul's assurance and boldness were based on his personal relationship with the living God.

Paul had staked his whole life on the trustworthiness of God. He had abandoned everything he had once counted as value for the sake of knowing Christ. But here at the end of the journey he had no regrets, no wavering; he had found God completely trustworthy. The phrase "I have believed" translates the Greek perfect tense and emphasizes the continuous nature of his assurance which began in the past but continues its vitality in the present. This living faith had given Paul the firm conviction that God is able to guard that which Paul had entrusted to Him. I think this sacred trust included Paul, his ministry, and his converts—everything he considered precious.

This is the firm conviction that stirs the flame in the midst of difficulty and suffering! It is the one truth that places this charge to Timothy in proper perspective.

Guard the Treasure *(vv. 13-14)*

Paul instructed Timothy to hold fast to the standard of sound doctrine and to guard the treasure. These are closely related commands. Paul presented his own teaching as a pattern of sound doctrine to which Timothy must hold fast. He also instructed Timothy concerning the manner in which he held to sound words. "Faith and love" qualify the act of holding. Thus, the manner in which orthodoxy is maintained is placed on an equal plane with the orthodoxy itself.

If our commitment to orthodoxy is always tempered by faith and love, the bitterness of controversy would be done away with. We can reject neither the demand for orthodox teaching nor the call for faith and love in our interpersonal dealings. The two must be kept in dynamic tension. Notice also that this "faith and love" are in Christ Jesus and thus we are brought back to the common ground of our salvation and our calling.

This precious treasure of the gospel must be guarded by young Timothy. Here Timothy's personal responsibility was stressed but even here it is obvious that Timothy could only do so through the Holy Spirit who dwells in us. What a precious charge! The rich heritage of God's plan for mankind is, in every generation, placed in our stewardship. Is it any wonder our desire must be that the gift within us would be kindled afresh?

About four years ago I had the unique privilege of flying to Boston and then returning to Norfolk aboard the aircraft carrier *John F. Kennedy*. It was a special cruise for dependents of the sailors. On our second day aboard, there was an air show in which they launched the various planes carried on board that vessel. All of the planes were impressive, but for me the star of the show was the F-14 Tomcat. A 35-ton beast that generates 60,000 pounds of thrust and has significant fire power. A "cat" launch is an impressive sight under any circumstances. Try to imagine yourself being hurtled from a standing start to a speed of 160 miles an hour in 2.2 seconds in a space no longer than a football field.

I don't think the adrenaline level of the pilots could have exceeded mine as I waited to watch the launching of the first plane. I was privileged to watch this launch from above the flight deck. In the same space, in a very prominent position, was a young lad. He was carried to this position of honor because he was unable to walk on his own. He had a degenerative disease of the bones which was diagnosed as terminal. I soon learned that his dad was the commanding officer of the Tomcat squadron aboard and that he would be piloting the first plane. My anticipation was transformed to awe as I tried to place myself in that young lad's place as this might be the first and only time he would see his dad fly.

The cat was loaded. The signal given and the plane was literally hurtled into the morning sky. Now I am a fan of war movies of most every kind and had seen enough launches from old carriers that I expected the plane to dip down slightly at the end of the deck, skim over the water and then emerge victorious. When this Tomcat left the deck, it appeared to me that we had launched a rocket as it took off in an almost vertical trajectory. I was significantly impressed. I soon discovered that everyone else around me, even old hands, were nearly as awed by the launch as I was. The silence of the moment was broken with the exclamation—"a full afterburner launch." This was not the run-of-the-mill practice launch. To demonstrate to his son the capacity of the plane, the father had pulled out all the stops.

As I watched subsequent launches, even my untrained eye could see the difference in that launch and others. My vantage point enabled me to look directly up the exhaust of the F-14 as it was launched. The plane with full afterburners glowed with a white-hot heat, in contrast to an orange intensity of those under military power. I later learned from an officer in my church that the afterburner launch was not normally used to impress, but to provide the additional power needed when a plane had a full load of fuel and was armed for combat. Then the extra flame, the white-hot flame, was a necessity, not a luxury.

In a similar sense we do not need the rekindling of our gifts to white-hot heat in order to impress but because the glorious truth of the gospel demands nothing less than full afterburners. May we be stirred once again by God's Spirit.

9
INTERPRETING THE BIBLE: NEW TESTAMENT
Grant Osborne

It is, indeed, with a profound sense of humility that I approach this paper in light of the vast breadth of this topic and the tremendous importance of this conference. It is not without reason that both the International Conference on Biblical Inerrancy and the Ridgecrest Conference followed a preliminary consultation on inerrancy with a conference on hermeneutics. No discussion on biblical authority can proceed very far without delineating the parameters for interpreting Scripture. The two aspects are intertwined.

The more I have studied the proliferation of articles and books on the subject of biblical authority the more illuminating I have found the parallels between debates on inerrancy and the current Christological controversy. In a recent article, Gerald O'Collins lists several areas where traditional Christology has been challenged.[1] I would like to take each as an introduction to many of the issues in bibliology we are facing in this conference.

1. A Christology "from above" (centering upon the divine aspect) has been challenged by a Christology "from below" (centering upon Jesus' humanity). In the same way inerrantists have been charged with a docetic approach to Scripture, stressing only its revelatory nature while ignoring its human origins.

2. An incarnation-centered Christology is being replaced by an Easter-oriented approach, stressing God's acts of power as well as Jesus' divine nature. Similarly, critics have argued that inerrantists have based their approach upon a speculative construct (theoria) rather than the dynamic power of the Word to change lives (praxis).

3. The philosophical problems of the Chalcedonian "two natures in one person" can result in a submersion of the human within the divine; modern Christologies emphasize more the intersubjectivity and self-awareness of Jesus' personhood. Similarly, modern approaches to bibliology look to the process of interpretation as speech-act or a fusion of horizons rather than as a communication of propositional content. Inerrantists are charged with bibliolatry, making the Bible a set of cosmic laws rather than a casebook for encounter with God.

4. Recent approaches speak of a "naive mixture of history, faith, and 'mythical' imagery" in traditional Christology and thereby differentiate levels of confession between the brute facts (e.g. Jesus' birth) and faith-statements (e.g. His

conception by the Holy Spirit). The trend in modern hermeneutics has also been away from a "naive" supposition that the Bible is free from error and toward a separation between the salvific (where authority resides) and the phenomenological (where errors may occur) spheres of biblical statements.

5. The ministry and deeds of Jesus more than later creedal interpretation by the early church (e.g. Phil. 2:5-11 or Col. 1:15-20) are seen as determinative for a doctrine of the nature of Christ. In similar fashion recent critics have demanded that an inductive (what the Bible actually does) rather than deductive (what later theorists have formulated) approach must be taken to the doctrine of Scripture.

6. Modern interpreters refuse to differentiate between Jesus' person (Christology) and His work (soteriology). To subordinate the latter to the former is erroneous. The same charge is made of inerrantists, who are said to ground all dogma upon a view of an inerrant Bible. The latter is given inordinate importance and the actual phenomena within the Bible is artificially harmonized on the basis of a theoretical construct.

7. Modern theorists are no longer willing to develop a diachronic or even synchronic delineation of Christological themes in the first century but are contextualizing that data on the basis of the needs of the present context. Such is true, for instance, of materialist or liberation Christologies. The same is true of recent approaches to the Bible. Many modern practitioners argue for a dynamic rather than static view of inspiration. Paul Achtemeier sums up this school when he applies inspiration to the original event, the later tradition-development of that event leading to its codification in the canon and to later interpretations of that event in Scripture, church history, and today. The interpretation of each community on the basis of its needs is valid and from God.[2]

Current debates regarding the human and divine aspects of scriptural formulation, the static and dynamic approaches to biblical authority, and the propositional versus experiential elements of scriptural communication are, therefore, not new. The same debates were ensuing in many areas of theological inquiry and parallel controversies throughout the history of the church. Further, these debates are necessary components of any valid search for truth and must be addressed. However, we must be careful to avoid the disjunctive fallacy, that is, the tendency to make an either-or out of a both-and and to dismiss a view without valid reasons. In *The Unfettered Word* I was especially impressed with the article by Fisher Humphreys, "Biblical Inerrancy: A Guide for the Perplexed."[3] However, I found myself agreeing again and again with both sides. The criticisms by noninerrantists have a certain validity to them. The appeal to the original autographs, while necessary on one level, is distracting and obscure when made a final arbiter. Since text critics have produced a text about which we can be 99 percent certain, the inerrantist does not need to make this a pillar statement. Furthermore, concern for the static or propositional aspect of revelation can lead to a preoccupation with trivial details of dogma and a resultant denigration of the dynamic aspects of discipleship and obedience. Finally, such a static view fails to separate between original meaning and current interpretation, so that opinions on issues like eschatology or the charismatic debate are elevated to inerrant positions. Such an approach runs counter to the Reformation principle of the priesthood of the believer and the Baptist heritage of soul competency. However, while some inerrantists fall into these traps, not all do. Nuanced inerrantists like Packer, Kantzer, and Erickson certainly avoid these pitfalls.

The purpose of this paper is to provide a hermeneutical bridge between these options so that one can see inductively how the New Testament views and treats itself as well as deductively how we may approach Scripture in a way that is cognizant of these internal dimensions. Therefore, I will approach the topic in three stages: first to trace the modern hermeneutical debate and to suggest a way out of the dilemma of author-text-reader; second, to develop a hermeneutical approach which will preserve both the static or propositional content and the dynamic or existential relevance of the text for our lives; and third to apply these to the genre of the New Testament, especially to narrative, epistle, and apocalypse, in order to demonstrate the hermeneutical perspective concretely in actual texts. The problem will be to accomplish all this in a relatively short paper, so the reader will have to forgive certain over-generalizations.

The Modern Hermeneutical Debate

There are three components in the act of interpretation: a source (S), a message (M), and a receiver (R). The process of interaction between these elements is called interpretation, and for biblical study it involves a text (S) and a reader (R). However, where does meaning (M) reside? Traditional hermeneutics has taken an author-text approach; the task is to discover the author's "intended" meaning in the text. Friedrich Schleiermacher, the father of modern hermeneutics, believed that we can understand the author better than he understood himself.

Movement Away from the Author

Karl Barth also had a text-centered hermeneutic but added a dynamic twist which moved the goal away from the purely cognitive one of understanding the text. For Barth the Bible is not so much the Word of God as it *becomes* the Word of God when God addresses us through it. Barth and Brunner made biblical authority relational rather than propositional, oriented to encounter more than belief or understanding. Bultmann went a step further when he developed an existential approach to biblical relevance. The New Testament (hereafter NT) perspective is based upon the religious experience of the authors, which itself was mythical at the core. The modern reader comes to the text with a different set of presuppositions and so must "demythologize" the message in order to derive its existential core. Yet Bultmann's is still a text or author-centered hermeneutic,[4] though for him the conscious presuppositions of the reader play a much greater role.

The first true movement away from the author-text approach came with the New Hermeneutic and specifically with Hans-Georg Gadamer. Ernst Fuchs and Gerhard Ebeling developed a linguistic theory of the New Testament as "speech event" or "word event." For them it is the "word" rather than the text itself which constitutes meaning. Rather than the reader interpreting the text, the "hermeneutical circle" means that the text interprets the reader.

Gadamer in his magisterial *Truth and Method* calls this a "fusion of horizons," namely the horizon of the text and that of the interpreter. Interpretation does not involve reconstructing the past meaning of the text but establishing a dialectic with the text in the present. In the act of writing "meaning has under-gone a kind of self-alienation" and must be "stated anew" or reawakened to spoken language in a new relationship with the reader.[5] At the same time, according to Gadamer, interpretation is a historical act determined by the "temporal distance" between subject (interpreter) and object (text). This distanciation makes one's preunderstanding the key to meaning: The interpreter's prejudgments interrogate the text and in turn are interrogated by the text. The openness of the text must be paralleled by the openness of the interpreter as the historically conditioned horizons of both merge in the act of coming-to-understanding. It is important to realize here that Gadamer never denies the place of objective or scientific method. Rather he argues that such can never truly recreate the "original" meaning but must become part of the new aesthetic dialogue between text and reader.

A movement further away from the priority of the text occurred within structuralism, more particularly the post-structuralist school of semiotics. This school built upon Claude Levi Strass's theory that interpretation is a linguistic phenomenon depending not upon the "conscious" but the "unconscious" meaning in the deep structure underlying a text.[6] The key is to recognize the closed system of "signs" which determine the author's view of reality and which subsist at the subconscious level. A story such as John's version of the triumphal entry is first decomposed or broken up into its basic narrative units, then examined in terms of the binary opposites or structural codes in these units and finally is recomposed on the basis of transformational rules. The triumphal entry in John would be seen as a set of oppositions within the play of the text (e.g. Jesus' directions vs. the disciples' confusion, the crowds expectation vs. Jesus' acted parable, the donkey rather than a war horse) and these become codes for the interplay within the story itself and; thus, for the underlying or deep structure meaning.

Structuralists reject a diachronic approach to the past meaning of the text and utilize only a synchronic approach which seeks the present "meaning" for the community. Current biblical criticism, structuralists assert, centers upon the historical traditions rather than genre and plot development and, thus, sacrifices historical truth *(Geschichte)* on the altar of history *(Historie)*.[7]

However, dissatisfaction with inherent weaknesses in the system has led many to declare that structuralism per se has been superceded or is even "dead."[8] Their preoccupation with linguistics and their failure to lay a strong philosophical foundation coupled with a radical denial of history and its replacement by a closed system of signs are perceived by many as critical flaws. There is an inadequate foundation for the separate existence of "deep structures" in the mind. Primarily for us, the refusal to consider a text's historical horizon actually denies the synchrony of the text itself, since it originated not in a modern but rather in a past era. The lack of a rigorous methodology has thereby led to a reappraisal.

The post-structuralist movement which has made the greatest impact on literary criticism has been the "deconstruction" school of Jacques Derrida. For Derrida the "presence" of meaning in spoken language is excluded in the act of writing. The reason for this negation is the "difference" between the "signified" (the message to be imported) and the signifier (the terms or codes which impart that meaning). In the act of reading, meaning is transformed and cannot be transferred to the recipient.[9] Therefore, a text is open-ended at both ends (i.e. at the level of text and in the act of reading); the symbols can no longer be identified with their original intent. As a result "an infinite number of sign-substitutions come into play,"[10] as the varying interpretive playgrounds of readers lead to varying meanings.

Deconstruction is perceived as a "decentering" process in which the reader "deconstructs" the text from its historical referent and restructures meaning on the basis of the present encounter. John P. Leavey notes a two-step process of "reversal," which overturns the hierarchy of the text; and "reinscription," which creates a continual openness by transforming the old concepts and creating new interactions with the text.[11] The focus has now shifted entirely to the reader. The triumphal entry would consciously be removed from any historical referent, and each believing community would be free to restructure or unlock the narrative to new meanings for the present situation. This new interpretation would be achieved through a close reading of the text itself, allowing the text's own intertextuality to reform its own interpretation, that is to guide the readers to new understandings. In other words even in deconstruction the text is still the focus, but the reader's own analytical perspective becomes the guide through the text.

Similar to deconstruction (many would hold the two to be identical) is reader-response criticism which posits not only the autonomy of the text but also the veritable union of text and reader at the moment of response. The emphasis in interpretation has shifted from text to reader to response. Neither text nor interpreter has autonomy, for both fuse in the act of reading. David Bleich argues for a subjective criticism which replaces the text with individual identity.[12] The text is an object only in a physical sense; as meaning it exists only in the mind of the reader. Therefore, response unites the person with the text and is a subjective act leading to new meaning. In the moment of understanding, both text and reader are transformed into a new entity, recreated by the act of reading.

In the *Semeia* volume on the parable of the prodigal son, successive articles interpret the parable from the perspectives of Freudian psychoanalysis, Jungian archetypes, and structuralism respectively. Following this Susan Wittig provides a programmatic essay, "A Theory of Multiple Meanings."[13] She states that the presence of multiple meanings (technically called polyvalence) demands a new theory. Wittig calls for a "second-order" system in which an "unstated" significance in the surface structure itself compels an interpreter to complete it. The reader's own belief-system determines this meaning more than the signifier or text itself.

One dare not discount the influence of this movement. The New York Times recently published an essay on "The Tyranny of the Yale Critics," chronicalling the growing influence on American literature of deconstruction via the English department of Yale.[14] The output from this school is prodigious, and few departments of literature remain untouched. In biblical studies dozens of volumes appear every year, and it is fair to say that reader-oriented hermeneutics is winning the day over more traditional modes. For instance, Raymond E. Brown in his *The Critical Meaning of the Bible* recognizes the basic validity of seeking the original meaning but qualifies this by noting several stages in the "literal" sense: (1) the meaning it had when it left the author's pen; (2) the modified meanings given it by later redactors; (3) the sense it had when codified in the canon; (4) the meanings it had for later communities.[15] The church's interpretation might differ greatly from the original intent but is held in check by a dialogue with that literal meaning. In short the interactions of later communities are also formative of meaning. David Kelsey goes a step further, arguing for a "conceptual discontinuity" between textual meaning and theological formulation. It is the "aptness" rather than the accuracy of theological formulations which counts. Thus, exegesis is secondary to one's imaginative judgment, which controls the perspective and thereby the creative use of Scripture as normative.[16]

To react with anger or contempt, as so many have done, may result more from ignorance than knowledge. The difficulty in developing a hermeneutical blueprint for the interplay of author-text-reader in light of these challenges calls for careful consideration, especially when no one could deny a degree of truth in the centrality of the reader in the interpretive process. A great deal of what the reader-response critics argue actually occurs in many modern sermons and Bible study groups. The difference of course is that Derrida rejects the historical referent while the average evangelical merely ignores it. However the result (a subjective interaction with the text) is quite similar. Moreover, all of us who have argued with colleagues over eschatology or the ordination of women have said "Why can't they see the facts?" while failing to notice that our opponents are saying the same thing of us!

I agree with Tony Thiselton, who notes four levels at which the "illusion of textual objectivism" becomes apparent: (1) One's understanding exerts great influence over the interpretive act; (2) the differing situations between the recipients of a text as they interact make a purely objective approach impossible; (3) these problems are magnified when other factors intrude, such as narrative time, plot development, or dialogue; (4) meaning is never context-free but involves a large list of unconscious assumptions between sender and receiver.[17] It makes a great deal of difference whether one is a Southern Baptist, Methodist, or Presbyterian when studying a passage like the warning against apostasy in Hebrews 6:4-6.

An Attempted Solution

Most critical scholars agree that the author's intended meaning is a legitimate goal of historical-critical investigation but argue that it cannot be the primary goal since the contemporary world must construct its own meaning. The first mediator between the two sides is Ludwig Wittgenstein in his *Philosophical Investigations*. Here he added to the referential view of language in his *Tractatus* a functional approach. Wittgenstein argued that the multi-faceted character of language causes it to speak differently in various semantic situations or "games." Therefore, language cannot be expanded to abstract principles or universals but can only be applied to specific contexts. Meaning is not fixed but is subject to the laws of the particular language game.[18]

Thiselton applies this also to past language games in written texts. He has developed three classes of grammatical utterances: (1) "topic-neutral" statements which do not provide information and depend on the reader's understanding; (2) foundation statements which are unshakable axioms; and (3) linguistic recommendations which apply "institutional facts" to force a reappraisal of one's views.[19] The latter two demand a recognition of intentionality and are not as open to multiple meanings as are class one utterances. The language games in these instances contain rules which allow the interpreter to discover their intended meaning. Let us examine this further.

1. *Verification and Meaning: The Contribution of Analytical Philosophy.* On the basis of the verifiability principle, A. J. Ayer and other logical positivists argued that only sense data from the physical world can be empirically verified

and thus be valid. In response Frederick Ferré has developed a system of "interpretive realism" or "functional analysis" which expands the narrow limitation of "fact" to empirical data. Ferré conceives reality on the basis of rational thinking rather than mere sense-perception and seeks theories which correspond to reality.[20] The use of language in its own context becomes the basis of verification. Since religious language belongs to a metaphysical frame of reference, it is verifiable along analogical lines, namely its correspondence to interpretive (in keeping with the intrinsic meaning of the facts) and confessional (relation to personal beliefs) reality.

Analytical philosophy takes a functional view of language similar to that of the later Wittgenstein. There are a variety of speech utterances in the New Testament and they do not all operate on the propositional level. Hermeneutics must allow a variety of language games to take place between text and readers. John Searle argues that speech itself is referential; the sentence brings the hearer into a rule-governed arena so that meaning can be attained intrinsically. The object or reference exists in the rules of the language game and the sender or text supplies preparatory conditions or presuppositions as well as "excluders" which help the reader to identify the referential meaning on the basis of the linguistic relationships.[21] There are both performative and referential functions in biblical language, and these aid the interpreter to understand their original intent.

2. *Paradigm Structure and Intentionality*. T. S. Kuhn in his monumental *The Structure of Scientific Revolutions* examines the way paradigms or supertheories change in the scientific community. Change occurs when a community of scholars with their shared values come to consensus on the validity of a new paradigm. This has come under recent critical scrutiny in volumes by Frederick Suppe and Gary Gutting among others.[22] Here we will center upon Ian Barbour's application of this to religious paradigms. Agreeing with the importance of shared paradigms in a community (which parallels both reader-oriented criticism and analytical philosophy) and noting that observations are paradigm-dependent, Barbour argues that a continual dialogue between paradigm communities leads more often to "micro-revolutions" than to full paradigm shifts. Although all data are value-laden, observations can be controlled by independent criteria of assessment and even metaphysical assumptions are not immune to change. Religious commitment combined with critical reflection and dialogue between communities provide objective features that help to overcome subjective prejudices.[23] In other words, on issues like eternal security or the ordination of women, both sides can dialogue, examine the data (i.e. study the text afresh due to the challenge from the other side) and thereby come closer to the "truth."

The major problem is, of course, one's preunderstanding. On the basis of competing paradigms or systems, one interpreter may see coherence and adequacy in a Calvinistic understanding of John 10:27-29 and Hebrews 6:4-6, while another may reject this approach. Is there any way out of the impasse? Only if the competing paradigms are open to dialogue. If not, the original meaning may not be recoverable (both sides believe they have it!). D. A. Carson notes two types of preunderstanding: a "functional non-negotiable," an accepted position which remains open to the evidence; and an "immutable non-negotiable," a fixed position which is closed to contrary data.[24] Most of us would align with the former and on some issues would add a third category, a "negotiable" position which invites dialogue and continually seeks further data. In short, community dialogue and the possibility of countering one's preunderstanding through critical reflection in a pluralistic setting make it possible to experience change within a paradigm community. In fact, we evangelicals should add our contribution in light of this, a "hermeneutics of humility" which refuses to take itself more seriously than the text and seeks to learn from rather than merely triumph over one's theological opponent. We above all should be seeking truth rather than merely using the Bible to confirm our preconceived views.

When this is applied to the issue of intentionality, the results are interesting. Since the appearance of Wimsatt and Beardsley's classical essay, "The Intentional Fallacy," the debate has accelerated on both sides. Analytical philosophy has often addressed the problem, for instance in G. E. M. Anscombe's *Intention*. Approaching the issue through her mentor, Wittgenstein, Anscombe asserts that intention is a form of description which answers the question "why?" Therefore, it is connected to practical knowledge and is open to examination and interpretation.

Most who deny the viability of seeking the author's intention do so on the basis of certitude. For instance, deconstructionist J. Hillis Miller states, "It's not that no thing is referential, but that it is *problematically* referential" (italics his).[25] Probability theory has increasingly come to the fore in discussions of meaning transference and truth claims. In the 1967 issue of *Philosophy Review,* separate articles by R. Firth and J. L. Pollock argue for the priority of probability theory over necessary knowledge, stating that the demand for certitude negates the quest for knowledge before it can even begin.[26] The criteria for meaning centers upon adequacy, coherence and synonymy and this itself depends upon a theory of probability in decision making. Therefore, as competing communities interact and debate passages like 1 Timothy 2:8-15 (on the ordination of women), criteria of coherence and adequacy enable them to challenge and correct one another and thereby to move closer to the original intent of the text and its significance for today. Paradigm systems are not self-contained and mutually exclusive in any final sense. There must be dialogue between competing truth-claims based upon internal consistency (lack of contradiction), coherence, comprehensiveness (enveloping all experience), and congruity (the theory adequately accounts for new evidence); then one can move beyond multiple meanings to the probable intended meaning in a text.

3. *Propositional Truth and Dynamic Views of Inspiration*. It is increasingly popular today to deny that the New Testament has a static or propositional component which must be taken seriously. Yet it is difficult to deny that the New Testament contains assertive sentences and propositional content. An interesting paper read at the 1982 Northwestern Conference on Semiotics was John Morreall's "Religious Texts and Religious Beliefs." He stated that the semiotic disregard for questions of reference to reality in the Bible undermines the very nature of religious belief. Religious faith itself derives from assent to propositions. While the language of the Bible is, indeed, the speech-act, the most important speech-act is assertion. If the autonomy thesis applies, there is no referential dimension and no set of assertions which call for belief. We are awash in a sea of relativity with no ship of truth to save us.

Of course not all speech-acts in the New Testament take propositional form, Thiselton notes the "unhelpful polarization in the debate" and states that the issue of dynamic vs. static concepts of biblical truth is not an either-or but a both-and.[27] The presence of metaphor and parable is a case in point. In fact the whole discussion of narrative in the third section will demonstrate how narrative and proposition (dynamic and static) forms can blend together in a single genre.[28]

Figurative speech does not of itself entail polyvalence. Redaction criticism should teach us that. Even parables were placed into contexts for a purpose. Most polyvalent interpretations fail to consider the immediate literary context. For instance, the multiple dimensions of the prodigal son parable in Luke 15 are polyvalent when the parable is taken by itself but have clear parameters when studied in light of its immediate context. The father is God, the younger son refers to the "tax-collectors and sinners," and the older brother represents the "Pharisees and scribes" (see vv. 1-2).

Few scholars doubt that the Bible contains propositions; rather they question what these assertions entail. For instance James Barr charges evangelicals with categorical error, stating that they misunderstand the function of biblical statements, which are given not so much to provide cognitive information as to encounter the reader with the reality of God.[29] Barr and many modern critics deny a referential or propositional approach to divine revelation and prefer an aesthetic or poetic understanding which sees the New Testament message as internal or literary rather than external or historical. Yet again this is guilty of the disjunctive fallacy. We are arguing that the Bible has both a static, propositional message and a dynamic, aesthetic dimension.

Kevin Vanhoozer argues strongly for an informative as well as an affective aspect within Scripture's attestations. The key is to allow the "diverse literary forms" within the Bible to guide the interpreter. The genre or literary form provides a context within which the informative and affective dimensions can be clearly delineated. Following Wittgenstein and Hirsch, Vanhoozer points a way out of the impasse: genre provides a set of rules which help the interpreter understand the language game being played and to allow poetic and didactic portions to function according to their own forms.[30] Utilizing John Searle's discussion of illocutionary force (what one wishes to accomplish with words) in speech acts, Vanhoozer proposes that a text's genre provides a guide to both its propositional and illocutionary or affective purposes by allowing the reader to see it in all its manifold purposes.[31] In other words any proper hermeneutic must recognize both static (propositional) and dynamic (performative) dimensions in the New Testament.

4. *Conclusion—An Authority Grid*. A completely static view of New Testament revelation does injustice to the illocutionary force behind even the propositional statements. Even more it allows individuals to link their systems too closely to Scripture and to extend inerrancy to opinion as well as fact. A flow chart will help to demonstrate this:

Flow-Chart on Authority

Level I	text	implicit authority
	↓	↑
Level II	interpretation	derived authority
	↓	↑
Level III	contextualization	applied authority

As one can see the level of authority descends as we proceed from the text to interpretation to application. One's interpretation has authority only to the extent that it coheres with the text's intended meaning. Here I am consciously building upon everything said to date. First, the intended meaning of the text is a possible goal for interpretation. Second, it is valid to seek the intended meaning. Third, the New Testament demands that the reader understand (the propositional aspect of meaning) and respond (the affective aspect of meaning) to that message. Therefore, implicit authority resides only in the author-text and derived authority in one's interpretation. Multiple or competing meanings occur when different paradigm communities read the text on the basis of their systems and see different "truths" in it. Yet all do not have the same authority; each must ask whether the other may be "more true" or cohere more closely to the original meaning. That tension should lead to a critical realism which re-examines the text and one's interpretation in a constant reappraisal.

Hirsch's distinction between meaning and significance is seen in the application or contextualization of one's interpretation. The movement here is from "what it meant" to "what it means." At this third level multiple "meanings" operate in a valid sense. The text will have different significances in differing contexts. However the validity of the application will depend upon the extent to which it coheres with the interpretation.

A Field Approach to Hermeneutics

The paper thus far has demonstrated the validity of integrating the two major aspects, meaning (author-text) and significance (text-reader). The polarities which have clouded the hermeneutical debate over inerrancy—dynamic vs. static views of revelation, propositional vs. encounter theology, word vs. sentence vs. discourse models of communication, informative vs. poetic approaches to literature—are interdependent parts of a larger whole. It remains now to provide a hermeneutical grid for demonstrating this, i.e. to add the praxis to the theoria.

(1) A close reading of the text cannot be done without the perspective provided by one's preunderstanding. Reflection demands mental categories, and that is provided first by one's basic world-view and then by the paradigm community, for us the Southern Baptist community. Since neutral exegesis is impossible, there will always be differences of opinion. However, as I have said, this does not necessitate polyvalence or multiple meanings. Probability theory allows critical interaction, as long as the communities are open to dialogue. The key is to follow Paul Ricoeur's suggestion and to place ourselves "in front of" the text rather than "behind it," so that the text can draw us into its own world.[32] This critical reflection will enable us to determine which types of preunderstanding are valid and which are not.

(2) Good hermeneutical principles will shape our exegesis and control our tendency to read our prejudices into the text. Historical-critical tools will make us aware of the need to center upon the biblical framework and grammatical-historical exegesis will allow the text to speak for itself. Peter Stuhlmacher calls for "methodological verifiability" (lest subjectivity control modern exegesis) combined with an "openness to transcendence" which keeps the interpreter continually open to the new possibilities in the text.[33]

(a) Note the genre or type of literature and interpret according to the proper rules of the language game. This is where the propositional and illocutionary aspects come to play. If the biblical statement is informative, one gives it intellectual assent; if it is commissive, one reacts with obedience. Vanhoozer provides an excellent discussion of infallibility and inerrancy in this light. "Logically . . . infallibility is prior to inerrancy. God's Word invariably accomplishes its purpose (infallibility); and when this purpose is assertion, the proposition of the speech act is true (inerrancy)."[34] Each passage is allowed to guide the interpreter in its intended direction, whether it be belief or action. This will be developed further in the next section.

(b) A delineation of structural development will provide a control against atomistic exegesis (the error of both form criticism and grammatical-historical exegesis). Rhetorical and narrative criticism has moved away from the parts to the whole. Meaning results from the symmetry of the passage as a whole not from the isolated parts. Moreover the context of the whole controls the meaning of the parts and provides parameters so the interpreter might choose between alternative proposals.

(c) Semantic research in this light is based upon synchronic and structural considerations rather than diachronic research. In the past word studies were universally based upon etymology and linguistic roots. However, human language is rarely cognizant of past meanings and linguists today note that the background of a word is a valid aspect of meaning only when there is a deliberate allusion, as in the New Testament use of the Old Testament.[35] Meaning is determined on the basis of the congruence of two factors, semantic field and context. One first determines all the possible lexical meanings of the term and then selects the meaning which best fits the context.

For instance, scholars have long debated the thrust of *ekenosen* in the Philippians hymn (2:7). The controversy has centered upon the exact thrust of "emptied," i.e. is Jesus' emptying himself of His deity (the kenotic school) or of the prerogatives of deity (the traditional approach). However, Gerald Hawthorne has recently shown that the intransitive form of the verb does not mean "empty" (no content is specified in 2:7) but "make law" and is synonymous with "humbled" in verse 8.[36] A proper use of semantics can solve a major theological problem and help one get much closer to the original meaning of the text. However, the blend of semantics and structure enables the interpreter to avoid static or atomistic approaches which lead to what James Barr calls "illegitimate totality transfer,"[37] i.e. erroneously applying all the possible theology behind a word to its use in an individual context. This is a constant mistake in Kittel's *Theological Dictionary of the New Testament*, in which terms are studied on the basis of biblical theology rather than context.

(3) A judicious use of background can help one avoid the opposite error, ignoring the historical aspect on behalf of the poetic. Scholars trained in modern literary criticism so stress the intratextual dimension that they deliberately cut the passage off from its historical moorings and as a result twist its meaning in an internal direction. The tendency is to say, "the text contains all the meaning there is." The problem, however, is that the New Testament author shared certain assumptions with his readers, and the interpreter needs to discover these underlying "givens" for properly understanding the text.

For instance, the letter to Laodicea in Revelation 3:14-22 builds upon two aspects of Laodicean experience, their water problem and their civic economic pride. In verses 15-16 the message depends upon the fact that Laodicea had no direct water supply. They lay between Colosse, known for its cold, clear water, and Hieropolis, famed for its hot springs. They had to pipe their water from Hieropolis, and it arrived lukewarm and mineral-laden, unfit for drinking. Thus when they are told "I wish you were cold or hot" and "I am about to spew you out of my mouth," it was a particularly forceful message. Interpreters unaware of the background have often made the mistake of reading "spiritually cold" (negative) and "spiritually hot" (positive) here.[38]

However, many practitioners of this method go too far in the other direction. The sociological school is often guilty of a revisionist rewriting of biblical history on the basis of modern sociological models. For instance, Norman Gottwald in *The Tribes of Yahweh* changes the conquest of Canaan from a migration into a Marxist-like internal revolt of disenchanted peasants against the rich Canaanite proletariat. There is a constant tendency to read speculative historical parallels into the text without asking whether they are true parallels rather than seeming parallels. As a result some have reacted negatively to the value of sociological analysis in biblical backgrounds.[39]

However, this is too extreme, and a balanced use is preferable, observing several cautions: (1) Make certain that the background material stems from the same era as the text; this is the error of both Alfred Edersheim and Strack-Billerbeck who applied Talmudic parallels indiscriminately to the New Testament without asking how many of the parallels reflected the pre-AD 70 situation. (2) Collect all the possible parallels; most scholars fail to differentiate between possible parallels and probable parallels. The research is often not broad enough to prove any more than an analogical link. This is the common error of the History of Religions school. (3) Apply all possible parallels and ascertain (on the basis of context) which best fits the data. Here one moves from a seeming parallel to a likely parallel; the means for determining this is the extent to which the contexts overlap. Does the Jewish or Greco-Roman custom actually explain the passage better than the other possibilities? Does it cohere with the data?

(4) One of the most vociferous debates has occurred regarding biblical and systematic theology. Many critics have doubted the very validity of a biblical theology since it stems from a propositional view of Scripture. Hence the new biblical theology movement has stressed narrative theology, centering upon the interactions between Jesus and His followers and between Paul and his churches. In other words this new emphasis is a reflection of the dynamic view of the New Testament and comes from an encounter theology rather than a content-oriented faith. Again we have argued that the two are not dichotomous and that a true biblical theology will bridge from the informative to the personal as the data indicates. For instance Hebrews and James warn and command obedience far more than they inform.

Biblical theology begins at the descriptive level, collating the results of the exegesis done at the earlier stages. Here the interpreter tries to draw together the plan and emphases by book and then by author, noting for instance the interplay between Christology and discipleship in Mark and Matthew and between Christology and soteriology in Luke and John. Again both static and dynamic aspects are noted as indicated by the data. The next step is more controversial, depending as it does upon prior decisions regarding unity and diversity in the New Testament.[40] However, at the deep structure level (i.e. the level of theological underpinnings) differences of language and emphasis are not so great as to preclude a deeper paradigm unity.[41] Therefore, archetypal patterns can be discovered which bridge not only the books but also the testaments (demonstrated for instance in the work of Gerhard Hasel and Brevard Childs).

Systematic Theology is a contextualization of biblical theology according to the world view and thought patterns of our day and our culture. The data is supplied by biblical theology and the issues are noted first as they have appeared throughout the history of dogma and second as they speak to the modern situation. The content is filtered through exegetical and biblical theology, but organization and form stem from the current era. After the collation of the biblical data, one traces both the propositional/dogmatic and the performative emphases of the individual books then notes patterns which emerge from the progress of revelation through the biblical period. These provide the major themes studied analytically as they tie together the major themes of God's revelation. Finally, one can reorganize or package this data (again noting the interaction of theoria and praxis) on the basis of cultural norms. For instance, if one were to develop the doctrine of the perseverance of the saints, one would see how the theme is stressed in the covenant passages of the Pentateuch then trace it through the relationship between Yahweh and Israel in the Old Testament and between Christ and the church in the New. Apostasy and perseverance would be studied as they appear in Luke and John, as well as in Romans and Hebrews, then the passages on both sides (apostasy and perseverance) would be studied to develop the balance between sovereignty and perseverance and to decide which "system" best fits the data. Finally, the material will be reworked in order to explain and apply (the static and the dynamic aspects) the issue for our day.

Yet there is another side to biblical issues: Every exegetical decision has political ramifications. If some of you were to change your mind on issues discussed here (with an irenic spirit), you could be fired from your pulpit! People can feel very strongly about such positions as women in the church, the rapture question, or the perseverance of the saints. We need a biblical perspective for theological debate.

A Perspective on Theological Debates

Aspect	Attitude	Action
Cardinal Doctrine	⟶ Intolerance ⟶	Discipline

Middle Position: Denominational Distinctives

Non-cardinal Non-essential Doctrines	⟶ Tolerance ⟶	Dialogue

Criterion: The Word of God
Control: The history of dogma

Whenever an issue comes up on our church, we need to ask first what our attitude should be—tolerance or intolerance. If it is an issue calling for tolerance, we will "agree to disagree," and the resultant action will be dialogue. On that topic the paradigm communities will interact and challenge one another with mutual respect. If the issue calls for intolerance, we will have to discipline the offender—either ask him to stop teaching or, if it is serious, remove him from the church roll. How do we decide this? The difference is whether we are dealing with a cardinal doctrine, which is defined as an essential doctrine on which Scripture is clear and firm (such as the deity of Christ or substitutionary atonement).

Yet how do we differentiate a cardinal from a non-cardinal doctrine? All would agree that the Word of God is the sole criterion. Yet the problem is that everyone with a hobby-horse issue believes the Bible makes it essential. Therefore, we need a control, and that is the history of dogma. Any issue which arises is studied in light of church history. Cardinal doctrines have been settled for centuries and are challenged only by those who deny the Word of God. Issues which have continued to be the source of debate among those with a high view of biblical authority are shown to be non-essentials. Let us consider the debate over women in the church. Many have linked that with inerrancy, stating that all who allow women's ordination deny Scripture. Yet we have seen here that many inerrantist do, indeed, believe that the Bible allows women's ordination (see below). Further, many Baptist groups (as well as other evangelical denominations) have had women pastors or deacons in the recent past. Therefore, this is a matter for tolerance and dialogue, not for discipline.

Finally, we must note a middle position. Some denominational distinctives may well fall into the tolerant camp but for reasons of denominational history are distinctives. In my denomination an example would be the premillenial return of Christ; within the SBC an example would be eternal security. We can be tolerant of those who hold opposing views but still recognize a denomination's right to elevate a doctrine to a higher level for the sake of unity.

(5) Hermeneutics is incomplete until the material has been contextualized or applied to our own lives. This, in fact was one of the most frequent criticisms of inerrantists in the first Ridgecrest Conference.[42] The theory itself was developed by missiologists who sought hermeneutical guidelines for cross-cultural communication of the gospel. Yet it applies to any proclamation of Scripture. The task of hermeneutics is not complete until we have wedded our exegesis of the Word to an exegesis of our world. Yet the debate continues. How free is our communication? If the New Testament is primarily functional and personal rather than dogmatic, the current context will control our interpretation and one would develop an "indigenous Christianity" (the approach of the liberation theologian). If there is a propositional core (as we have argued), one would maintain a "form" and "content" distinction, that is, the content will remain inviolate but the form by which it is expressed will differ depending on the culture. A diagram may help us to visualize the hermeneutical process.

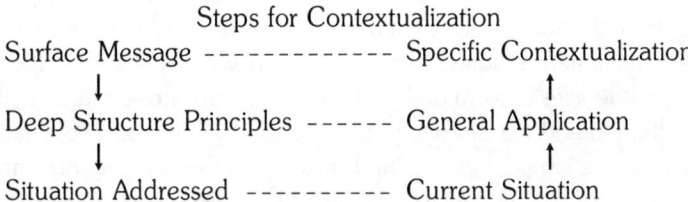

Steps for Contextualization

Surface Message ------------- Specific Contextualization
↓   ↑
Deep Structure Principles ------ General Application
↓   ↑
Situation Addressed ---------- Current Situation

The "deep structure" is the larger theological foundation from which Paul or another writer "contextualized" (see the discussion of "Epistles" below), the material he stressed for his readers. The "situation" is the *Sitz im Leben* ("situation in the life" of the church) which led to the particular emphasis. Through exegesis the interpreter proceeds from the surface statement to the underlying theology to the situation behind the passage. This becomes the basis for the contextualization. First one identifies a parallel situation in the life of the church (or one's self) today and then applies the passage at either the general or "deep" structure level or at the level of the surface or specific teaching. For instance, 1 Peter 1:6-7 actually addresses a persecution situation; but since the language applies to many "diverse" trials (cf. Jas. 1:2-4 which uses the same catechetical language in a more general sense), the preacher can apply it to more general "trials" today as well as to specific persecution.

In conclusion hermeneutics must deal honestly with both the cognitive and the functional sides of the New Testament. If the propositional element is ignored, the New Testament will degenerate into merely the outdated religious experience of an ancient people, the early Church. If the commissive side is ignored, New Testament religion becomes sterile and irrelevant. As James says, "Be doers of the Word and not merely hearers, deceiving yourselves" (1:22).

New Testament Genres

Narrative

Nearly 60 percent of the New Testament consists of narrative material, yet this is the least understood of the literary types. Traditionally evangelicals have stressed the historical side of the material and liberals the theological. However, a new movement has developed from literary criticism, asserting that neither is adequate and that we must approach it as literature. The dictum of this school is "the text and only the text"; however, what is usually meant by this is a close reading of the text applying the theories of reader response and deconstruction espoused earlier in this paper. As Kenneth Dauber puts it, "The Bible is not a text to be interpreted; rather, . . . interpretation is the text itself. No subject engages no object to be read. 'Relationality,' prior to both, defines subject and object according to itself."[43] In other words one does not "interpret" in a traditional sense but establishes an encounter relationship with the text.

At the outside this radical denial of the historical dimension seems confusing. Within New Testament studies, however, it is a valid reaction to the radical historicizing tendencies of form and tradition criticism. Those critics divided the text into authentic and inauthentic pericopes on the basis of a speculative reconstruction of the original events and in so doing entirely ignored the final form of the text. Redaction criticism did little better since it accepted the results of tradition criticism and simply reversed the emphasis by centering upon the evangelist's additions to reconstruct a "theology" of Matthew or of Mark. So the narrative critics have rediscovered the text. In itself this is a healthy development. However, we dare not ignore the radical rejection of history *(Historie)* in favor of a fictive dimension *(Geschichte)*. As John J. Collins states:

> The rediscovery of biblical narrative has been largely a consequence of the negative results of historical research. This point has theological importance. Many conservative biblicists have invoked literary criticism as a way of avoiding unwelcome historical conclusions . . . It should be clear that such evasions will not work . . . "Story" is not "history." It is essentially fiction, material which has in some measure been invented.[44]

David Rhoads in similar fashion asserts that "the integrity of the narrative" demands that we consider the gospel "story" as "a literary creation of the author with an *autonomous integrity* quite apart from any resemblances to the real world of Jesus' time (italics his)."[45]

However, I agree far more with Joanna Dewey, who argues that "the procedure is in a sense arbitrary; one can enter the circle of literary criticism at any point," adding that "the two approaches, rhetorical-literary and redaction-critical, are complimentary. Both seek to understand the Gospel, and they can aid each other in the task."[46] Certainly there is a fictive dimension in the

Gospels—plot, structure, narrator, characterization, dialogue, narrative, time—all are present in the Gospels' story form. However, this does not mean that the stories have no connection with the originating events behind them. The two—original event and Gospel retelling—are interdependent. In fact there are several components which interact together to produce meaning: the event, the author, the story and the reader.

Hans Frei decries "the eclipse of biblical narrative" and argues that we must return to a pre-critical "realistic" reading, by which he means a recognition of the "history-like" character of Gospel narrative. In so doing, however, he differentiates this from a referential approach which links the originating historical event and its depiction in the Gospels. For Frei the narrative shape *is* the meaning, for the events point to the reality of the person.[47] Frei's is an interesting and helpful corrective to the radical negation of history in modern narrative criticism, but he does not go far enough. Meir Sternberg (discussing Old Testament narrative) rejects any dichotomy whatsoever saying "it is a pity indeed . . . that enthusiasts about the 'literary' approach to the Bible should preach as historical doctrines whose brief heyday has long passed and which were never quite literally meant, let alone practiced, even by their New Critical originators."[48] For Sternberg, the literary and historical approaches exist side-by-side and inform one another. Therefore biblical narrative, though fiction-like in its character, cannot be linked in any sense with fiction. It is both literary and historical.[49]

I will go one step further than Sternberg and argue that hermeneutics must blend the historical and the literary features in order to get to the meaning of the text. As a literal re-presentation of events (note the claim of Luke 1:1-4 to be an "orderly account" of "eyewitness" testimony),[50] the background behind the text is important, especially since it often reflects shared assumptions between the author and his first century readers. Nevertheless, the text as a literary enterprise controls the study and the interpreter should not go beyond it in recreating the event (i.e. in the act of interpreting the text). Hermeneutical criteria will help us do so.[51]

1. First ask how the four Gospels relate to one another and to the events that surrounded the historical Jesus. They are not chronological in essence but literary; none of the four give us a month-by-month chronicle of the events. Rather each evangelist was free to draw from the many potential stories those he wished and to arrange, highlight, and color them so as to bring out certain nuances or theological emphases. These could differ greatly from Gospel to Gospel depending upon the emphasis of the evangelist. For instance, the feeding of the five thousand and walking on the water scenes conclude quite differently in Mark (6:52) and Matthew (14:33). Mark ends with "their hearts were hardened" (comparing the disciples with Pharaoh) while Matthew concludes with a Christological confession ("Truly you are the Son of God"). Greater polarization in two versions of the same story is difficult to conceive. However,

Mark decided to contextualize at a point two-thirds through the story (omitting the positive ending) in order to stress discipleship failure, while Matthew adds the scene with Peter walking on the water to demonstrate how Jesus' presence brought the disciples to understanding. The same emphases are found after the feeding of the four thousand (Mark 8:21; Matt. 16:20) so the differences are due to theological themes and do not constitute a historical difficulty.

The critical aspect is closely related to the theological. When does a historical discrepancy become an error? The example from Mark 6 and Matthew 14 is not an error, for there is no historical discrepancy. Rather there is an editorial choice, and omission does not constitute an error.

The doctrine of inerrancy does not demand that we have the ipsissima verba (the exact words) of Jesus but rather the ipsissima vox (the authentic voice), as Paul Feinberg's classic article on inerrancy demonstrated.[52] This is important, for it means the evangelists were free to paraphrase and put Jesus' sayings in their own style. For instance, J. I. Packer in last year's conference used this to solve the dilemma of the different styles of Jesus' sayings in the Synoptics and in John, saying, "Reportorial conventions are not errors."[53] Similarly, let me respond to an example used by Alan Culpepper in *The Unfettered Word*, to show that "Jesus did not use the Scriptures inerrantly." He cited Mark 2:25,26, which says that David took the shewbread from the Temple "when Abiathar was high priest." In reality Ahimelech, Abiathar's father, was high priest (1 Sam. 21:1-6).[54] However, the Jews often telescoped together both passages and events in order to make a point. I believe it is more likely that Jesus deliberately telescoped the later situation into the earlier in order to remind his hearers of Abiathar's later exalted position. Again there is no need to posit error. I am an inerrantist not merely on deductive grounds but also on an inductive basis. In my years of studying the Gospels, I am unconvinced that any errors have been proven. The Gospels are the proving ground for all theories of biblical authority, for they present the greatest challenge due to the four differing versions of the life of Christ.

2. Do a close reading of the text, noting the narrative flow. While inductive Bible study has stressed this approach for years, narrative critics have added refinements which greatly aid the interpreter.[55] For example, the concepts of implied author and narrator help one to identify how the story is told; in the Gospels there is an omniscient author who knows all and can comment upon the significance of details. Also the "implied reader" enables the interpreter to note the audience and effect the text wishes to make. I call this "reader identification," i.e. asking what the text asks the (implied) reader to do with the story. This is a crucial step to contextualization. The development of and dialogue between the characters guide one to the plot and purpose of the story. The narrative world is the thought-world of the text which draws the reader into itself and calls for interaction. The interactions within the story compel the

reader to respond in ways dictated by the text itself. All these elements combine to compel the reader to react and fill in the "gaps" in the text, and this leads to understanding at both the theological and dynamic levels.

3. Do a source-critical and redaction-critical study comparing the Gospels. Many doubt that there is any propositional element in narrative; however, redaction criticism for all its pitfalls[56] has proven the presence of a biblical theology in the Gospels. The consensus position, with which I concur, is that Mark was the first Gospel and Matthew and Luke used his Gospel as well as their own sources and a Q source containing sayings of Jesus. On the basis of this, I will compare the Gospels and note the omissions, expansions, and paraphrastic emphases. This does not produce the meaning, for that comes out of the narrative as a whole. However, it does present a crucial control to guide the theological emphases of the writer. For instance, Matthew's Beatitudes center upon spiritual qualities (5:3, "blessed are the poor in spirit") and Luke's upon the economic aspect (6:20,24, "blessed are you poor . . . woe to you rich"). In both cases they fit the major theological emphases of each Gospel.

4. Trace the extent to which the points are theological threads running throughout the Gospel. We tend to forget that individual episodes or sayings are not meant to be taken in isolation but are part of a larger context. This is why modern scholars see the parables as polyvalent. By themselves they are, for they can be used in diverse contexts. However, Jesus (and the Gospel writers) always placed them in contexts. Therefore, they do have a basic meaning in those contexts and that meaning is available to the interpreter.[57] For instance the parable of the rich man and Lazarus (Luke 16:19-31) has two emphases: a stress on salvation (due to the larger context of chs. 15-17) and an economic thrust (due to the narrower context of ch. 16). Moreover both are major threads linked together in the Gospel as a whole.

5. Use background as part of the detailed exegesis of the text. The narrative by itself can be misunderstood unless placed consciously within the historical parameters of Jesus' day. Background data not only provides good illustrations for explaining the text but also functions as an aid to interpretation. Unless one understood the ceremony of the Feast of Tabernacles, one could not understand how Jesus replaced both the water and the candle ceremonies in the feast with Himself as the source of "living water" and as the "light of the world" (7:14,37-39; 8:12). Parables are the best example of the value of backgrounds. Only by uncovering such could the reader catch the option that the so-called "unjust steward" (Luke 16:1-8) may have been lowering not the loan itself but either the interest[58] or his own commission.[59] Of course background information can be overdone so that the text is either rewritten or overwhelmed. A good example of this is Kenneth Bailey who treats Jesus' parables in Luke as real events and adds details hardly intended either by Jesus or Luke.[60] Nevertheless, when used in a nuanced fashion, historical background

is essential to the meaning of the text. The key is that the text controls, and sociological or background exegesis never becomes an end in itself but rather is utilized as a means to elucidate the text.

The Epistles

At first glance one would think that Epistles almost interpret themselves. Most of us have cut our spiritual teeth on Paul's Epistles, and they seem much simpler to understand than narrative or apocalyptic. However, they have their own problems, not only for Paul's garbled syntax and incredibly complex theological concepts but also for the whole issue of contextualization or cross-cultural exegesis. All recognize that the Epistles in some fashion were occasional letters sent to answer specific problems in local congregations. Nearly all fall within the Greco-Roman epistolary pattern of salutation, greeting, thanksgiving and prayer, body, closing greetings.[61] However, several do not follow this format: Hebrews lacks the first three elements; James, 2 Peter and Jude lack the closing greetings; and 1 John lacks both opening and closing. By form these could be called treatises or general tracts meant for the whole church. However, by content those most frequently discussed in this light are Romans, Hebrews, and James. On the whole all the New Testament Epistles are recognized as specific letters which were also meant for the whole church. Hermeneutically, this is important because of the tendency of most evangelicals to "proof text," that is to prove doctrines by appealing to isolated verses. Here we need to remember the earlier breakdown between the surface message and the deep structure theological principle. Individual passages or statements in the epistles are contextualizations which stress one aspect of a larger biblical theological principle in order to meet a specific need. Therefore, we should not overly dogmatize but build theology only out of the whole fabric of passages on an issue. Individual passages provide the parts, biblical theology the whole, and out of this we construct our dogma.

This is important also for the other debated aspect, the question of cultural relativity. There are certain situations—footwashing, slavery, temple feasts, head covering, meat offered to idols and so on—which belong in the first century and seem to have little to do with us. Some have gone to an extreme and posited a Scripture which was authoritative primarily at the macro-structure level (the deep structure level of salvation) more than at the micro-structure level (the surface level of the culturally relative text).[62] However, this is reductionistic, for too many passages are clearly meant for the church down through the ages. Of course incidental references like Paul's command to Timothy to bring his cloak and scrolls (2 Tim. 4:12) can hardly be applied. Few if any argue that all commands are automatically applicable to all cultures throughout the ages. For instance even those which practice footwashing or the holy kiss do so only at the eucharistic celebration and not in the sense of the original command. In my own baptistic heritage and in Southern Baptist churches, women do not have to pray with their heads covered (1 Cor. 11:2-16 is cultural) but are not allowed to teach men in an official church capacity (1 Tim. 2:11-15 is normative or supracultural).

This is an important principle. In our own heritage we recognize that there are culturally relative passages but that many are normative for all ages. The problem is identifying such hermeneutically. Some do in fact argue against any such division. J. Robertson McQuilin has argued that only those passages which are explicitly overturned in the New Testament should be considered culturally relative.[63] This, however, is problematic for there are many passages which are implicitly if not explicitly tied to the first-century culture (like meat offered to idols) and which must be applied at a secondary level if they are to be applied at all.[64]

However, this does not establish a canon within a canon or determine first-class and second-class passages. It is a matter of contextualization, that is deciding whether the passage must be applied at the surface level of the specific command or whether it may be applied to the deep structure level of the broader theological underpinning. Let us take 1 Timothy 2:11-15 as an example. The question is whether the surface command (women cannot teach men) or deeper theological foundation (submissiveness—see below) is mandated for today. Let us note some hermeneutical principles for making this decision, using 1 Timothy 2:11-15 as a test case. Before we begin, however, it is important to realize that the very fact that we consider 1 Corinthians 11:2-16 to be cultural means that we must be open to the *possibility* that 1 Timothy 2:11-15 is cultural. On the surface they are too similar to allow dogmatism to control the discussion.

1. Note the extent to which it is tied to the culture of its day. Women in the first century were not allowed to speak in public. Even the Roman matrons, those wealthy, influential Roman women, seldom functioned as public orators. Among the common people and among Jews such was scandalous. Many also believe that these women were among the false teachers at Ephesus and the passage should not be applied further than this. This latter is somewhat speculative since there are no specific indicators as such. Moreover, there is no cultural language such as found in 1 Corinthians 11 ("scandal," "custom," "nature"). Nevertheless, there is a strong tie to the first-century situation, and Western culture today is quite different, affirming the equality of women and their leadership role.

2. Determine the eternal principle which underlies it. In 1 Timothy 2 there are two passages looking to creation and the fall. Many believe this is enough to make the command normative; however, it is important to realize that creation underlies 1 Corinthians 11:2-3 on the headcovering. Only if one considered both 1 Corinthians 11 and 1 Timothy 2 to be normative could this be valid.

However, both the Genesis passages behind this teach submission and are only applied to the issue of women teaching men in 1 Timothy 2. Nevertheless, the presence of creation and the fall are pointers toward normative status.

3. Determine whether there is any distance or difference between the surface command and the deep structure theology behind it. The greater the difference, the greater the likelihood that it is culturally relative. For instance, there is quite a distinction between footwashing as a cultural expression and the servanthood that lay behind it in John 13; at the same time there is no distance between the teaching that homosexuality is unnatural and its underpinning as sexual deviation in Romans 1. In other words, footwashing is relative and homosexuality as sin is normative. The passage in 1 Timothy 2 lies between these examples. There is considerable distance between the command to submission and its application to women teaching men. In an earlier article I argued that this favored a decision that the surface command is culturally relative.[65]

An important issue for this conference is that the issue of women in the church is not ground for intolerance; inerrancy is not at stake. We are asking simply how to apply a notoriously difficult passage which has experienced a tragic amount of acrimonious debate in recent years. We must challenge each other from both sides on issues like this. Above all, the decision does not entail a culturally relative New Testament; it functions at the level of application and asks simply at which level we align ourselves with the text.

Apocalyptic

A few years ago I taught a Doctor of Ministry course on the Book of Revelation and the morning it began was told that one-third of the class was dispensationalist, one-third of the post-tribulation persuasion, and one-third amillenialist. I walked into that course with fear and trembling, expecting civil war. Instead it was one of the most satisfying teaching experiences I have ever had because at virtually every point in the book, we discovered we could all agree on *the author's intended meaning;* when we could not (as on 20:1-10, the millenial passage), we discovered we could respect the other's opinion, learn from one another, and "agree to disagree."

This is a daunting book. From the realistic world of the Gospels and Acts and the practical exhortations of the Epistles, we are transported into a mythological world of dragons and many-headed beasts, of unbelievable supernatural powers and cosmic war. In a sense it is "Star Wars" and "Apocalypse Now" rolled onto a single canvas. At the same time, when approached properly it is an immensely satisfying book, filled with exciting theological truth and soul-gripping challenges (the static and dynamic aspects).

Apocalypse means "to reveal" and is both a genre or type of literature with formal features and a set of concepts or world-views describing the mind-set behind the text. Therefore we need to consider each aspect in turn. There are five formal features:

(1) It is first of all a revelatory communication, distinguished from prophecy primarily by being a literary work rather than an oral presentation and employing esoteric symbolism. Therefore, it has a much more stylized form.

(2) Angelic mediation is a necessary aspect, for the symbolism often has the writer confused. An angelic guide will take the prophet on a "tour" (Ezek. 40; Zech. 1; Rev. 17) or explain the vision (Dan. 7—8; Rev. 7).[66] This is utilized to stress the intersection of the natural realm by the supernatural.

(3) Discourse cycles control the literary form. These often comprise a series of dialogues between the seer and the angelic interpreter with stylized rhetorical techniques. In Revelation the controlling factor is the seals, trumpets, and bowls, and I follow those who see these as comprising not a "successive sequence" of events but rather a "progressive intensification" of repeated cycles.[67]

(4) Ethical discourse clarifies the purpose of the visions. In most apocalyptic works, this is a call to endurance and righteous living in the face of overwhelming evil. R. H. Charles calls the book "essentially ethical" in the sense of exhorting the saints to an awareness of and faith in the God who controls present and future.[68] The key term is "overcomer," which occurs at the end of each of the seven letters and is reflected in the exhortation of 21:7,8.

(5) Esoteric symbolism is the most visible feature. These symbols were drawn not only from numbers and the experiential world (locusts, horses, stars) but also from fantasy (dragons, mythological creatures combining the animal world). However, the important thing for us is to realize that the symbols were taken from a common stock understandable to people of the first century and were conventional symbols which communicated to the readers. There is no need to see the "eagle" as a reference to America and the "bear" to Russia. If we believe in authorial intent (the theme of this paper) we must ask what it meant for John and his readers *before* we apply it to ourselves.

At the same time there are five characteristics:

(1) A pessimism toward the present dominates most apocalyptic works. They were developed in times of crisis and peril; the situations were usually so desperate that there could be little hope for the present. Therefore, the symbolism was intended to turn the attention to the God who was in control of history, past as well as future. This is the meaning of the title "Alpha and Omega" (1:8; 21:6; 22:13) which means Christ is Lord of the beginning and the end as well as of all in between. Only he could bring order out of this chaos.

(2) The promise of salvation or restoration is the other side of the same coin. In both Daniel and Revelation the theme of divine restitution is central. In Revelation 6:9-11; 8:3-5 the prayers of the saints for retribution are answered in

the outpouring of God's wrath and the passages on the agony of the "earthdwellers" are paralleled by those on the glory and joy of those martyred for Christ (the "heaven-dwellers").[69]

(3) A view of transcendent reality centering upon the divine presence and control provides the means by which this salvation will occur. In fact, the emphasis in the Apocalypse of John is more upon the hopefulness of the future than upon the hopelessness of the present. While it may have seemed that God had disappeared from the scene, He in fact is sovereign over history and will bring it to a close in His own time.

(4) A determinism is clearly observable, for all of history is completely under God's power. The future course of this world has been predestined by God, and apocalyptic is in fact the "revelation" of this pre-ordained future history. The triumph of the wicked is temporary and illusory, and true triumph is held in reserve only for those faithful to God.

(5) A modified dualism is seen in the doctrine of the two ages (this age and the age to come). This age is characterized by the total opposition between God and Satan, between good and evil. Yet this unceasing war between the opposing forces is not an actual dualism, for the forces are not equal. Satan's power is a mere illusion, and all he can do is imitate the perfect plan of God (e.g. the sealing of the saints, 7:3; imitated by the mark of the beast, 13:16; and the Triune Godhead imitated by the false trinity, 16:13). A major theme of the book is the futility of Satan, who can only rage in frustration as he sees his plans thwarted (e.g. 12:17).

The major hermeneutical task is obviously the interpretation of the symbols. The traditional dichotomy between literal and symbolic is breaking down. Not even the most ardent dispensationalist takes a completely literal approach, for the descriptions of the locusts in 9:7-8 or the many-headed beast in 13:1-2 obviously must be interpreted. Further, many amillennialists like Anthony Hoekema recognize that apocalyptic does point forward to literal events.[70] In other words there are both literal and symbolic features in the symbolism employed in the Apocalypse of John. Moreover we must seek the author's intended use of the symbol in the first-century context before we try to apply it to our day. This will protect the interpreter from speculative errors like identifying 666 in Revelation 13:18 with this individual or that. Both the symbol and the idea it represents stem from the first century. My own belief is that the number probably did not refer to an individual (though the letters behind "Nero Caesar" in the Hebrew do add up to 666) but referred to the ultimate personification of the depravity of man in the antichrist (the number 6 is the number of man).[71]

In moving from the symbol to the reality it envisages, the reader should seek first the biblical background behind such symbols and then utilize this to interpret later allusions. The use of the beasts in Revelation 13 parallels Daniel 7 and the meaning of the two are intertwined. Yet while the past use of a symbol is a pointer to its meaning it is not determinative in and of itself. Symbols rarely become fixed and in actual fact symbolism is an extension of metaphor as the multiple senses behind the figurative use of a term. There are many sources for the symbols. David Aune, for instance, argues that ancient magic (seen in Merkarah mysticism within Judaism and in the magical papyri of the Greco-Roman world) is relevant for interpreting the symbols.[72] One must study all possible interpretations and then see which best fits the passage seeking "a dynamic equivalent" understanding based upon the use of the symbol in the whole context.

In summation, one must study the Book of Revelation from the standpoint of its literary artistry and of its developing message. Every technique described in this middle section of the paper will be utilized on the basis of the rules of the apocalyptic language game in order to determine the intended message of God through his Seer, the Apostle John. The propositional theology as well as the dynamic exhortation of that message to our own day will be the result.

Conclusion

In all three sections I have sought to remove all dichotomy between fact and value and between the New Testament text as propositional truth and as dynamic encounter. A nuanced view of inerrancy must work within these parameters to link the divine revelation of God in His Word to the life of obedience and faith in the church which results. In each New Testament genre this goal is not merely possible but demanded by the text itself. Neither static nor dynamic dimensions dare become an end in itself, lest the interpreter become mixed in the sterile reconstruction of the past or the subjective encounter of the present. The literary artistry in all three genres must be understood in light of the poetics of the biblical authors within their historical framework. In one sense, the literary and the historical are inexplicably linked; a speech act as communication is only discernible if one can draw upon the historical situation within which it occurs. Therefore, in another sense the literary is dependent upon the historical referent. Divorced from its historical context, the literary intent is betrayed. Indeed, both aspects must be wed together if the New Testament is to be preserved as inspired revelation from God, His Word from the past addressing our world in the present so that we may live for Him in the future.

Notes

1. Gerald O'Collins, *What are they Saying about Jesus?* 2nd ed. (New York: Paulist Press, 1983), pp. 5-12. The seventh area is my own; see my "Christology and New Testament Hermeneutics: A Survey of the Discussion," *Semeia* 30 (1984): 49-50.

2. Paul J. Achtemeier, *The Inspiration of Scripture: Problems and Proposals* (Philadelphia: Westminster, 1980), pp. 57-75.

3. Fisher Humphreys, "Biblical Inerrancy: A Guide for the Perplexed," in James B. Robinson, ed., *The Unfettered Word: Southern Baptists Confront the Authority Inerrancy Question* (Waco, TX: Word Books, 1987), pp. 47-60.

4. For a good brief discussion of this aspect of Bultmann's hermeneutic see Josef Bleicher, *Contemporary Hermeneutics: Hermeneutics as Method, Philosophy and Critique* (Boston: Routledge and Kegan Paul, 1980), pp. 104-107.

5. Hans-Georg Gadamer, *Truth and Method*, 2nd ed., trans. G. Borden and J. Cummings (New York: Crossroad, 1982), pp. 354-55.

6. Claude Levi-Strauss, *Structural Anthropology*, 2 vols. (New York: Basic Books, 1963, 1976) 1:32-34.

7. See Josué Harrari, *Textual Strategies: Perspectives in Post-Structuralist Criticism* (Ithaca, New York: Cornell University Press, 1979), pp. 20-22.

8. See Robert Detweiler, *Story, Sign, and Self. Phenomenology and Structuralism as Literary-Critical Methods* (Philadelphia: Fortress Press, 1978), p. 166; and Edith Kurzweil, *The Age of Structuralism: Levi-Strauss to Foucault* (New York: Columbia University Press, 1980), pp. 229-230, 240-245.

9. See Jacques Derrida, *Writing and Difference*, trans. A. Bass (Chicago: University of Chicago Press, 1978), pp. 29-30.

10. Ibid., p. 280.

11. John P. Leavey, "Four Protocols: Derrida, His Deconstruction," *Semeia* 23 (1982): 50-55.

12. David Bleich, "Epistemological Assumptions in the Study of Response," Jane Tompkins, ed., *Reader-Response Criticism* (Baltimore: The Johns Hopkins University Press, 1980), pp. 134-163.

13. Susan Wittig, "A Theory of Multiple Meanings," *Semeia* 9 (1977): 84-92. J. D. Crossan follows Wittig with "A Metamodel for Polyvalent Narration" (pp. 105-143) and applies Derrida's concept of "play," arguing that "freeplay" in the text removes any possibility of a final or ultimate deciphering of its meaning. Interpretation is open-ended rather than representative. All literature is read on different levels depending upon the "perceived perceivers" and their perspectives.

14. Colin Campbell, "The Tyranny of the Yale Critics," *New York Times Magazine* (February 6, 1986): 21-27, 43, 47-48.

15. Raymond E. Brown, *The Critical Meaning of the Bible* (New York: Paulist Press, 1981), pp. 23-44.

16. David Kelsey, *The Uses of Scripture in Recent Theology* (Philadelphia: Fortress Press, 1975), pp. 186-187, 192-193, 197-207.

17. A. C. Thiselton, *The Two Horizons: New Testament Hermeneutics and Philosophical Descriptions* (Grand Rapids: Eerdmans, 1982), pp. 1-4.

18. Ludwig Wittgenstein, *Philosophical Investigations*, trans. G. E. M. Anscobe (New York: Macmillan Press, 1953), sect. 11.

19. Thiselton, pp. 386-407.

20. Frederick Ferré, *Language, Logic, and God* (New York: Harper and Row, 1961), pp. 42-52.

21. John Searle, *Speech Acts: An Essay in the Philosophy of Language* (New York: Cambridge University Press, 1969), pp. 19-21, 42-50, 77-80.

22. Frederick Suppe, ed., *The Structure of Scientific Theories* (Urbana: University of Illinois Press, 1977); and Gary Gutting, ed., *Paradigms and Revolutions: Applications and Appraisals of Thomas Kuhn's Philosophy of Science* (Notre Dame: University of Notre Dame Press, 1980).

23. Ian Barbour, "Paradigms in Science and Religion" in Gutting, pp. 223-245.

24. D. A. Carson, "A Sketch of the Factors Determining Current Hermeneutical Debate in Cross-Cultural Contexts," in *Biblical Interpretation and the Church: The Problem of Contextualization* (Nashville: Thomas Nelson Publishers, 1984), pp. 12-15.

25. Campbell, p. 48.

26. R. Firth, "The Anatomy of Certainty,"; and J. R. Pollock, "Criteria and Our Knowledge of the Material World," *Philosophy Review* 76 (1967): 3-27, 55-60.

27. Thiselton, pp. 411-415, 433.

28. See the excellent discussion of non-literal or figurative meaning in George B. Caird, *The Language and Imagery of the Bible* (Philadelphia: Westminster Press, 1980), pp. 183-197.

29. James Barr, *The Bible in the Modern World* (London: SCM Press, 1973), pp. 123-127.

30. Kevin Vanhoozer, "The Semantics of Biblical Literature: Truth and Scripture's Diverse Literary Forms" in D. A. Carson and John Woodbridge, eds., *Hermeneutics, Authority, and Canon* (Grand Rapids: Zondervan, 1986), pp. 78-85.

31. Ibid., pp. 85-91.

32. Paul Ricoeur, "The Task of Hermeneutics," *Philosophy Today* 17/4 (1973): 112-128.

33. Peter Stuhlmacher, *Historical Criticism and Theological Interpretation of Scripture*, trans. Roy A. Harrisville (Philadelphia: Fortress Press, 1977), pp. 83-90.

34. Vanhoozer, p. 95. See also Thiselton, pp. 432-438.

35. But see Moises Silva's cautions here in *Biblical Words and Their Meaning* (Grand Rapids: Zondervan, 1984), pp. 56-73.

36. Gerald Hawthorne, *Philippians*, Word Commentary Series (Waco, TX: Word Publishing, 1983), pp. 85-86.

37. James Barr, *The Semantics of Biblical Language* (London: Oxford University Press, 1961), p. 222.

38. For an excellent discussion of this, see Colin Hemer, *The Letters to the Seven Churches of Asia in Their Setting* (Sheffield: JSOT Press, 1986), pp. 178-209.

39. See Cyril S. Rodd, "On Applying a Sociological Theory to Biblical Studies," *Journal for the Study of the Old Testament* 19 (1981): 95-106; and Edwin M. Yamauchi, "Sociology, Scripture and the Supernatural," *Journal of the Evangelical Theological Society* 27/2 (1984): 169-192.

40. See James D. G. Dunn, *Unity and Diversity in the New Testament* (Philadelphia: Westminster Press, 1977); and for a more conservative approach, D. A. Carson, "Unity and Diversity in the New Testament: The Possibility of Systematic Theology," D. A. Carson and John Woodbridge, eds., *Scripture and Truth* (Grand Rapids, Zondervan, 1983).

41. See Richard Gaffin, "Systematic Theology and Biblical Theology," J. H. Skilton, ed., *The New Testament Student and Theology* (Philadelphia: Presbyterian and Re-

formed, 1976), pp. 35-50; and C. K. Barrett, "What is New Testament Theology? Some Reflections," *Horizons in Biblical Theology* 3 (1981).

42. See *The Proceedings of The Conference on Biblical Inerrancy, 1987* (Nashville: Broadman Press, 1987), pp. 64-65, 74-76, 107, 137, 159, 209-210, et al. Note too that both moderates and inerrantists make this point.

43. Kenneth Dauber, "The Bible as Literature: Reading Like the Rabbis," *Semeia* 31 (1985): 27.

44. John J. Collins, "The Rediscovery of Biblical Narrative," *Chicago Studies* 21 (1982): 47-48.

45. David Rhoades, "Narrative Criticism and the Gospel of Mark," *Journal of the American Academy of Religion* 50 (1982): 413.

46. Joanna Dewey, *Markan Public Debate: Literary Technique, Concentric Structure, and Theology in Mark 2:1—3:6* (Chico: Scholars Press, 1980), pp. 9-10.

47. Hans W. Frei, *The Eclipse of Biblical Narrative: A Study in Eighteenth and Nineteenth Century Hermeneutics* (New Haven: Yale University Press, 1974), pp. 10-16.

48. Meir Sternberg, *The Poetics of Biblical Narrative: Ideological Literature and the Drama of Reading* (Bloomington: Indiana University Press, 1983), p. 70 (cf. also pp. 15-23).

49. Ibid., pp. 24-35. Here he opposes specifically Alter's depiction of the Bible as "fiction," cf. Robert Alter, *The Art of Biblical Narrative* (New York: Basic Books, 1981), pp. 23-24. For this criticism see also Tremper Longman III, *Literary Approaches to Biblical Narrative* (Grand Rapids: Zondervan, 1987), pp. 53-58.

50. Against those who interpret the preface along salvation-historical lines rather than historiographical, see I. Howard Marshall, *The Gospel of Luke* (Grand Rapids: Eerdmans, 1978), pp. 39-40.

51. Here I draw upon my earlier article, "Round Four: The Redaction Debate Continues," *Journal of the Evangelical Theological Society* 28/4 (1985): 399-410; Gordon D. Fee and Douglas Stuart, *How to Read the Bible for all its Worth* (Grand Rapids: Zondervan, 1981), pp. 103-121; and Scot McKnight, *Interpreting the Synoptic Gospels* (Grand Rapids: Baker Book House, 1988).

52. Paul D. Feinberg, "The Meaning of Inerrancy," in N. L. Geisler, ed., *Inerrancy* (Grand Rapids: Zondervan, 1979). He says "with regard to the sayings of Jesus, what would count against inerrancy? The words in the sense of ipsissima vox were not uttered by Jesus, or the ipsissima verba were spoken by our Lord but so used by the writer that the meaning given by the writer is inconsistent with the intended meaning of Jesus."

53. *Proceedings of The Conference on Biblical Inerrancy, 1987*, p. 211.

54. Alan Culpepper, "Jesus' View of Scripture" in Robinson, pp. 31-32.

55. For extensive discussion see Alan Culpepper, *Anatomy of the Fourth Gospel: A Study in Literary Design* (Philadelphia: Fortress Press, 1983); and for a more concise presentation, note Terence J. Keegan, *Interpreting the Bible: A Popular Introduction to Biblical Hermeneutics* (New York: Paulist Press, 1985), pp. 93-106.

56. In addition to the article mentioned in n51, see my "The Evangelical and Redaction Criticism: Critique and Methodology," *Journal of the Evangelical Theological Society* 22/4 (1979): 305-322, and the bibliography noted in the two articles.

57. On parables see Craig Blomberg, "New Horizons in Parable Research," *Trinity*

Journal 3/1 (1982): 3-17; and Robert H. Stein, *An Introduction to the Parables of Jesus* (Philadelphia: Westminster Press, 1981).

58. See J. D. M. Derrett, "The Parable of the Unjust Steward," *New Testament Studies* 7 (1961): 198-219.

59. See Joseph Fitzmyer, "The Story of the Dishonest Manager (Luke 16:1-13)," *Theological Studies* 23 (1964): 23-42.

60. Kenneth E. Bailey, *Poet and Peasant* and *Through Peasant Eyes*, combined ed. (Grand Rapids: Eerdmans, 1976, 1980).

61. For an extended discussion see Stanley K. Stowers, *Letter Writing in Greco-Roman Antiquity* (Philadelphia: Westminster, 1986); for a more concise presentation see Fee and Stuart, pp. 43-49.

62. See James Olthuis, "On Interpreting an Authoritative Scripture: A Proposal for a Certitudinal Hermeneutic," paper delivered at the 1981 Toronto Conference on "Interpreting an Authoritative Scripture."

63. J. Robertson McQuilkin, "Limits of Cultural Application," *Journal of the Evangelical Theological Society* 23/2 (1980): 113-124. See also D. A. Carson in *Biblical Interpretation and the Church*, pp. 19-20.

64. Fee and Stuart, pp. 62-64 argue that some passages like the meat offered to idols are "not comparable" and should not be applied at all.

65. Grant Osborne, "Hermeneutics and Women in the Church," *Journal of the Evangelical Theological Society* 20/4 (1977): 337-352.

66. J. J. Collins, "Apocalypse: The Morphology of a Genre," *Semeia* 14 (1979): 12-13, who makes this the basis of his breakdown of apocalyptic into two types: those which include an otherworldly journey and those which do not.

67. See Robert W. Mounce, *The Book of Revelation* (Grand Rapids: Eerdmans, 1977), pp. 45-47.

68. R. H. Charles, *The Apocrypha and Pseudopigrapha of the Old Testament*, 2 vols. (Oxford: Clarendon Press, 1913) 2:16.

69. E. P. Sanders, "The Genre of Palestinian Jewish Apocalypses," in David Hellholm, ed., *Apocalypticism in the Mediterranean World and the Near East* (Tübingen: J. C. B. Mohr, 1983), p. 456, believes that this is the one essential peculiarity of the movement. This is certainly an overstatement, since the promise of restitution can be found in prophetic and wisdom writings as well. Nevertheless it is a major characteristic of apocalyptic.

70. Anthony Hoekema, *The Bible and the Future* (Grand Rapids: Eerdmans, 1979).

71. For a list of options see Mounce, pp. 264-265.

72. David Aune, "The Apocalypse of John and the Problem of Genre," *Semeia* 36 (1986): 82-84.

10
BIBLICAL INTERPRETATION AND THEOLOGY: BRINGING THE BIBLE TO LIFE

Robert Johnston

If you are asked by one of your church members to state what is the meaning of Jesus Christ's death on the cross, how would you respond biblically? Would you say that Jesus made expiation for our sins as a merciful and faithful High Priest (cf., Heb. 2:17)? Would you explain that Jesus Christ through His shed blood bought us our freedom (cf., 1 Cor. 7:23)? Or might you quote Galatians 3:13: "Christ redeemed us from the curse of the law"? Some of you might speak of Jesus, through His death, destroying "him who has the power of death, that is, the devil" (Heb. 2:14). Others might simply quote John 3:16: "For God so loved the world that he gave his only begotten Son, that whosoever believeth in him should not perish but have everlasting life." All of these answers (and more!) are given in Scripture. All are "the gospel truth!" All are necessary for a mature understanding of a biblical theology of the cross.

In any given generation, however, one or another of these multiple biblical word pictures that are given to convey aspects of the mystery of the cross will be emphasized by the church and others will be viewed in a secondary light. And certainly your hypothetical church member is not looking for ten answers, but for a sure, direct answer from God. For those in Anselm's day, "satisfaction" became the interpretive key for understanding a biblical theology of the cross. Here is how Anselm would have addressed his parishoner, for chivalry and personal honor were paramount. For those in Sweden in the early twentieth century, "Christus Victor" summarized the gospel's intention. Those Pietists knew that God was more powerful than their present church had taught. For evangelicals in America, the theological description of Christ's death on the cross has most often had the character of "penal substitution."

I wish to explore with you your theology of the cross. I do this for three reasons. First, as Paul summarized, as Christians, our task is to "preach Christ crucified . . . Christ the power of God and the wisdom of God" (1 Cor. 1:23-24). Thus, if our study of biblical interpretation cannot help us with regard to the cross and its intended meaning, it is of marginal use. Secondly, I have chosen the cross as a case study in biblical interpretation, for this topic forces the biblical reader to consider the significance of multiple texts simultaneously. How do we interpret larger groupings of Scripture? In seeking as pastors and teachers to make the cross "gospel"—good news—for our church members and students, we must decide how to ejudicate multiple biblical emphases. God's love and God's justice co-adhere in the cross, but our understanding of them will necessarily flow from the concept of love toward that of justice, or vice versa. Choices are forced upon us as interpreters who come to the biblical data.

Thirdly, I am convinced that there is within the evangelical church today a growing dichotomy between our theology of the cross and our proclamation of the cross, that is, between our theory and our preaching. To the degree such tension exists, it must be understood and corrected lest the intellectual foundations of our biblical faith be undermined.

Let me, then, present a contemporary evangelical theology of the atonement as a case study in the practice of biblical theology. How can we bring the Bible to life? As in any theology, one must ground his or her understanding in Scripture which alone is authoritative. But one need not always begin with Scripture. Just as James Packer illustrated as he prefaced his theology of creation with a discussion of natural science and his theology of the role of women in our secular society and in our church life, it is often theologically advantageous to come to the biblical text with an understanding of how the church context, the Christian tradition, our personal experience, and/or the wider culture bear on the issue.

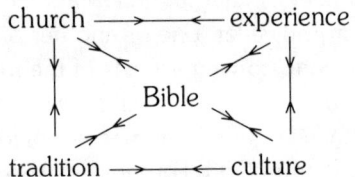

This is even more the case, as with an understanding of the cross, when we are dealing with multiple texts, not just a text. I begin, therefore, not with a discussion of Scripture but with a description of the contemporary American evangelical church. Does it provide hindrance or help for articulating the gospel of the cross in our day?

An Evangelical Theology of the Atonement

Our Church Setting

James Davison Hunter has studied American evangelicalism's recent turn from objective to subjective categories of thought. This has led him to label this phenomenon "Accommodation: The Domestication of Belief."[1] His thesis is that evangelicalism, as a result of its interaction with modernity, has undergone subtle but real change. There has been concession and compromise. In documenting this conclusion, Hunter analyzes the titles of evangelical literature published in 1980 from eight leading houses. Although the omission of Eerdmans, Inter Varsity, and Baker (presses with more traditional academic interest) skews his findings, it is nonetheless telling that 12.3 percent of all the titles surveyed were oriented toward "understanding the emotional complexities of human experience from an evangelical perspective."[2]

With other Americans, evangelicals are asking, "Who am I?" Of the books Hunter examined which focused on the human, a third dealt with one's emotional and psychological maturity, with self actualization. A slightly smaller percentage emphasized the need both to understand and to solve emotional problems (pressure, fear, loneliness, etc.). And another 28 percent were oriented toward "Christian" forms of narcissism and hedonism. Hunter's examples include books such as *Dare to Live Now, Life without Limits,* and *Living the Adventure.* To be sure, such "hedonism" expressed within an evangelical world-view did not have the same quality as that found in secular literature. Self-infatuation and vanity were not the foci. Nevertheless, Hunter found in this literature "the conviction that human experience should be characterized by unfathomable inner joy and happiness and the unquenchable expectancy of good things."[3] Perhaps some of you have read James Packer's *Hot Tub Religion* (1987) which offers a critique of our propensity for pleasure. Here is a theological critique of what Hunter, a sociologist, had earlier attempted to describe.

In his most recent book, *Evangelicalism: The Coming Generation,* Hunter provides a second illustration of this "accommodation" to modernity, quoting from Robert Schuller's book, *Self-Esteem: The New Reformation* (1983). In this book which was sent free of charge to one quarter of a million religious leaders across America, Schuller criticizes reformational theology for not being a "well-rounded, full-orbed, honestly-interrelated theology system." Traditional Protestant theology, thinks Schuller, has wrongly centered its definition of sin on "rebellion against God." Such a notion for Schuller is not incorrect as much as it is shallow and insulting to the human being. The core of sin is in reality "a lack of self esteem." In this light, salvation means

> to be permanently lifted from sin (psychological self-abuse with all its consequences as seen above) and shame to self-esteem and its God glorifying human need-meeting, constructive and creative consequences. . . . To be saved is to know that Christ forgives me and now I dare to believe that I am somebody and I can do something for God and for my fellow human beings.[4]

We must not risk further assault on the person, argues Schuller, by continuing to teach humankind's lack of worth in God's sight.

Schuller provides Hunter his paradigm. How has the traditional judgmental aspects of evangelicalism's soteriology found acceptance in a socially and religiously tolerant society such as America? "How is it that so exclusivistic a group can experience such broadly based social acceptance in any modern society?" There has been, thinks Hunter, "a softening and polishing of the more hardline and barbed elements of the orthodox Protestant world view." The doctrinal core has remained unchanged, but it has been culturally edited for the sake of civility. In the words of Hunter:

> The civilizing process entails a deemphasis of evangelicalism's more offensive aspects: The notions of inherent evil, sinful conduct and lifestyles, the wrath of a righteous and jealous god, and eternal agony and death in hell. The deemphasis has been more quantitative than qualitative. The offensive elements are, in the main, neither substantively devalued nor glossed over as unimportant. They are simply not referred to as much as they have been in the past. These elements have not lost their doctrinal centrality, but have lost a stylistic centrality once taken for granted in the preaching and teaching in this tradition.[5]

Here, then, is a thesis concerning American evangelical church life. Acculturation has taken place under the press of modernity. Efforts at cooperation have inevitably necessitated concession. Like most other Christian movements that have dared to open themselves to engage the world, evangelicalism finds itself civilized, and yet compromised.[6]

Acculturation or Inculturation?

Is Hunter correct? Is the subjectivism which he chronicles the sociologically inevitable compromise that has resulted from neo-fundamentalism's encounter with modernity? Examples can surely be given where this is the case. Schuller's redefinition of sin would seem to be one, although his background is not fundamentalism. A theology of prosperity which equates Christianity with success would be another. But could not evangelicalism's recent recasting of Christianity in terms of the human subject have a more complex basis as well? Rather than being rooted simply in civil religion, could it not be based praxiologically in the dialogue between Scripture and society, God's story and our own? Rather than judging our turn toward the human as simple acculturation with its resultant blurring of the apostolic faith, could not evangelicalism's positive focus upon humankind represent initial, largely intuitive efforts at inculturation, the contextualizing of the gospel?

When John Piper's *Desiring God: Meditations of a Christian Hedonist* appeared (1986), it created controversy. Published by the conservative Multnomah Press, the book would seem to illustrate Hunter's thesis. Piper, a General Conference Baptist minister who has taught at Bethel College, states his intention as offering an interpretation of the catechism, namely: "The chief end of man is to glory God *BY* enjoying him forever." Our motive for Christian service and church-going should be, he thinks, our desire for happiness or pleasure.

Since Piper understands happiness to be a basic human need, there is no moral judgment attached to such an observation. If anything the problem facing humankind is not "in the intensity of our desire for happiness, but in the weakness of it."[7] To be sure, Piper warns against making a god out of pleasure or of viewing God instrumentally as a means of worldly pleasure. Rather, humankind's highest joy is found only in the worship of God and our happiness in sharing with others His love. It is not our seeking after happiness, but the object of that happiness, which is the central problem for humankind today.

Piper's book is shaped around a meditation on Scripture. It owes much to the thought of Jonathan Edwards who is Piper's constant theological companion. Yet when asked why he has picked up and made central those traditional, biblical themes of happiness and joy, Piper turns not to Scripture or tradition, but to an assessment of contemporary life. When asked why he adopts the controversial terminology of "Christian hedonism" rather than repeating the straightforward biblical command, "Believe in the Lord Jesus and you will be saved," Piper says it is because belief in Jesus has become an empty phrase in America. "Millions of unconverted people . . . say they believe in Jesus."[8] In order to effectively communicate the gospel, Piper argues for a biblical focus on Christian hedonism. In serving God you will find your true happiness.

Piper's focus on happiness/hedonism attempts to be responsive both to Scripture and to our contemporary age. If the gospel is to mean anything, it must connect with the lives of its hearers. One can question whether the term *Christian hedonism* has meaning beyond its shock value. Negative connotations intrude. But Piper has recognized that the topic "glorifying God" can best be addressed today from the viewpoint of its subject and not its object, from a discussion of *our* desire for God. Whereas ontologically, glorifying God has priority for Piper, epistemologically he believes happiness to be the central concern. Hunter might think this a compromise, a simple example of civil religion, of cultural accommodation. But *Desiring God's* attempted cultural translation of biblical truth is more complex.

Where Hunter's critique of books like Piper's provides more insight is in his observation that evangelical literature dealing with contemporary human sensitivities remains *at the doctrinal level* largely immutable. That is, a larger, rational theological structure is maintained, even if it is not emphasized. For Piper this finds expression in his discussion of the cross. Although Piper's exploration of Christian happiness led him to discuss that topic from "below," from the standpoint of humankind, no parallel presentation of the atonement is provided. Rather than selecting those biblical images concerning the cross which speak of humankind (e.g., we are *received* into the family of God, we are *freed* from slavery, our relationship with God is *restored*, etc.), Piper remains traditionally "objective" in his analysis: "The death of Christ is the wisdom *of God* by which the love *of God* saves sinners from the wrath *of God,* and all the while upholds and demonstrates the righteousness *of God*."[9] The atonement as *God's* righteous act remains the theological focus for Piper, even while his desire to foster a living faith in his readers causes him elsewhere to stress the importance of human happiness. Understanding the cross as primarily God's transaction, Piper largely ignores its reality or its implications for his topic, Christian happiness. The two topics inhabit largely different worlds.

A more successful attempt at developing a contextualized understanding of the gospel which includes the cross has been made by William Dyrness. Like Piper, his concern is with communicating and extending the Christian faith. In fact the title of his most recent manuscript is *How Does America Hear the Gospel?* Theology, particularly in North America, has become professionalized, abstracted from life. As a result it is too often reduced to reflection on previous thinking. For Dyrness American evangelical theology has lost its essential nature as biblically informed reflection on life.

Dyrness desires his theology to be "both biblical and American." Recognizing that American culture is diverse, he nonetheless concentrates his thinking initially on certain core values of white, middle-class America, allowing other voices into the conversation as critics and foils. He isolates three complexes of values: "Americans' materialist bias, their tempermental optimism and their individualism." He then asks "how these values enhance or impede our understanding of the Gospel." Only by knowing how we hear God's Word today can we become more effective in our mission and more vital in our theology.[10]

Because Americans have come to believe that the good life is their right, the gospel must be presented first in those terms, thinks Dyrness. Moreover, there is in America "the dominant feeling that things are going to turn out alright. This surely must be dealt with . . . this cultural optimism." One approach which Dyrness rejects is to insist that people be made to know first that they are sinners, so that they then can believe in salvation. No, awareness of sin will be for many Americans a result and not the precondition for encountering God's love in Jesus Christ. If effective communication is our goal, then Christians will need to make the love and goodness of God their entrance to the gospel.

Ultimately, suffering will need to be seen; sin exposed. And it will. Dyrness believes that the gospel will challenge many of our fundamental values. God's holiness and justice will be understood as complementing His love. There is not only an ethos of privilege but an ethos of need. We are not only individuals, but part of a community. This movement in repentance toward Christian maturity, however, will be for most Americans in the direction from love toward justice, from privilege to need, not vice versa. Dyrness summarizes the options: "The one begins with enmity and hears the challenge of Christ's death as reconciliation; the other begins with individual fulfillment and hears the Gospel as a fellowship of suffering."[11]

Our Cultural Context

The observations of Dyrness are preliminary but point in the right direction, toward an evangelical, biblical theology of the atonement. In a class at New College Berkeley, which I jointly taught with him in 1986 and in three subsequent class situations at North Park Seminary, students responded to the question, "Do you expect your world to be good and pleasant or evil and difficult?" by saying it was supposed to be good. Although they might experience a variety of frustration along the way, they expected to succeed. This is surely not the only answer one could have given. Think how different such an ethos is than that found in most Negro spirituals, for example. But it is consistent with what we have been led to expect by such analyses of the American character as Daniel Yankelovitch's *New Rules* and Robert Bellah's *Habits of the Heart*.

When these same students were asked what Americans consider their primary goal to be, self-fulfillment was the answer. Our heroes are those like Abraham Lincoln who overcame a nervous breakdown, failure in business, and repeated defeat in public elections only to become the president of the United States. Such perseverance continues to be given popular expression in box office hits like the play "Starlight Express," where the old reliable steam engine overcomes adversity and setbacks to defeat both the electric (modernity!) and the diesel (the devil!) engines in the big race.

While success is admired, most hope it will come with a minimum of pain. Like Horatio Alger, or Benjamin Franklin's Poor Richard, we desire a more consistent course from rags to riches than Lincoln had. In fact, the Lincoln "myth" must compete in the American mind with another—Superman. We would have our success presented to us as a given and expressed through power, not death. Consider Rambo.

When asked what Americans consider "evil," the answers my students gave centered on anything which stands in the way of one's personal fulfillment. Thus, as an American society today, we often believe that divorce will help us. As Christians we regularly shop for another church where "I'll be ministered to." It is difficult to think of the common good apart from that which will make my own life better the majority of times. *It is not the language of accountability that resonates with the American ethos, but that of fulfillment.*

Our Biblical Foundation

What has this to do with a theology of the atonement? Since the beginnings of the church, Christians have declared that "Christ died for our sins in accordance with the Scriptures" (1 Cor. 15:3; cf, Phil. 2:7-8). But these early confessions and hymns of the church were not meant to provide theories of the atonement so much as testimonies to its reality and to the new life which believers had experienced in Christ.[12] Under the Spirit's continued inspiration, a variety of images were used to explain the meaning of the cross. None of these descriptions was meant to explain fully the mystery of the atonement they had experienced, but all were faithful to its reality.

The biblical writers turned for their language concerning the cross both to the Old Testament and to their contemporary experience.[13] As in their *Temple worship,* Jesus was portrayed as a high priest, offering himself as a sacrifice, once for all, to accomplish our redemption. The Epistle to the Hebrews, in particular, developed this understanding of Christ's death (Heb. 2:17; 9:12-14,26; cf., Mark 10:45). Behind such imagery is Jesus' own acceptance of his identification with the suffering servant of Isaiah 53: "Behold, the Lamb of God, who takes away the sin of the world!" (John 1:29). Complementing this description was another taken not only from the Old Testament but from *contemporary commerce.* We have been ransomed as salves from the auction block, "with the precious blood of Christ" (1 Pet. 1:18,19). We have been "bought with a price." As such, we are not again to "become slaves of men" (1 Cor. 7:23).

The apostle Paul was particularly fond of turning to the *law courts* for his metaphors concerning the meaning of the cross. We are "justified by his blood" (Rom. 5:6-11). "Christ redeemed us from the curse of the law" (Gal. 3:13). Although the necessary penalty for our sin is death, the free gift of God in Christ Jesus our Lord is eternal life (Rom. 6:23). If such language suggests images of God as judge, other biblical metaphors focus instead on Christ as a mighty warrior. On the *battlefield,* Christ entered into conflict with the devil and triumphed (Heb. 2:14). Reflecting Jesus' own definition of his ministry in terms of a battle against evil powers, the New Testament writers saw the cross and resurrection of Jesus as the decisive victory.

Elsewhere in the New Testament, the cross is understood as accomplishing reconciliation, the restoration of relationships both with God and between people. "All this is from God, who through Christ reconciled us to himself and gave us the ministry of reconciliation" (2 Cor. 5:18). Drawing its meaning in part from *family life,* this image finds in love the power to heal. As John expresses it, "We love, because he first loved us" (1 John 4:19). Driver points out that the word *reconciliation* means literally to "re-concile," to bring people into council again.[14] The image is at times *political.* Through the cross, a new humanity has been formed from all nations (Eph. 2:16). "For in him all the fullness of God was pleased to dwell, and through him to reconcile to himself all things whether on earth or in heaven, making peace by the blood of his cross" (Col. 1:20).

When speaking of the cross, the context of family life proved helpful to the New Testament writers in still another way. The metaphor of *adoption* was used to describe how we have been brought into God's family. Just as Jesus addressed God the Father as "Abba," so can we through the cross: "God sent forth his Son . . . to redeem those who were under the law, so that we might receive adoption as sons. And because you are sons, God has sent the Spirit of his Son into our hearts, crying, 'Abba! Father!'" (Gal. 4:4-6)

With these and other word pictures, the New Testament writers have spoken to us of God's act of salvation. Neither redemption nor ransom, justification nor triumph, reconciliation nor adoption tells the full story of the cross. John Driver is correct: "The plurality of images used to understand the work of Christ is essential. The apostolic community allowed all to stand in a complementary relationship rather than attempting to reduce them to a single theory or dogmatic statement."[15] Often the images overlap, as in the fourth chapter of Galatians where Paul combines our redemption from slavery with our adoption as sons (Gal. 4:1-7). Sometimes several will come near to being conflated (cf., 1 Pet. 1:18,19). But the crux of the gospel cannot be reduced to one image. There remains an overflow of meaning.

Our Traditional Theology

Evangelicals have often not been comfortable with this plurality of meaning. In particular, the images having to do with the law court and the vocabulary of justification have been made to dominate. In his lecture this morning, for example, Grant Osborne called "substitutionary atonement" a cardinal doctrine and therefore, of the essence of our faith. Typical, as well, is J. I. Packer's Tyndale Lecture in 1973, "What Did the Cross Achieve? The Logic of Penal Substitution."[16] In itself a model of both scholarship and faith, the lecture can nevertheless be questioned. Packer states his task to be that of explicating a belief which is "a distinguishing mark of the world-view evangelical fraternity: namely, the belief that Christ's death on the cross had the character of *penal substitution*, and that it was in virtue of this fact that it brought salvation to mankind." We are, in other words, to understand biblical atonement by focusing first and pre-eminently on the image of the law court.

Packer understands his viewpoint to be similar to the reformers, a redefinition of Anselm's notion of Christ's *satisfactio* (satisfaction). Packer admits there are a variety of other biblical images and models used to describe the work of Christ. Moreover mystery will remain in any discussion of the atonement. Nonetheless, Packer argues that penal substitution be understood as the central theological model for the cross. He wants to avoid caricature. His model is meant to convey the meaning of the cross not its mechanics. It might best be viewed, in fact, as a dramatic idea:

> The notion which the phrase "penal substitution" expresses is that Jesus Christ our Lord, moved by a love that was determined to do everything necessary to save us, endured and exhausted the destructive divine judgment for which we were otherwise inescapably destined, and so won us forgiveness, adoption and glory.[17]

One notes that other models have, in fact, been combined by Packer with that of the law court. "Love," "forgiveness," "adoption," and "glory" all suggest other primary word pictures. It is the law court which provides the integration, however.

Here is my question to you? Should the image of the law court still provide integration for all other primary biblical word pictures concerning the meaning of the cross?

For Packer, the word *penal* is there not to create questions about guilt. It is not meant to imply an impersonal, external God responding to the law. It is certainly not intended to describe the means by which the punishment for humankind's sins was transferred to Jesus. Rather it is meant by Packer to evoke awareness that Jesus bore the judgment I deserved because he loved me. Although the term *penal* is extra-biblical, Packer believes it communicates biblical truth.

The question must be asked, however: Does *penal* vocabulary continue to highlight for modern Americans the character of Christ's redeeming love? Does it communicate biblical truth today? If it does not, then Packer himself says it "stands self-condemned."[18]

A Contemporary, Biblical Restatement

While Packer would have us believe that traditional Christian language can still communicate effectively to contemporary humanity if it is adequately explained and qualified, the preceding discussion would cause one to question this. Dietrich Bonhoeffer suggested from his prison cell during World War II that our theological language of redemption has lost something of its force and meaningfulness within contemporary society. Bonhoeffer even believed that in a post-Christian age, the church might for a time be reduced in its witness simply to prayer and righteous action.[19] This judgment has proven hyperbolic, but its insight retains validity. Christians today are being called to demonstrate through renewed worship and service that their faith is real. In addition Christians are exploring the use of other less traditional theological vocabulary including other biblical models of the atonement. The church needs to speak in a language more atune to where modern women and men live. If mission is our goal, communication must begin with where people are.

Could it be that many secular Americans are rejecting the message of the cross today because they lack any strong cultural model for understanding it? If I am correct that it is not the language of accountability that most easily resonates with the American ethos, but that of fulfillment, then should we not shape our communication of the gospel accordingly? There are other biblical images of the cross which can communicate to moderns in ways more understandable and convincing than that of the law court.

Our most effective evangelism has recognized intuitively the need to present the gospel in the context of images of human fulfillment. For example, Bill Bright's "Four Spiritual Laws" begin, "God loves you and has a wonderful plan for your life." Similarly, when evangelical collegians and seminarians were asked by James Hunter how they would try to persuade someone to become a Christian, sixty-seven percent said they would first talk to a nonbeliever about either "the sense of meaning and purpose in life" that comes from being a Christian or the fact that "God has made a difference in my life." Only one in ten said they would speak first of the judgment or wrath of God.[20]

Some will object that such "subjective" interpretations of the gospel represent a danger. John Stott, in his excellent book *The Cross of Christ* (1986) states that it is his intention to make clear once again for our generation the distinction between an "objective" and "subjective" understanding of the atonement. The meaning of the atonement is found "in what *God* did when in Christ on the cross he took our place and bore our sin."[21] This is surely the case. Criticism of subjectivist theories of the atonement has validity if such models deny the objective meaning of the cross as God's action on our behalf. The love of God enfleshed in Jesus Christ is more than an example of sacrificial love to be imitated by the Christian. It is the objective basis for the "ransom" which has been paid, the "sacrifice" which has been accomplished, the "victory" which has been won and the "relationship" which has been secured. "We love, because *he first loved us*" (1 John 4:19). But it is also the case that "*we love.*" One need not juxtapose objective and subjective understandings of the cross. The cross reflects both.

Criticism of subjectivist theories go back as far as Bernard of Clairvaux who charged Peter Abelard with teaching that Christ lived and died *only* to point out the limits which our love should go. If such was, indeed, his position, Abelard deserves criticism for understanding the cross in sub-biblical terms. The atonement accomplished more than providing a compelling example of the love of God. But scholarship today recognizes that even in Abelard, his soteriology centering on our responsive act of love went beyond the mere arousal of love for God within humankind. There was an objective, theocentric side to Abelard which his critics have chosen to overlook.[22] Abelard is not to be criticized for failing to understand reconciliation as ontologically God's action toward us, but for denying the validity of such other biblical models as "propitiation" and "justification." Recognizing a tendency toward legalism and abstraction in the dominate theological discussions of the atonement in his day, he wrongly reduced the multiple descriptions of the cross to one. The language of righteousness in Romans, for example, was transposed as reconciliation.

What is questionable about the explications of the meaning of the cross which Packer and Stott provide is not their objective doctrine. It is biblical and sound. What is problematic, however, is their language and emphases. Both theologians are reacting to abuses perceived within subjectivist interpretations of the atonement. As such their constructive statements are perceived by some to be disconnected from the dominant American ethos. The biblical exegesis of these leading evangelical spokesmen has the same high standards that we have come to expect from other of their writings. But despite their best intentions, their emphasis upon legal metaphor, upon divine satisfaction, causes a distantiation from the modern reader. The discussion remains somehow abstracted and intellectualized.

My own church, The Evangelical Covenant Church, has its origins within the free church pietistic renewal of Scandinavia, which occurred a century ago. In that setting, orthodox theology had been reduced to formal dogmatic statement, lifeless and nontransforming. As in that context when revivals swept through Sweden, there is the need today in evangelical discussion of the cross "for a new *picture* with its own distinctive feeling tone."[23] Evangelical theology risks communicating with regard to the cross a sterile orthodoxy. Many of the readers of evangelical theology today understand God to be standing over against sinful humanity in righteous wrath needing His holiness to be satisfied in order that relationship can be restored. This is the case, protestations of caricature not withstanding, for contemporary Americans have heard the cross discussed in the language of accountability through ears atuned to images of fulfillment. If the gospel is again to evoke faithful response, we need to help modern men and women see a biblical understanding of the cross as revealing the extent to which God our Heavenly Father has expressed His love so that we might be reconciled to Him and to His world.

It is the imagery of family life, of restored relationship, which holds the greatest initial promise for effective communication today. Only as this biblical model is grasped will others (including that of the law court) take on new relevance and possibility. There is a plurality of meaning biblically with regard to a theology of the cross. And each image presented is crucial for a full-orbed theology. Nevertheless, as William Dyrness recognizes, "Communication takes place from the known to the unknown."[24] It is not surprising that John 3:16 is often viewed as a contemporary "gospel in a nutshell." For there we hear of both God's love and His justice, our accountability and our fulfillment. The entry point, however, is the love of God. Here is a message that is both biblically sound and culturally relevant.

In his summary of the origins of The Evangelical Covenant Church, Donald Frisk recalls that the favorite text of these revival people was the parable of the prodigal son. What they heard in this story was the amazing reality of the father's love. Salvation for them became "a joyous and life-changing entrance into personal relationship with God."[25] When the Swedish church leader P. P. Waldenstrom attempted to express this fact theologically, Covenanters argued whether such a subjective view of the atonement as his was correct. (And they still do!) There is no doubt that a stress on the atonement as "for our benefit" such as Waldenstrom suggested can cause one to lose sight of the fact that it is accomplished by God through the death of Jesus Christ. But Waldenstrom could not have been clearer that this was not his intention. Waldenstrom was attempting to confront those who would reduce the atonement to a transaction God had accomplished which we could then ignore. His mission was nothing less than the revival of his church. If a like mission is to continue to characterize the wider evangelical church, might we not need to take again today a similar task?

Notes

1. The title of chapter six, James Davison Hunter, *American Evangelicalism: Conservative Religion and The Boundary of Modernity* (New Brunswick, N.J.: Rutgers University Press, 1983).
2. Ibid., p. 41.
3. Ibid., p. 45.
4. Robert Schuller, *Self-Esteem: The New Reformation*, pp. 145-146, 65, 98-99, quoted in James Davison Hunter, *Evangelicalism: The Coming Generation* (Chicago: University of Chicago Press, 1987), p. 70.
5. Hunter, *American Evangelicalism,* p. 87.
6. For a similar analysis of the history of Fuller Theological Seminary, see Terry Muck, "Waiting for the Second Coming," review of *Reforming Fundamentalism* by George Marsden (Grand Rapids: Eerdmans, 1987), New York Times Review of Books, January 24, 1988.
7. John Piper, *Desiring God: Meditations of a Christian Hedonist* (Portland: Multnomah Press, 1986), pp. 14-16.
8. Ibid., p. 42.
9. Ibid., (underlining added).
10. William A. Dyrness, *How Does America Hear the Gospel?* unpublished manuscript, no pages.
11. Ibid.
12. Cf. John Driver, *Understanding the Atonement for the Mission of the Church* (Scottdale, Penn.: Herald Press, 1986).
13. An excellent summary is provided by Donald C. Frisk, *Covenant Affirmations: This We Believe* (Chicago: Covenant Press, 1981), pp. 92-96.
14. Cf., Driver, *Understanding the Atonement,* p. 26.
15. Ibid., pp. 15-19.
16. J. I. Packer, "What Did the Cross Achieve? The Logic of Penal Substitution," *Tyndale Bulletin* 25 (1974): 3-45.
17. Ibid., p. 25.
18. Ibid., p. 42.
19. Dietrich Bonhoeffer, *Letters and Papers From Prison,* ed. Eberhard Bethge (New York: Macmillan, 1955), pp. 151, 190-191.
20. Hunter, *Evangelicalism: The Coming Generation,* pp. 39-40.

21. John Stott, *The Cross of Christ* (Downers Grove, Ill.: Inter Varsity Press, 1988), p. 9.
22. Cf., Allister McGrath, "The Moral Theory of the Atonement: An Historical, and Theological Critique," *Scottish Journal of Theology* 38, No. 2 (1985): 207.
23. Frisk, p. 99.
24. Dyrness, no pages.
25. Frisk, p. 100.

11
WHAT IS THE GOSPEL?
Romans 1:16-17

Jon Stubblefield

Whenever the message of Romans has been taken seriously, spiritual awakenings have occurred and lives have been transformed. On the afternoon of May 24, 1738, a broken, despondent John Wesley went to Saint Paul's Cathedral where the choir sang the words of Psalm 130: "Out of the depths I cry unto thee." That evening he went "very unwillingly" to a meeting held on Aldersgate Street. A man stood and began reading the preface to Martin Luther's commentary on Romans. Imagine that! Wesley described what happened next in his *Journal:* "About a quarter before nine, while he was describing the change which God works in the heart through faith in Christ, I felt my heart strangely warmed. I felt I did trust Christ, Christ alone for salvation; and an assurance was given me that He had taken away my sins, even mine and saved me from the law of sin and death."[1]

This day marked a new beginning for John Wesley. For the next fifty years he traveled four to five thousand miles a year, mostly on horseback, and preached over forty thousand sermons.

The powerful message of Romans was rediscovered in 1918 when a young Swiss pastor named Karl Barth published a commentary on Paul's letter. He wrote in his preface: "The reader will detect for himself that it has been written with a joyful sense of discovery. The mighty voice of Paul was new to me: and if to me, no doubt to many others also. And yet now that my work is finished, I perceive that much remains which I have not yet heard."[2] However, what Barth heard he wrote down, and the first edition of his *Römerbrief* fell "like a bombshell on the theologians' playground."[3] It signaled the death of Old Liberalism and a serious return to the study of God's Word.

Our focus is on the powerful message of Romans which declares the meaning of the gospel of Jesus Christ. The theme is set forth in 1:16-17 and developed throughout the rest of the letter. Paul wrote: "For I am not ashamed of the gospel: it is the power of God for salvation to every one who believes, to the Jew first and also to the Greek. For in it the righteousness of God is revealed through faith for faith; as it is written, 'He who through faith is righteous shall live.'"[4]

Paul boldly declared he was not ashamed of the gospel. What about us? Are we ashamed to share it or do we boldly declare it? One of my vivid childhood memories is a worship experience in my home church in Fayetteville, Arkansas. A big, redfaced fullback who played for the Arkansas Razorbacks sang, "Jesus is all the world to me." When I looked into his face and heard him sing, I somehow believed he meant it. He was not ashamed of Christ.

In his declaration Paul used the technique of understatement to increase the effect *(litotes)*. We do this in such statements as, "Pete Rose has been a pretty good baseball player" and "Billy Graham is a better than average preacher." What we mean is they are the best! Paul certainly was not ashamed of the gospel; he gloried in it! Elsewhere he wrote: "But far be it from me to glory except in the cross of our Lord Jesus Christ, by which the world has been crucified to me, and I to the world" (Gal. 6:14).

Paul was not ashamed of the gospel because "it is the power of God for salvation to every one who has faith" (Rom. 1:16). The gospel is powerful in its *effect* and universal in its *extent*. It is much more than a philosophy or a system of belief. It is something dynamic, "the power of God." The word is *dunamis* from which we derive our word dynamite. The gospel is explosive in its effect. It can change lives.

What is the extent of the gospel? It includes "every one who has faith." God wants a big family! Nobody is excluded because of position or past sin in his or her life. Both a seeking intellectual like Nicodemus (John 3) and a sinful Samaritan woman (John 4) can experience the life-changing power of the gospel. "Every one who calls upon the name of the Lord will be saved" (Rom. 10:13).

During a revival, the pastor and I visited a retired couple. They had moved from a northern state seeking the warmer climate of the South. We shared the plan of salvation. When we finished both bowed their heads and received Christ into their lives. The revival concluded Easter Sunday morning. The couple came forward during the invitation. They announced to the congregation: "All our lives we knew something was missing; now we know what that something was." The transforming power of the gospel had made a decisive difference in their lives!

But what is the gospel? What is its content? Paul stated four tremendous truths in his letter to the Romans. The gospel affirms something great about the character of God, something tragic about the human condition, something wonderful Christ has done, and something challenging about Christian living.

Something Great About the Character of God

In Romans 1:17 Paul declared "the righteousness of God is revealed" in the gospel. That God is righteous is not something Paul discovered on his own. He did not figure it out or arrive at this conclusion through speculation or human wisdom. Rather, God revealed it. The word used is *apokaluptō* and means "to uncover what has been hidden." God took the initiative, pulled back the curtain, and allowed His righteousness to be known.

What is the righteousness of God? This is an important concept in Romans. Righteousness is an *attribute* of God. He is right and not wrong. He is good and not evil. His nature is to be just and upright. However, the concept means much more as Paul used it. The righteousness of God is primarily an *activity*, what God has done to save sinners. Righteousness is God's grace at work whereby as sinners we receive a new standing before Him and are offered a new way of life.

Picture a courtroom scene. As guilty sinners we stand before a holy God. Instead of pronouncing sentence, God declares us acquitted. He pronounces us to be righteous and actually makes it so. He accepts us although we are not acceptable.

This righteousness is received by faith. Faith is life-changing relationship. It is our response to the divine initiative. Faith is emptying our lives of selfish concerns to make room for God. It is affirming the words of the gospel hymn, "Nothing in my hands I bring, simply to thy cross I cling." We recognize our own resources are woefully inadequate to provide authentic life, so we thrust ourselves upon the mercies of God.

God's righteousness is a gift. It cannot be merited or earned. The son of a miner learned this truth centuries ago. His name was Martin Luther. Luther's father wanted him to become a lawyer. However, a bolt of lightning during a violent thunderstorm moved his life in another direction. Young Luther came close to death, and it frightened him. He made a vow to serve God, became a monk, and entered a monastery.

Luther aspired to be a model Christian. To find salvation he chose the path of self-help. He fasted and prayed for days at a time. He threw his blankets aside and nearly froze to death in an effort to atone for his sins. But the guilt remained.

Then Luther visited Rome. Surely, he would find peace of mind there. While in the eternal city he plunged into a frenzied routine of saying confession, celebrating the mass, visiting the catacombs, and touching every sacred relic he could find. On his knees he climbed the *scala sancta* thought to be the steps from Pilate's palace in Jerusalem where Jesus was condemned to death. Despite his efforts, peace still did not come to his troubled heart.

Returning to Germany, Luther began to lecture at the University of Wittenberg. He focused on the Psalms, Galatians, and Romans. One day while reading Romans 1:16-17 the truth suddenly dawned on him, "There I began to understand that the righteousness of God is that by which the righteous lives by a gift of God, namely by faith. . . . Here I felt that I was altogether born again, and had entered paradise itself through open gates."[5] The gospel affirms something great about the character of God: He is righteous.

Something Tragic About the Human Condition

The gospel sounds a tragic note about the human situation: We are sinners. We cannot escape this reality. In Romans 1:18—3:20, Paul pointed to the universality of sin. Jew and Gentile were in the same predicament. The Jew had known greater privileges and was under heavier accountability, but Jew and Gentile alike were judged impartially, each in terms of the light he possessed. Both were aware of the disclosure of God in creation and were "without excuse" in their rejection of Him (1:19-20). Furthermore, the Jews had the advantage of knowing God through their covenant relationship with Him (chap. 2).

Paul concluded that all people are guilty before God and are "under the power of sin" (3:9). He added, "There is none righteous, not even up to one" (3:10; author's translation of the Greek). Indeed, all have "missed the mark" and "fall short of the glory of God" (3:23).

Picture two men boarding a train. One is evidently a successful businessman dressed in his tailored suit, expensive shirt, and silk tie and carrying a leather briefcase. The other is a drunken bum, unshaven, smelly, wearing clothes that are dirty and torn. As they sit beside each other, the differences are striking. Suddenly, both men look out the window and discover they are both on the wrong train going in the wrong direction.[6] The gospel affirms something tragic about the human condition: We are all sinners!

Something Wonderful Christ Has Done

In Romans 5:1-2 Paul declared, "Therefore, since we are justified by faith, we have peace with God through our Lord Jesus Christ. Through him we have obtained access to this grace in which we stand, and we rejoice in our hope of sharing the glory of God." How confident Paul is! Through faith in Christ we have been made right with God and have a new standing before Him. This is the wonderful work Christ has accomplished for us!

"Peace with God" signifies alienation has been overcome by reconciliation. The very form for the word peace *(eirō)* means "to bind up the pieces or fragments into a whole." Christ is able to bring wholeness and completeness to lives marred and broken by sin.

A young man burst through my study door and fell face down on the carpet. He had run with the wrong crowd. Alcohol and drugs had almost ruined his life. He blurted out, "Can God forgive me for what I have done?" I pointed him to Christ who has provided a place of beginning again! His life is now whole. He has peace with God. Moreover, he teaches a Sunday School class of teen-aged boys!

Faith in Christ opens the door to "access" to God. The Greek word *(prosagōgē)* pictures a person being ushered into the presence of royalty. Jesus Christ opens the door, ushers us in, and introduces us to God. Before God we find salvation, not condemnation; hope, not despair. In Christ we are given the freedom to become who we are. The word for "access" also denotes the place where ships come in to harbor. Life's storms can easily overwhelm us. In God's presence we experience protection and care.

Paul was certain our salvation was made possible only by the redemptive work of Christ. It was "at the right time" while we were "helpless" and "ungodly" that Christ died for us (5:6). This act of supreme sacrifice demonstrated God's great love for us (5:8). Christ died in our place. Sydney Carton in Charles Dickens's *A Tale of Two Cities* offered his life to save a man he thought was better than himself. Whereas, Jesus Christ who is much better than anyone who has ever lived offered His life for sinners. The gospel affirms something wonderful Christ has done: He has given us a new standing with God!

Something Challenging About Christian Living

Paul's letter to the Romans concludes with a challenging affirmation about Christian living. In Romans 12:1-2 he declared that we are saved to serve! According to Paul, the *indictive*, what God has done in Jesus Christ to save sinners, always is followed by the *imperative*, the evidence of our lives committed to Him in faithful service. Orthodoxy (right belief) must lead to orthoproxy (right practice). Our Lord demands a belief that behaves, a faith that functions.

On the basis of the "mercies of God," we are to "present" our "bodies" to Christ as a "living sacrifice" (12:1). The word "present" was used of bringing a sacrifice to the temple. "Bodies" involves the whole person or total being. A "living sacrifice" not a dead one is required. God desires a bold commitment of our lives to Him as the only acceptable act of "spiritual worship." The lines between sacred and secular have been erased. The whole of life is holy and must be dedicated to God. Such a radical commitment to God includes a decisive transformation (i.e., a metamorphosis) whereby our entire outlook on life is changed. We must refuse to be "conformed to this world" or to permit others to determine our agenda. Convictions will not tolerate compromise in doing the will of God.

In Romans 12:3-8 Paul described the church as "one body in Christ." As such, it has many members who perform different functions. The Holy Spirit has bestowed charismatic gifts upon all believers to equip them for service to build up the church. The church is a vibrant, living organism set apart to carry on the Lord's mission in the world.

The work of the church may be described as the continuing incarnation. *Incarnation* is the theological term that points to the reality of the divine becoming human, God coming into the world in flesh and blood in the person of Jesus of Nazareth. We need to remember, however, that God came into human life in the incarnation never to leave it. Luke began the book of Acts with these words, "In the first book, O Theophilus, I have dealt with all that Jesus began to do and teach, until the day when he was taken up" (Acts 1:1-2). The language means Jesus would continue doing and teaching all that He *began* to do and teach. But how could this happen following Jesus' ascension to the Father? The answer is that the church continues the work of Christ as the incarnation. As followers of Christ we are to continue doing and teaching all that Jesus began to do and teach! We are to embody the message of the gospel in word and deed.

J. Winston Pearce has related an interesting story that illustrates the meaning of the continuing incarnation. His wife, Winnie, was a mountaineer. She was capable of speaking in a brogue common to her upbringing.

Once Winnie did some work in religious drama at a great university. During the school year her group was invited to put on a play for the entire campus community. The play chosen had as its principal character an old mountain woman. Students began reading lines and trying out for the parts.

A problem arose when the professor responsible for the production tried to cast the old mountain woman. Nobody could imitate the exact speech required of the chief character. In desperation, the professor asked students in the class to read the lines. At last Winnie's turn came and she simply lapsed back into the language of her beloved hills. "Eureka!" shouted the professor, "we have our mountain woman." Little did he realize she was doing what came naturally!

Opening night came. Just before the curtain went up, the professor came backstage and startled the cast with the announcement that the author of the play had just come into the theater and was seated in second row front! There was no time for panic. The show must go on!

Following the final curtain call, the professor brought the author of the play backstage. He had kind words for the members of the cast. Then, he came to Winnie Pearce. He took her hands in his, looked deeply into her anxious eyes and said, "My dear, tonight you put into flesh and blood the woman I dreamed on paper."[7] When we stand before God one day, may He be able to say to each of us, "You lived out in flesh and blood the person I had in mind when I created you and gave you life."

What is the gospel? It declares something great about the character of God: He is righteous. It reveals something tragic about the human condition: We are sinners. It affirms something wonderful Christ has done: He has given us a new standing with God. It offers something challenging about Christian living: We are the body of Christ, the continuing incarnation.

Notes

1. *The Journal of John Wesley* (Chicago: Moody Press, 1952), pp. 63-64.
2. Karl Barth, *The Epistle to the Romans*, 6th ed., trans. Edwyn C. Hoskyns (New York: Oxford University Press, 1968), p. 2.
3. The phrase is attributed to the Roman Catholic theologian, Karl Adam, according to F. F. Bruce, *The Epistle of Paul to the Romans*, Tyndale New Testament Commentaries (Grand Rapids: Wm. B. Eerdmans Publishing Company, 1963), p. 60.
4. Scripture quotations, unless otherwise indicated, are from the Revised Standard Version.
5. John Dillenberger, ed., *Martin Luther: Selections from His Writings* (Garden City: Anchor Books, 1961), p. 11.
6. Adapted from Emil Brunner, *Our Faith*, trans. John W. Rilling (New York: Charles Scribner's Sons, 1954), p. 41. The illustration was suggested by Peter Rhea Jones, "Preaching from Romans," *Review and Expositor*, LXXIII:470, 1976.
7. J. Winston Pearce, *I Believe* (Nashville: Broadman Press, 1954), pp. 110-112.

12
THE CHALLENGE OF BIBLICAL INTERPRETATION: ESCHATOLOGY

James I. Packer

As I attempt to deal with eschatology, I am trying to offer you a viable, overall synthetic, biblical view of the matter. I cannot discuss the academic minutia of any of the texts with which I deal because I am trying to cover a great deal of territory. While I admit candidly that my synthesis is not definitive, I trust it is viable. I want to show you at least one way of putting it all together which is coherent, which takes account of all that is in the Scriptures, which doesn't require one to turn one's back on any of the biblical material and doesn't oblige one to say, "Well, Scripture is irrevocably in contradiction with Scripture at this point or that point or the other point."

Eschatology is the study of last things. It is a very important field of study, for its real theme is the Christian hope, and hope is integral to the New Testament Christian life. Indeed, hope is integral to all life that is worthy of that name. Existence without hope is something less than really living. So the study of the Christian hope is important in itself, essential indeed to those who would proclaim the gospel in its full glory. My subject is the objective given content of the Christian hope. I would like to set what I am going to say under the authority of a single phrase found in 1 Timothy 1:1. It is a little phrase of four words which, to my mind, really says it all. The phrase is this: "Christ Jesus our hope." Everything that I say will, one way or another, be revolving round that phrase and seeking to illuminate it in different ways. Christ Jesus is our hope. Let us explore this theme of eschatology and see what that means.

To begin I want to explain a limit which I have set myself. There are three matters often discussed when eschatology is the theme among Bible believers about which I am not going to speak at all. They are, first, the state and prospects of the country now called Israel, the country which of course is still relatively young, the country now inhabited by several hundred thousand. I think it is about 2 million unbelieving Jews (when I say unbelieving, I mean they are not Christian) who have made themselves a power in the Middle East, as you well know. I will not say a word about the place and the prospects of the state of Israel. Nor will I address the rapture of the saints before Christ appears. Nor, thirdly, will I deal with a great tribulation, greater than any has hit the world before that is expected by some at the end of the age before the public reappearance by the Savior. The reason I will not address these three themes is a simple one. As I understand the Bible, it says nothing about any of those three matters. The belief that it does say something about these three matters rests, I believe, on the misinterpretation of a whole series of texts. Such a conclusion is bound to offend someone, but I want to share my position honestly.

By way of introduction, we must first consider the subject matter of eschatology. It is the Christian hope; I can say a little more than that. The theme of eschatology, the study of the last things, God's future, is God's fulfillment of His purpose of perfecting His creation by eliminating from it the disorder brought into it by sin and reconstructing everything into its final perfect form. Further, the biblical presentation of this great theme is like an ellipse with two foci, an oval figure with two points each of which is just as central in its significance as the other. The two foci are *global eschatology* (which has to do with the future of Jesus Christ and this whole world) and *personal eschatology* (which has to do with the future of the individual Christian and the individual unbeliever).

One can go on further and say that the biblical perspective, as the New Testament in particular presents these two themes, is what is called inaugurated eschatology, that is, the belief that the kingdom of God is here and the powers of the kingdom are at work already. The gospel is the good news that heaven has already begun here on earth for those who are Christ's. The gospel is the good news that the prophesied king of Old Testament prophesy has come. He came in lowliness as the servant Savior of men. Now He is risen and enthroned, and from His throne He still comes to men by the personal presence by His Holy Spirit. One day He will come again publicly in glory as the world's judge, and those who are His are already risen with Him out of their spiritual death into the life of His kingdom, the life for which eternal life is the New Testament name. We are risen with Christ. We live with Christ. That is our eternal condition. It will always be so in life, in death, in resurrection, through judgment and on beyond; those who are Christ's will be with Him and He with them in love and joy and glory. That is the truth about the destiny of the Christian believer.

We live, according to the New Testament, in the last days. That means the period between the Lord's first coming and the Lord's second coming. Not everyone who uses the phrase "last days" realizes that that is the biblical lexicography of it, but in fact it is, and it would only take two or three minutes with a concordance to verify. In these last days, this era of Christ's kingdom and Christ's church and Christ's gospel and the outworking of Christ's saving purpose for those for whom He died, there is constant conflict between the devil and his forces opposing Christ. This is how it is going to be in an increasing measure, so it seems, from certain texts until the Lord comes again. This is the biblical perspective of inaugurated eschatology. Already the Lord is transforming His own people in His own way. He transforms them from the inside out.

That is to say, he changes heart and character, though our physical body, that eternal physical aspect of a personal being which is given us for our expression and communication, remains for the most part unchanged. But one day when the Lord comes again, when we are taken from this world to glory, we who already have been changed inside will be given bodies to match, bodies that are true and adequate expressions of the new persons we are in Christ. That will be the fullness of our personal redemption. All around us when Christ comes again, we shall find that in a moment the whole cosmos, glorious as it is in its present form, will have been remade into yet greater glory. New heavens, new earth, call it what you will, it will be a wholly new order of things, and the word *perfection* will be the only word that will then describe it. That's the biblical perspective. The fulfillment and completion of what God has already started. Come then to the study of eschatology with this overall point of view clearly in your mind. What we are going to study is the details within this frame of reference.

Let me make a further introductory remark: Never underestimate the theological significance of eschatology. In the schools, very often eschatology has been the poor relation in the theology courses. Coming last it has often been, to speak frankly, skimped in teaching. Partly, I think, this is because professors have not always known what to say. In addition, everyone who works in the classroom knows things tend to take longer to teach than you anticipate, so that the final bit of your course nearly always get skimped. That's universal teaching experience. But it is a very sad thing that eschatology should ever be skimped because, as you can already see, it is a matter of enormous importance, very much a part of the glory of the gospel and very important for every Christian to understand. Several points add weight to what I am saying about the significance of eschatology.

Eschatology is first the key to understanding the unity of the Bible, which is a book of hope, Old and New Testament both looking forward to a final consummation, finding its unity in all the lines of thought and teaching and of divine action, too, which will bring in that final consummation towards which God is working. Eschatology is, further, the clue to understanding the nature of the Christian life. It is essentially a life of hope, a life in which nothing is perfect yet but the hope of perfection is set before us, a life in which one forgets what is behind and reaches out to what lies ahead and presses towards the mark for the prize of the high calling of God in Christ Jesus. One of the things we modern Christians are very bad at, it seems to me, is remembering what the whole materialist culture around us encourages us to forget, that there are two worlds not just one, two lives not just one, and heaven really is more important than earth, for that life is the goal for which this life is preparation. Martin Lloyd Jones published a tract containing a sermon of his on the early verses of the twelfth chapter of Hebrews called "Life's Preparatory School." It is a perfect title, taking you right to the heart of the Christian life as the New Testament views it. Life is preparation for something more glorious that is ahead of us in the future. We need, then, to understand the Christian hope in order to understand the Christian life.

Third, eschatology is the key to understanding the shape of world history now. The Bible has a clearly articulated view about world history. The people of God, the church as we New Testament believers call it, are at the center of the world history. It always was, and the way to read the book of world history is in terms of the life, work, fortunes, and the battles of the church of Christ. That is a helpful perspective to bring to the bewildering confusions of world affairs today. Remember that the church under the sovereign hand of God is the real center of what is going on and always will be. That is the Bible view. Finally, eschatology is supremely relevant for teaching the gospel in these days, considering what we are up against. On the one hand are utopian hopes, false hopes of different kinds offered by different people—some of them Marxist with secular false hopes, some of the simply American optimists but again with secular hopes that may prove false. We need a clear and firm grasp on the hope that God sets before us in the gospel. We are opposing utopian false hopes just as we are opposing a great deal of pessimistic hopelessness, the views of people who feel that they have seen through the false hopes of society and themselves now have no hope at all. To me one of the most pathetic things, and this of course becomes increasingly poignant to me as I grow older, is to observe so many folk of my age and a little beyond who see and feel their life as mere progress into the increasing darkness of a tunnel with no exit. Their physical strength is going. Their health is going. They have nothing to which to look forward. Their career is behind them. They are lonely. They are hopeless. We have to minister the gospel to many, many folk in that state of mind. We need to speak loudly and clearly about the glory of the Christian hope. The world needs to hear that word from our lips.

For the first nineteen Christian centuries, personal eschatology was central in the church's thinking about the Christian hope. The four last things of medieval preaching (death, judgment, heaven, and hell) occupied most of the attention of the Lord's people. Not much thinking was done about what the New Testament calls the *parousia,* quite literally the royal visit, the return of Jesus Christ to His world. But in the nineteenth century and even more in this twentieth century, the pendulum swung to the opposite extreme. Global eschatology, the future of Jesus Christ and the world, has become central in people's attention.

A number of factors have contributed to this development. Bible believers have insistently affirmed the parousia of hope against liberals in the church who have denied that we need ever expect to see Jesus Christ again. In addition, the future of the world and of the human race has become increasingly an existential question for everybody. Now that we have it in our power to blow the world up by nuclear means and run the risk of destroying the world by ecological folly, this has become a central question for everyone, and it is no wonder that the future of the world and the future of Jesus Christ in this world has become a central matter of Christian reflection, debate, and study. In this twentieth century when all the emphasis has been on the parousia and the future of the human race, not much thinking has been done about individual destiny. Because of this, what I say about individual destiny may seem a little old fashioned, and it is the case that nearly everything that I have to say on the subject was being said one hundred and more years ago.

Concentration on one of the foci in eschatology with insufficient concern for the other focal point is always going to produce unbalanced thinking. I want to try and set the balance right. There are interpretative difficulties as one comes to the text for three reasons at least. First, the events and experiences to which eschatology points are in the nature of the case unimaginable. Therefore testimony to them, I mean biblical testimony to them, is inevitably open-textured and elusive. We cannot with any certainty imagine what coming events and coming experiences are going to be like. We can use phrases that refer to them, but cannot really imagine them. They are beyond us. That means that indepth understanding of the biblical testimony to them is difficult to achieve. Second, the Bible is an Oriental book, and scriptural testimony to the future is given in Oriental fashion. It is given in a pictorial, evocative, evaluative, imaginative way rather than in a sort of repertorial prose which is informative in the way that a newspaper report of things is informative. This is the way that the Oriental mind, through which God gave us His Word, focuses things, formulates things, presents things. We have an abundance of very evocative imagery, but again and again you have problems in imagining what the reality to which those images refer will really be like. The world that doesn't die. The fire that isn't quenched. The crowns on the heads of God's people. The white robes that they wear. And in Revelation 21:16-21 the city of God, new Jerusalem, which comes down from heaven as a bride adorned for her husband, which has walls, foundations, and gates of jewels (lists of jewels are given), and which is as high as it is broad and as it is long. It is a perfect cube, and the breadth of it is 12,000 stadia which is 1500 miles, and the length of it is 12,000 stadia which is 1500 miles, and the height of it is 12,000 stadia, 1500 miles. Imagery is being used. This is the Oriental imagination through which God is presenting this vision of final glory, and as with so many of the details the sort of imagery that is used enables us to understand the significance of what is being presented. It is perfection in a dozen different forms without enabling us to envisage what it will look like and feel like in specific detail. God thought it good that we should have His Word given to us via the Oriental imagination. What we have to do is to learn to appreciate this material for what it is.

A third point follows from the second: Much scriptural testimony on the future is given in the idiom of Jewish apocalyptic. It is a highly imaginative form of communication which to us in the modern West comes across as a quasi-poetic code. It's prose, but there is so much imagery, so much fantastic imagery, that we feel that this hardly is prose of an ordinary sort. This is quasi-poetic. Imagery is being used to create a sense of significance, but we simply cannot look through the imagery to envisage the events to which the imagery refers. When apocalyptic or Oriental imagination really goes into high gear, it expresses thoughts which I call "visuals" (that is visual imagery), which are often incompatible with themselves and are often further decorated with additional visuals that are there to indicate importance rather than to add to our knowledge. For an example of visuals that are intrinsically incompatible, though glorious in their meaning (I move for a moment out of apocalyptic into the world of simple imaginative vision) I cite Revelation 7:14. "Who are these? These are they who have washed their robes and made them white in the blood of the lamb." Now if you have ever cut yourself, you know that blood does not make linen white. You know the theology that this phrase is expressing and you glory in it as I do, but when you analyze it it is a couple of visuals (blood and dirty robes being washed white). The visuals in literal terms contradict each other. We understand that the Bible is not contradicting itself, of course, because we understand that this is a phrase expressing a theological thought. But it is expressed in terms of two visual elements which actually contradict each other, which actually don't fit. This is how the Oriental imagination works.

A further example, and one taken from the world of apocalyptic, is Acts 2:16-21. I have to do this so that you will understand something of the grammar of apocalyptic, that is the way that apocalyptic is put together. Peter on the Day of Pentecost begins his sermon by saying, "This is that which was spoken by the prophet Joel. In the last days it shall be, God declares, that I will pour out my spirit on all flesh. Your sons and daughters shall prophesy. Your young men shall see visions and your old men dream dreams. On my men servants and maid servants in those days I will pour out my spirit and they shall prophesy." This is that, says Peter. But he hasn't finished his quotation yet. He goes on in verse 19, "And I will show wonders in the heavens above and signs on the earth beneath, blood and fire and vapor of smoke. The sun shall be turned into darkness and the moon into blood before the day of the Lord comes, the great and manifest day. And it shall be that whoever calls on the name of the Lord shall be saved." Is this which has just happened on the Day of Pentecost the outpouring of the Spirit that which was spoken of by Joel in chapter 2, verses 19-21? As Peter cites the passage, yes, it is. What are we to make of it then?

On the Day of Pentecost there were not cosmic convulsions. The sun was not turned into darkness and the moon into blood on that day. No, this is decoration added to the main thought in the way that all sorts of small decorations were added to the main structure in medieval cathedrals, added to enhance the dignity and the glory of the main thing. What details? The sun turned into darkness, the moon into blood. What does that mean? It is an imaginative way of expressing the thought that what happens when God pours out His Spirit is something so momentous that the world is never the same again. That is the thought being expressed by this fantastic imagery of the sun turned into darkness and the moon into blood. There is much of this in apocalyptic, and in interpreting apocalyptic you have to remember to ask constantly what is the main thought and what is the supportive decoration. That is the only way to get out the meaning that is being expressed. In the vision in Revelation 21 of new Jerusalem, the details of the precious stones of which walls and foundations are made are also decoration. The specifics are put in in order to underline the thought that the city is a glorious city with every glory that you can imagine being a part of it. But if you said each of the twelve different sorts of Jews must stand for some specific excellence in the city, you would be misunderstanding the way that the grammar of apocalyptic works. All these things have to be understood, or any amount of what the Bible says about the future will be misunderstood in detail.

Turning to personal eschatology, consider first and briefly the biblical certainties and then second the biblical questions, where again I shall have to be more brief than I wish. There are two central biblical certainties. The prospect for believers who already are alive in Christ, indwelt by the Holy Spirit who is God's seal upon them, marking them out as His, is that He one day will come to claim us. Meanwhile His Spirit in us is His seal indicating ownership. We who through the Spirit manifest His fruit and His gifts and experience the witness of the Spirit assuring us that we are children of God and heirs of glory with Christ, we and all other believers with us have before us a prospect of glory. We are assured of animation by Christ in resurrection (John 5:28-29; Phil. 3:20-21). In addition, we can count on acceptance through Christ at whatever judgment we may face in that day. We must all appear before the judgment seat of Christ, says Paul. That could mean loss in some sense for some Christians, but it won't mean loss of salvation. The way to express justification is to say that it is God's last judgment passed on believers here and now in time, assuring us of our eternal security with him. That last judgment will never be retracted or reversed. So acceptance with Christ is guaranteed through that final accounting and whatever lies beyond it.

In addition, we expect association with Christ forever. We shall be forever with the Lord (1 Thess. 4:17). Remember Jesus' prayer in John 17:24, "Father, I will that those whom you have given me be with me where I am that they may behold my glory." To the Christian, and this is really a very good test of a Christian, the prospect of being forever with the Lord Jesus, whom we love because He loved us, is glorious, thrilling, and nothing better could be imagined. To the unbeliever it would be a different story, but we are only talking about the destiny of the believer now. So animation by Christ in resurrection, acceptance through Christ at future judgment, association with Christ forever, and finally adoration of Christ as the height of love and joy (Rev. 22:3-5; etc.) are the thoughts, the theological thoughts, that make up the New Testament picture of the prospect that awaits the believer. The crowns and the white robes are trimming, decorations in the picture. The relationship with Jesus is the heart of it. That's what it all means, and you can spell it out under these four headings as I have done.

By contrast, and this is the second certainty regarding personal destiny that the New Testament teaches us, the prospect of unbelievers and apostates is awful, fearful. It has only two elements, resurrection to judgment for condemnation. Read again what Jesus says about that in John 5:28-29: "All that are in the grave shall hear the voice of the son of man and come forth, some for the resurrection of life and others for the resurrection of condemnation" or judgment. And following that resurrection, the condemnation comes, being relegation to a condition described in Matthew 25:41 as eternal punishment and in Revelation 20:15 as the lake of fire. Imagery? Yes, but clearly this imagery is pointing to something fearsome. So the prospect for believers according to the New Testament is something very good, and the prospect for unbelievers and apostates according to the New Testament is very bad. That is stark stuff. I simply lay it on the table and move on, for I now want to look at three biblical questions relating to the destiny of individuals.

First question: Is the resurrection body given at death? It has been argued that perhaps it is. The argument has been based on 2 Corinthians 5:1-4 where Paul expresses the Christian hope in terms of not wanting to be unclothed, that is to be deprived of our present physical dimension of life altogether, but rather to be clothed upon, further clothed, so that what is mortal may be swallowed up in life. Paul goes on to say, "He who has prepared us for this very thing is God who has given us the spirit as a guarantee." There are three possible lines of interpretation at this point. There is first the common view that bodily resurrection, further clothing, clothing upon, is awaited by the Christian dead who are consciously and joyfully sustained in what we call the intermediate, that is the disembodied, state by the Holy Spirit. God's gift of the Spirit as a guarantee, referred to in verse 5, remains with us through the intermediate state. Though in one sense we have lost because temporaly we have no body through which to express ourselves, in another and more fundamental sense we will have gained because we will have departed to be with Christ, which as Paul said in Philippians 1:21 is far better. He means far better than life in this world ever can be. This is a common view, and I am not sure that I want to depart from it.

An alternative view is preferred by such scholars as F. F. Bruce and Murray Harris: Resurrection bodies are actually received at death, but manifested only at the parousia. That is why Jesus is able to say that those that are in the graves will come forth, some to the resurrection of life, others to the resurrection of condemnation. The resurrection bodies, whatever they are, will only be manifested at the parousia. Then there is a third view, namely that resurrection is experienced by the believer as immediately following death, either because unconsciousness intervenes between the day of death or because the dead, in effect, are now outside of time. I am not sure what that last phrase means, so I hesitate to embrace this view. But a biblical scholar like T. F. Torrence has argued for it.

It is healthy to remember that when we look into the future, some things are certain. Some things are not certain. What is uncertain here is where and how our future enhanced bodily existence becomes real for us. There is an uncertainty as to how this biblical data should be interpreted. What is certain, however, is that we, creatures of God, need a bodily form of existence for expression of ourselves. We need a face with which to smile. We need hands with which to wave and hug people. We use our body for purposes of expression. We need a bodily form of existence for communication. God who made us with a bodily form of existence for these two purposes will one day raise us into a perfected bodily existence in which expression and communication will also be perfected. What it will be like is beyond us to imagine. But that it will be so is a matter of divine promise. Many texts could be brought in here, such as 1 Corinthians 15. It is going to happen; it is certain. It is the resurrection hope, even if we are not quite certain as to when and how the gift will be given.

The second biblical question: Is it possible, as more and more today wish to think, that universalism might be true? I am going to be quick, blunt, and even brutal in dealing with this one, for it seems to me that the question is one to which the Scriptures return a very blunt, firm, and brutal answer. And the answer is *no*. No text, to start with, unambiguously asserts universalism, and many texts seem to deny it. Many texts speak of the impossibility of salvation without faith. "He who believes not shall not see life. The wrath of God abides on him." This is just one of many at the end of John 3. Therefore, those who wish to affirm universalism have to embrace some doctrine of a second chance for those who leave this world in unbelief, and that is a matter of unbiblical speculation in itself. The supposition that those who are unconverted in this world will be converted in some future life is entirely speculative and altogether hazardous.

Three biblical questions can be asked which together are fatal to the universalist's speculation. Question 1: Does not universalism fly in the face of the biblical evidence on the decisiveness of this life's decisions? What is so awful about Jesus' threat to the Jews that if they do not believe that He is the one who should come, they would die in their sins (John 8:21), if indeed they are going to be converted in some future life and weaned away from their sins there? What did Jesus have in mind, supposing that universalism is true when He said in Matthew 12:32 that whoever speaks against the Holy Spirit will not be forgiven either in this age or in the age to come? What did Jesus have in mind when in the story of the sheep and the goats, that vision of future judgment, He speaks of the sheep being welcomed into eternal life while the goats are banished into eternal punishment. Eternal life, the life of the age to come, is at the least life that will never end. What then about eternal punishment? What are we going to make of the Lord's words about Judas in Matthew 26:24, "The Son of Man goes as it is written of him, but woe to that man by whom the Son of Man is betrayed. It would have been better for that man if he had not been born"? Do you think Jesus would have spoken that way of someone He knew would be converted in a future life? And what is Paul saying when he says in Galatians 6:7 that those who sow to the Spirit will of the Spirit reap eternal life but those who sow to the flesh reap corruption? Are not all these texts stressing that this life's decisions really are decisive for eternal destiny. If that is so, how can the universalist's hypothesis stand?

Second, the universalist's hypothesis impales those who embrace it on the horns of a dilemma from which, I think, they cannot escape. Supposing that universalism is true, was the preaching of hell for unbelievers by Jesus and the apostles inept ignorance or immoral bluff? If universalism is true and Jesus and the apostles did not know it, it was inept ignorance. If universalism is true and they knew it, then their warnings to turn from the prospect of hell and final misery were simply immoral bluff, the kind of things of which evangelical preachers are sometimes accused.

The third question: Is not universalism contrary to each man's own conscience? Charity prompts it. But hear this word from James Denney, Scottish theologian of ninety years ago. "I dare not say to myself that if I forfeit the opportunity this life affords I shall ever have another. And therefore I dare not say so to another man." Don't you agree with me that that is good thinking. If I am not prepared to risk my eternal destiny by being spiritually negligent in this life because I hope that there will be a second chance in another life, it is not really charity for me to suggest that other people may warrantably do so. But that is what the affirmation of universalism does suggest. It is holding out a hope for others that I dare not hold out for myself. Surely Denney was right. And surely no honest man, no person who allows himself or herself to keep thinking as the impulse of charity stirs their mind, can embrace the universalist's speculation for others while not daring to embrace it for one's own soul.

What is certain here is that there is no salvation without faith; there is no salvation without turning to Christ. According to the consistent witnesses of Scripture, the decisive decision is made in this world. I dare not go beyond that. I do not find universalism a comfortable doctrine with which to live. I find it an unbiblical doctrine which is impossible in good conscience to accept.

Let me ask a third question which has a link with the second one, and here again I am dealing with something which is becoming increasingly popular in Christian circles. Is it possible that annihilationism or, as it is sometimes called, conditional immortality is true? That is, is it possible that those who leave this world in unbelief are simply snuffed out by God, so that there is no eternal distress for them? They simply cease to be, and the only human beings for whom unending life is provided are those who were Christ's and rise to the glory of heaven with him. Again, no text unambiguously asserts this dogma, and many seem to deny it. How one can squeeze this idea out of the New Testament's fire and destruction imagery is not clear. Jesus speaks of the worm that does not die, of the fire that is not quenched. And the language of eternal destruction refers (This is lexicography.) to being permanently unfit and unable to fulfill the purpose for which one was made in the way that a total car is destroyed. All the bits and pieces are still there, but they are so mangled that the car won't run anymore, never will, never can. The idea of eternity does seem then to be there in the awesome things that the New Testament says about the future of unbelievers.

A theological argument is offered that preserving the lost in endless punishment is needless cruelty on God's part. The conditionalists are trying to save God from the suspicion that He is cruel. This argument, however, fails. It boomerangs in the following way. If it is right to suppose that any preservation of unbelievers in being after this life is needless cruelty on God's part, then you have to say that His preserving them to the day of judgment, which the New Testament clearly says that He will, is itself needless cruelty on His part. Already, the conditionalist's hypothesis has proved God guilty of that of which it wants to clear Him. But in the New Testament, and this is the second argument which applies to the Old Testament also, the demonstration of God's retributive justice is praised as in truth integral to His glory. That is not needless cruelty. This is God displaying His righteousness in a way that makes for His praise. So we have in the nineteenth chapter of Revelation the loud voice of a multitude in heaven crying, "Hallelujah, salvation and glory and power belong to our God for his judgments are true and just." He has judged Babylon, the great harlot. Once more in verse 3, "They cried, 'Hallelujah. The smoke from her goes up forever and ever.'" A passage like this shows that so far from our being in a world of needless cruelty, we are in a world of divine justice. That is what we are talking about when we think of eternal punishment. That is the consistent witness of the New Testament. It seems certain and inescapable that any speculation diminishing the awfulness of the prospect of a lost eternity frustrates the purpose of all that gruesome New Testament imagery, which is gruesome precisely to serve as a warning, a red light flashing, a means therefore of begging and alluring folk not to travel along the road that leads to destruction. What we don't know is how the saved will think of the lost in the life to come. We know, however, that they will be praising God eternally for His manifested justice in judging those who merited judgment. There again is something that seems clear in New Testament theology and needs to be underlined as we preach the Christian hope and the Bible doctrine of the future of the individual in these days.

Briefly, let us consider now the issue that most eschatologists have concentrated on in this century: global eschatology. There are certain biblical certainties here. The parousia, that is the personal return of Jesus, will be a bodily return, a visible return, a sudden return, a triumphant return. It will interrupt. It will expose. It will change everything that is going on in the world at the moment when it occurs. It's purpose is threefold: judgment, renewal of the cosmos, and the bringing of the saints into their final joy forever with the Lord. Prior to this public manifesting of Jesus Christ, the judge come in glory, there will have been signs. Signs showing grace in action. The specific signs here are the worldwide preaching of the gospel, Mark 13:10, and the coming in of the fullness both of the Gentiles and of Israel, Roman 11:25-29. Also there will have been signs, that is, significant events showing satanic opposition, opposition to Christ and His kingdom in action. There will have been anti-Christs. There will have been apostasy. There will have been persecution.

There will, third, have been signs showing divine judgment in action, such as wars, earthquakes, famine, and the destruction of Jerusalem. See the little apocalypse, so called, Mark 13:21, Matthew 24, Revelation 6 among other passages. Here, too, there are uncertainties about which questions may be asked. In the interest of brevity, I must only paraphrase the things I wished to discuss more fully.

Question 1: How should we understand the imminence of the parousia? Be also ready; the Lord may come any time. That seems to be a motif running through the New Testament. How are we to understand that? Summarizing, the point of the imminence language in the New Testament is twofold. First, since the coming is certain, we should hope for it steadily. And since the date is unannounced, we do need to be ready for it every day, starting now. But Matthew 24:48 and following hint at the possibility of a longer wait than anyone bargained for. The parable speaks of the servant who says, "My master delays his coming" so he begins to become slack and go wild. And recall how in 2 Peter 3 the apostle has to minister to folk who are already discouraged at the time of writing because the Lord hasn't returned already.

On to a second question: How should we understand "all Israel" in Romans

11:26 where the words of Paul's argument are, "So all Israel shall be saved before the day of grace closes." I should observe first that Paul is discussing the method of grace, the method of God in saving Jew and Gentile. Rather than extending his discourse beyond that point, what he is showing is that just as the Gentiles have been first of all shut up in sin and saved by grace out of sin, so the Jews are going to be saved out of sin, the sin of unbelief in which they are now shut up. So the method of grace is the same for Gentile and for Jew, and all the praise for salvation in both cases will be God's because it was the salvation in each case of sinners who deserve nothing other than final rejection. That is all that's unambiguously clear in these verses.

There are three ways of taking the words "and so all Israel shall be saved." The first way is to understand the phrase "all Israel" to mean elect Gentiles and to take the word *so* as looking back to the reference to the full number of the Gentiles coming in, which is the last phrase in verse 25. If this is the case, Paul is saying that through the coming of the full number of the Gentiles, Jeremiah's prophesy of the deliverer coming to Zion and banishing ungodliness from Jacob will be fulfilled. The second view is that the entire Jewish race that is alive when the full number of the Gentiles is made up is what Paul has in view, the eschatological conversion of the whole body of Abram's genealogical descendents. Then the word *so* is prospective rather than retrospective. It is looking forward, and it means then that through this blessing which brings in the fullness of the Gentiles all Israel, all the nation, will be brought in in the last days. The third view is that the reference of the phrase "all Israel" is to elect Jews in all ages, who right through the gospel era are being brought to faith through the mercy that God has shown to the Gentiles. Paul's reference on this view is to the continuing incoming of those whom God has chosen among his own people. I think that the third view gives weight to the phrase "partial heartening has come upon Israel" in verse 25, and I do not think that the other two views give full weight to that phrase. But there are the three options, and it is for us to decide which we think fit the context better. The certain thing here is that the only future Paul is foreseeing for Jews is in the Christian church, in the one olive tree in which Jews were originally the natural branches, from which they have been broken off in unbelief but into which they could be grafted back again, and all Israel will be grafted back again through the sovereign grace of God.

How does all of this apply to life for the Christian? All that is said about the Christian hope, the hope for the world, the future prospects for the Lord Jesus, and the prospects for the individual believer, is saying to us is learn to live each day packed up and ready to go. One day Christ will come for each one of us. Whether we belong to the terminal generation and will see Him in the great public parousia, that unimaginably glorious event that is promised, we cannot say. But heart-stop day may come to any of us at any time. And heart-stop day should be understood as an appointment on the Lord Jesus' calendar. It is the day when He will come for us personally to take us to be with Himself. One way or another, He is coming for each one of us and should not find us unprepared. As children preparing for the holidays pack up and get ready well in advance, so should we. Keep short accounts with God and live each day as if thy last, just as the hymn says. While life does last, let us work and pray for the advancing of the kingdom. When Christ appears publicly in this world, in what posture should He find the church? Praying for revival and planning world evangelism surely. Let us see that when He comes for us, whether it is soon or late, those are the tasks in which he finds us engaged.

13
INTERPRETING THE BIBLE: GOD'S WORD FOR OUR DAY
Panel Discussion

EDITOR'S NOTE: *The panel discussion has been left essentially in its original form. Editing took place only where clarity was in danger of being lost. The participants were John Newport (moderator), James Packer, Grant Osborne, Walter Kaiser, and Robert Johnston.*

NEWPORT: They say that the last part of a Baptist program is like the Hebrew who arrives on the battlefield and the last Philistine has been slain. But I don't think that's true because there are already questions coming in, and I want to join with Dr. Honeycutt and the other presidents in expressing appreciation. Dr. Dilday asked me to go to the conference on inerrancy in San Diego, and when I first heard Dr. Packer I had resonance with him. I knew that we needed to have him at our school and needed to have him before Southern Baptists. I think you'll agree that he has made a contribution. Dr. Robert Johnston is an unusual man. He grew up in the West Coast, went to Stanford University, was Phi Beta Kappa, then went on to Fuller and then to Duke. He has an unusual background of understanding the whole discussion that's gone on about conservatism and fundamentalism in our country.

Dr. Walter Kaiser, as we know, has the leadership of one of the great schools of our country, some 1,500 students, more students than in all eleven or twelve of the theological institutions in that geographic area. We know him as a fine Old Testament scholar. In going to the American Academy of Religion meetings, the Evangelical Section, I've admired Dr. Grant Osborne through the years as I have listened to his discussion. So, we do have some outstanding persons here.

Let's have two or three guidelines. Limit yourselves to questions, not orations or speeches please if possible. I reserve the right to limit you to one question until others have had an opportunity. Third, you can direct your question to a particular person or ask a question and I will direct it or ask the panel who would like to answer it. Of course, the panel members may have some questions. I have one or two questions which I think are of general interest that we will probably end on. We have two or three questions that have come in, and I might start on those as you get ready to come to the microphone. Here, Dr.

Johnston: In the doctrine of the atonement, is it proper and necessary to designate one metaphor as primary controlling. If so, why and which metaphor is it? If not, why?

JOHNSTON: It's a key interpretive question and is probably the one that divides Jim Packer and myself. We talked, and Jim might also want to talk. He's convinced that the biblical record on its own terms suggests a controlling image or model based on substitution. I myself, in reading those documents, would see that the Bible has talked about the meaning of the cross in more than one way, so that reconciliation and redemption are equally valid, equally true, wonderful for us, but you don't help yourselves by conflating them. There are different points of view. One is the restoring of relationship with Christ, with God; the other is the forgiveness of sins. My own perspective in looking at the text is to see the text talking about the cross in multiple ways. But the answer to why or why you wouldn't have one is whether the text itself provides one or doesn't it? And at that point, interpretors disagree.

NEWPORT: Dr. Packer would you like to comment?

PACKER: Well, Dr. Johnston is quite right in thinking that I differ from him at this point. I think that there is a single, fundamental category of thought underlying all the imagery that is used about the cross in the New Testament. And, that category I believe to be—there's more than one way I can say it—penal substitution if you like that phrase, substitutionary retributive judgment, if you prefer that one. Certainly the thought of retribution can be substituted for the word *penal* in order to explain what is going on, and I think perhaps should be because the associations of the word *penal* are not always helpful. I believe that in the thought of Paul, for instance, the cross, there's a kind of hierarchy in concepts. The cross is redemption, that is an act of saving us from jeopardy because it's reconciliation, an act of bringing us back into peaceful fellowship with God, and its reconciliation because it's blood sacrifice, and blood sacrifice makes propitiation, that is to say it averts the wrath of God, the wrath of God being sin in my understanding of the New Testament, a semitechnical phrase for the certainty of judicial retribution, both present and future from God for sin, you see. And, it's propitiation because it is penal substitution because it is the diverting onto Christ of the curse of the law which was our due. Christ redeemed us from the curse of the law by becoming a curse for us. I would argue that position exegetically, and obviously Dr. Johnston and I don't quite agree about whether the text presents matters altogether in that way. I think they do, and he queries it. But among inerrantists this kind of difference relating to the precise nuances of biblical testimony, even to crucial things like redemption, is legitimate. It's to be expected; we all of us see as through a glass darkly; we are all of us advancing in our Bible study and our understanding of God's name. There would be something perfectionist in the expectation that all Bible believers would be able to agree about absolutely everything right now in this world. So, Dr. Johnston and I, in case you wonder, continue friends and we shall go on talking I'm sure for many years yet.

NEWPORT: All right, thank you very much. We appreciate these getting right to the point, and we have one for Dr. Kaiser. You did not address myth history. Will you give a few sentences on your views, specifically do you agree with Dr. Packer's allowance of the possibility of the thirteen-billion-year-old cosmos?

KAISER: Briefly?

NEWPORT: That's why I said that because I knew you could talk an hour.

KAISER: Yes, from here to eternity. But, briefly, there is a biblical date, and I am sure that if Dr. Packer had additional time he would want to say something about that very critical phrase "in the beginning." We are not in a dualistic system or pluristic system; it is everything that is here wasn't here until the Lord spoke the word, and that seems to be, ought to be, so fundamental that the psalmist celebrated it in Psalm 33:6 and 9, "By the Word of the Lord were the heavens made." Hebrews 11:3, which was cited is similar. Now, if you ask me what is the biblical date and what will I go down for fighting to the last, it's "in the beginning."

If you ask me to clarify that a little bit more and be a little bit more precise, now it's on that point that we get into mischief, and I have no problems with a five- to fifteen-billion-year-old universe. I don't see that the text has ruled that out. The evidence that comes from the biblical text and the evidence that comes from scientists' hands ought to be the same. If it is truth, it is owned by my Lord. There are no facts on which the devil has copyright. They are all owned by the Lord. And, therefore, if the various tests for the age of the universe are reflecting realities that are there, and I have no reason to doubt that the various dating methods that are used like uranium, potassium, argon, and other things of that sort do, indeed, point us adequately to a ballpark figure for when the universe was created. So, I'm very happy with those kinds of dates, and I do not think that our current rage over a young earth is rightly pitched and aimed. I hope you'll not feel badly about me for that. I think that that is becoming one of the great tests of those who really believe in inerrancy, and I think it's unfair. I don't think that that is playing cricket with the material, and, therefore, I would like us to come back and to listen to the text. Let's affirm as Bible believers that it was "in the beginning." That's the theologically sensitive point. The other point is to go gently with one another in terms of our BC calendar. There will be seminars in heaven, I'm almost sure, and we can check that one out later on.

NEWPORT: Amen. Thank you very much. This is a very important point because in our fellowship of Southern Baptists there are many people into creation science. I was with Dr. Morris for a week in one of our prominent Southern Baptist churches and he holds to what, ten, twelve, fifteen thousand years?

KAISER: At the maximum, I think he would say 12,000 or 15,000. By the way, I have been on panels and have been put on the opposite side from Dr. Gish and others in that, though I feel that they are my brothers and they are my kind. Yet, on the other hand we happen to differ very much on that point.

NEWPORT: All right, thank you very much. We have one other question here and then we're going to turn to the microphones. I'm going to ask one question of Dr. Osborne and then we'll turn to you, Dr. Packer. Regarding your comments on creation and women, it seems as if the presuppositions you carried to the text should rather have been conclusions based on the text. For example, consider your theology of creation and your understanding of the created order regarding women. In other words, your presuppositions were unwarranted at the point in the process during which they were introduced and, therefore, unfairly binding on the text.

PACKER: This was a problem of exposition. I wanted to major on Genesis 1 and 2 when talking about creation because it is there that so many pitfalls of exposition are found. But in order to do that, I had to establish a frame of reference, and so without citing a string of texts, which I could have cited, I formulated a theological notion of creation which would provide a frame of reference within which we could work. In the case of women, well, I wanted to survey the overall biblical teaching about women, Old and New Testaments together as part of a single revealed plan and pattern of God, and I wanted to get through all that in the time alloted, therefore, I established a frame of reference. I said that this was me sharing with you my answers to some, or rather my hermeneutical disposition on, certain matters. I would defend myself by saying I don't think that I, in my estimate anyway, mishandled or fudged any of the texts that I appealed to, and I don't think that an alternative frame of reference for them could be validly established from Scripture. In other words, the things that I took for granted I'm prepared to spell out in footnote style if the specifics are put to me. And I am prepared to challenge any other overall frame of reference for the material that I dealt with, in moderate detail anyway, if such an alternative is proffered. I don't think I can say fairer than that in a short answer to the question.

NEWPORT: Thank you very much. Of course, he did have a restriction of time, obviously. Dr. Osborne, some in our constituency are opposed in general to higher criticism of the Bible. As a scholar, conservative scholar, what are the strengths and weaknesses of higher criticism or the importance of higher criticism, so called?

OSBORNE: Yes, well, of course, higher criticism is actually that which is done on the text from above, rather than of course, lower or text criticism. Higher criticism technically simply tries to recover what the text originally was, especially in terms of its referential dimension. Therefore, I think in terms of some larger debates of referentiality, that is of historical background to the Old and New Testaments. This higher criticism is very helpful in reminding us that there is a referential dimension. There is a history behind the texts, and there were events that were being discussed, and I find that higher criticism can be very helpful when the negative presuppositions are removed. That's where the debate really occurs. Many evangelicals argue that you cannot remove the negative presuppositions. By that I mean, the use of higher criticism to differentiate between authentic and inauthentic texts, between those texts which for instance go back to the historical Israel and the historical Jesus and those texts which were later additions by the community, either Israel or the church, and were not historical. This is where I think the negative results of higher criticism have come from, and I find it on the whole an unnecessary presupposition of higher criticism. When higher criticism, both in terms of form and redaction, is used positively, to recover and uncover the actual meaning of the text (For instance, form criticism is that which relates to the various forms of the Gospels and of the Epistles; it's form criticism that for instance discovered the hymns and the creeds and the Pauline Epistles, etc.), then it can be extremely helpful. When redaction criticism helps us see how the evangelists used their sources, how they dealt with the traditions which they had and how they used them to highlight and to bring out and to further take the life of Jesus and contextualize it for their own churches, then it can be very helpful, so I think that it depends on what presuppositions are yours.

NEWPORT: An example of that was Earl Ellis on our faculty who used higher criticism to establish the Pauline authorship of the pastorals.

KAISER: Yes, exactly.

NEWPORT: I think that's an example of a positive use of higher criticism in a very exciting way. All right, is there a question from the floor? I have some others here; is there anyone who wants to go to the microphone now before we go on with some of the other questions? If so, make your way and we'll go on with another question here. Dr. Johnston, a very controversial subject in our constituency is the problem of abortion and, to a minor degree, the problem of homosexuality from a biblical perspective. Some people in our constituency believe that it's part of orthodoxy to have no abortion for any reason except the mother's life. What is the biblical approach to the problem of homosexuality, you dealt with that I believe in your book *Evangelicals at Impass*.

JOHNSTON: On abortion or homosexuality?

NEWPORT: Well, abortion. Start with that.

JOHNSTON: Again, it's an issue that often causes more heat than light. Our own denomination The Evangelical Covenant Church has had four different years of discussion at the national assembly trying to come up with a formulation which all of us could buy into. It's very clear that there is a wholesale misuse of abortion in our country and a cheapening of human life. However, as soon as you move in absolute terms to try to take some of the Old Testament passages and affirm with confidence that human life begins with conception, you've ended the discussion. Because, in fact, if you knew that human life began with conception, everything would be murder and there would be no discussion. And the fact that there is discussion in our churches, even the Southern Baptist churches, suggests to us that those texts are not as crystal clear as any one of us might like. If, in fact, it is not exegetically certain that human life begins with conception, then in fact we're into areas of larger theological discourse, and at that point I would plead that we join together as prolifers or as Christians concerned with the excesses to slow down the misuse of abortion. It seems to me as the church argues and splinters, it wastes all its ammunition on each other and doesn't get on with the task of trying to do something to address a social problem.

NEWPORT: Thank you very much. Would anyone else on the panel like to speak to that?

KAISER: I can't let that one go by. It's one of the most serious things in our day. I know we're deeply divided over it, and while the theological community still continues to argue, the medical community is rolling in evidence of enormous proportions. The medical community is far ahead of the theological community. The second thing is that I don't think that the text is as opaque as we had thought that it was. It is only that it is found in a spot where we are weakest in our interpretive armour, that is the Old Testament. And, it is certainly to be found at least in the Exodus passage in the covenant code; it is there also to be found in Psalm 139. It is my own private fear, having worked on this, now that we have reached since Wade-Row some 20 million known abortions that we have many cases where it wasn't for the saving of the life of the mother, but rather just out of personal predilection, that we were using as a way to further our own interests and preferences. It looks to me as if we are close now to quadrupling Hitler's record. He sent six million up the chimney; we are close to putting four times that in a bucket, and if God judged the Third Reich for doing that to the Jews, then I don't know what keeps the grace and mercy of God on the United States tonight. I don't. I think we should be careful; I know we differ. On the other hand, I don't think the Lord is saying, "I don't know what I'm going to do about this issue. I haven't made up my mind yet." I have an idea He has a view.

JOHNSTON: Let me dialogue with Walt just one further bit to say though that if the texts are clear that he mentions then it's not at all clear that saving the life of the mother is the priority. I mean we're dealing with life and life at that point. We agree totally that abortion in the interest of one's own pleasure or ease is wrong and other than God's intention. But how far do we push it? As soon as you make an exception whether it's for the mother's life or for incest or for rape, all of those have justification, it seems to me you're into problem areas in regard to the Old Testament texts.

KAISER: Then the answer seems to me is, Rob, to come back to that in the text itself. Of course, on these life issues, there were supplied even the very rationales that we are trying to see here, and even in the capital offenses that were put within the texts to show the seriousness for some twenty crimes in the Old Testament, there comes a particular text that says, with regard to the case of murder for example, you should take no ransom, no substitute. There was to be in this case an exclusion, and the history of interpretation both in the Jewish and in the Protestant realm had always been to say that this one is put in a separate category. Even though we have capital offenses for some eighteen to twenty crimes, yet this one is put in altogether a different situation for which there was no substitution. Now, I would begin making categories that it seems to me help the current community as it tries to approach these very same kinds of things. For example, the prohibition against murder is clear, yet if a person comes through the window at night and you are protecting your household, you should probably, use a pipe to part his hair first and ask questions later. And, that's legitimate in the biblical text, and there were no questions asked about that.

NEWPORT: All right maybe we better go on from that now and thank you for this. Dr. Packer, following up on what you said about women in our Southern Baptist seminaries, there is some question on some of our trustees part about women teaching men or teaching in the School of Theology. Perhaps they could teach children, perhaps they could teach youth and education, but teaching theology or teaching other subjects in our schools of theology—how do you feel about that from your understanding of womens' rights at our time and privileges?

PACKER: I would rather discuss it in terms of womens' gifts than in terms of rights and privileges. I think that there are some women who have the ability to do it, and I see no biblical reason why they should not be employed to do it when they turn out to be, sometimes they do I dare say, when jobs are advertised "the best man for the job." (Laughter) At this point, I don't think that anything in Scripture can be invoked against the use of womens' gifts. I think there is more of a problem when it's an ecclesiastical office that's in view. I did say when I talked about women in ministry that I thought it showed disrespect to the order of creation to put a woman in an official role where in her own person and in her own right she has to order men around. That's now what womanly human nature was made for as I read Genesis 2. And other things being equal, surely we ought to be respecting the order of creation.

But you'll remember that I said that in a stranger way than some do because I don't believe that any New Testament passage can be quoted as forbidding the people of God or anyone else to put a woman into that kind of role. I think we ought to see the task here as having two facets. One is that all the gifts God has given are given to be used. If in the Christian community a woman has a teaching gift, that gift was meant to be used. That's what God gave it for. The other facet of the matter is to say that in general, in ordering ministry in the church and this is what I, well what really I haven't got the resources for saying properly because no one seems to me has done their homework and I don't think that I fully have either, but in structuring ministry in the church the clue that we ought to be following is that women's ministry will be womanly ministry. It will have a maternal rather than a paternal cast because women are women and they are not men in disguise. Therefore, we ought to be thinking much harder than we are about informal patterns of ministry which women can fulfill, often regularly better than men as a matter of fact, in the congregation and teaching and counseling individuals, supporting folk in trouble, giving the kind of maternal care to needy groups which mother gives in the family. We ought to be working toward a consensus whereby women who may be on the church staff working full-time in that kind of activity see their role as the true fulfillment of their womanly, maternal nature in Christian ministry and don't hanker to be doing the man's job in the man's role. We haven't got there yet. Please God, we shall move in that direction rather than moving in any other in this whole matter, which is troubled waters, as I said. All sorts of mixed motives are operating here, and we just have to accept that as we try to work our way through.

NEWPORT: Thank you very much Dr. Packer. We have two deans here and might get a brief word from them about this because they have the same problem that I have, that the other deans out here have, in the presence especially of the ultimate persons on this and other boards.

PACKER: Perhaps I ought to have said before either of them speaks, that I came to Canada from a college where there were two able women on the faculty teaching alongside of men. That I suppose is a hermeneutically significant fact and will be interpreted by some as biasing everything I have just said. (Laughter)

NEWPORT: What is your position on this Dr. Kaiser?

KAISER: I think that God has given gifts of leadership, gifts of teaching to women; I think that the biblical texts that have been used have come up recently. It's a phenomenon since 1975 in our circles that has been, I think, put into a hierarchial kind of framework. I think there is a job subordination, an economic kind of subordination just as there is within the Trinity, and that was the text you pointed to in 1 Corinthians 11:4. But I think God has put authority on the head of a woman, not the veil which is a symbol of authority; that's the corniest translation in the history of interpretation, and it's in all of the Bibles, and there will be a lot of translators in line on the final day. (More laughter) I say that as a participant in one of them. Then it seems to me that we must also recognize, I don't take the cultural interpretation, but it seems to me that the 1 Timothy passage is straight away saying there that, indeed, while men are lifting up holy hands in every place, in like manner, *osautos*, in the same way, women, women lifting up holy hands in prayer much as we have in 1 Corinthians 11, and that Paul does not wish them to teach or to exercise authority because they have not learned. His imperative there is let the women learn. That's the clear imperative, and then the subjunctive is that I would not wish, I would prefer that they not teach. Why? Because. And I have taken a point of view which I know only several of us hold: my wife, myself (laughter) and Paul (more laughter). The devil made me say that! Basically it seems to me that he gives as reasons that Adam was formed first, and I still continue to think that Paul chose his words deliberately. The word means that Adam was plasticized, molded, and formed, and it does have the meaning in some instances of being shaped spiritually and educationally. Then came Eve. So rather than arguing as my colleague does for the orders of creation (Which I'm not really convinced of in this case. I really don't see the orders of creation here being based on who's here first, or the animals should have primacy; they were here first.), I think that whole concept here is that man was shaped, walked, and talked with God in the garden and had the advantage of being instructed, but the woman was tricked.

She was deceived. That also impresses me. How do you rope someone in and trick them? It seems to me you trick them when they haven't been taught. Therefore, once they had been taught, and once the gift has been recognized, then they can have ministry, which by the way comes from a term related to our word *minus* and, therefore, is not the leader but is the person who takes the lesser role. The minister is in the lesser position, not in the hierarchy position, and, therefore, I'd like to see the church move toward that. I don't think she will. I think we have cultural problems, and, therefore, I would like to see the use of women in the seminaries at many points where we can have agreement without distorting the ministry and gifts which God has given to women and without distorting the ministry and work that is already in progress. It calls for judgment and wisdom and maturity and balance on both parts, men and women. And therefore, we moved as a seminary for a five-year plan in which we went for all the positions which we could agree upon at the present time where we will seek women for the positions. My own faculty is divided right down the middle on this. So we have to work very, very carefully when you're dealing with 49 full-time faculty members, and all of them have strong opinions, and they hold their conviction before the Lord, and they hold it with commitment to the truthfulness of Scripture. We've had to work carefully with each other, and it's going to take a lot of praying, and I'm sure the angels are smiling at the small progress we are making, and we keep on praying and working toward that. Our own denomination, The Evangelical Free Church, in June will be voting on whether to extend a secondary kind of ordination to women who are in the military and institutional chaplaincies, missionaries, and who are on associate staff, minister of women, minister of educational programs, and things of this sort, and to reserve the ordination for male ministry alone. That's a change in our church. For in 1950, the ordination vow said he or she. But they have now been changed, and I date it around 1976, and we work with it as best we can. Grant and I both happen to be on the same faculty and both share the same point of view.

JOHNSTON: You can see somebody who's right in the middle of that controversy, and Walt could keep talking about that for a long time. We're looking for a woman for New Testament professor right now; if any of you know one I'd be happy to talk to you afterwards. I concur with everything Walt said. I would like to push it in a couple of particular ways. I think the point of 1 Corinthians 11, argued in terms of its structure, is that when women are involved in ministry, in this case praying and prophesying, they should do it as women. What's being discussed there is the importance of maintaining your own creational identity as you exercise the gifts of God. A second point is found in the Genesis text. I continue to be fascinated by the second creation account which ends with a summary by the author. You're familiar with this summary; it says for this reason a man shall leave his father and mother and cleave to his wife and the two shall become one. Have you ever paused to think of how that would have been heard by the original reader? Did in fact, men leave their father and mother and cleave to their wives? Or was it the other way around? Was it a matriarchal or patriarchal society? Clearly the answer is that it was patriarchal. It must have been grating, it must have been upsetting in ways that we just slide right over it for those people to hear the story of Adam and Eve and then hear the conclusion that men should pick up and leave and join women as opposed to vice-versa. Why would the author do that? One possibility is to make sure that you didn't misread his intention in terms of a creational ordering in which somehow male first means priority and authority rather than co-relationship and mutuality of two who are different and yet one. And so to make sure the pattern of first-second isn't seen as the point of that text in Genesis 2:24, he goes second-first. Interesting.

NEWPORT: Thank you very much. Dr. Ferguson, I see you are ready to go there with a real good question, as usual.

FERGUSON: Dr. Newport, I'd like to hear from the panel some discussion about the significance of the mind of Christ, the paradigm who is Christ, the risen Lord in the midst of His church. We talk about the authority of Scripture, that's why we're here in this particular conference, in the context of the community of faith, under the impact of the inner witness of the Holy Spirit as our final written authority. If I understand the Scripture, it points us toward the ultimate word of God who is the risen living Christ. For instance, what does the mind of Christ have to say to the question of abortion, especially when we find people who are so anti-abortion and procapital punishment, in the same breath and in the same mouth, crying out against the taking of life and calling for the taking of life? What is the mind of Christ at this point? With reference to women and their role and status, a part from, not a part from, but above and beyond and feeling full the meaning of this particular text about which we are talking, what is the mind of Christ and the paradigm or the example of Christ?

NEWPORT: All right, I think the first one was the contrast of people who seem to be so strong on abortion, yet are for capital punishment, and are very much militaristic in some cases. Does somebody want to answer that?

JOHNSTON: I'll start. With the mind of Christ, there are a couple of comments that seem relevant and the panelists can add. The spirit of Christ speaks through and is consistent with the word that we have. The word incarnate, the word inscripturated, the word proclaimed, there has to be a continuity there. If the question is on particular issues there a conflict or tension between particular aspects of the mind of Christ and the larger pattern of being Christlike, showing love and grace and a passion for the gospel, not being lost in the trees and not seeing the forest and so on. I agree with you that oftentimes in our concern to be Christlike in the particular, we become less than Christian in the larger. It's a sin we need to confess.

NEWPORT: Thank you very much. Our time is just about gone. I wanted to ask one concluding question of each person here. Does anyone here have a special word you'd like to say briefly on this. I see . . .

KAISER: Let me say that in 1 Corinthians 2 it seems to me that Paul makes the point that no one knows the mind of a man except the man. No one knows the mind of God except the Spirit of God. And, the mind of Christ it seems to me is not known to us unless there is revelation of that. Revelation in a person, yes. Revelation in an event, yes. And revelation in its word, yes. We must say yes to all three. And, therefore, even when that revelation comes in what we believe and what the churches continue to point to in all of its fullness, while there may be specialities that affect us that are in topics for us at a particular time, if we are to minister the whole counsel of God it will take some courage for us to wander into some fields which are not popular to particular days. But for which the same Lord who has revealed His mind through the Word, will then hold us accountable on that final day too. (Tape unclear.) I do agree that there is a centrality of our Lord and of His mind and His person, and yet while we are making the point of Christocentrism, we must not be Christoexclusivists. That would be reductionistic, and that, too, would get us into a canon within a canon. And this we have always resisted. We have said *all* of the Word of God, and that we would try to understand it for our day as it was intended, for indeed it has a possibility to extend to all of those areas.

NEWPORT: Thank you very much. Our time is just about gone. Outstanding scholars, could you say a brief word? What do you see as the strengths and weaknesses of our seminaries. Start with you, Dr. Osborne. Which direction do you think we should go, looking at us from the outside? You've had some contact each of you with our seminaries.

OSBORNE: I was hoping you wouldn't start with me. It's always difficult to be the first. The first thing I would want to say is we cannot set ourselves up as judges. Certainly our prayers are with you. We realize the trauma you are going through. We realize the difficult days in which we live. We realize the tremendous polarization that is taking place, and I think my major concern is that there is an unhealthy polarization in which both sides seem to be taking polar opposites, and there's too little dialogue. My prayer is that, involved in the whole situation, we can see a greater openness and a greater dialogue. I think that the major thing that I've always felt in the Southern Baptist seminaries is the tremendous dynamic, the tremendous power and energy. Everyone looks, in a very real sense, with awe at the Southern Baptist seminaries and the growth, the energy, and I think that you have set a pace for all the rest of us in this regard. It's my prayer that in these very, very difficult issues that we're facing, certainly the issue of inerrancy, and the many, many others, I hope that the sides can begin dialoguing and that we can start seeing, instead of politics taking place, a mutual desire for rapport and understanding. My other hope, frankly, is that in a very real sense, what these Ridgecrest conferences are seeing, namely that we who are outside can come in and learn from you as well as dialogue with you will continue and not just be restricted to these three conferences. I've learned a great deal. We've all tremendously enjoyed this week and I pray that it will continue.

NEWPORT: Thank you very much. Dr. Packer, you've had experience with us.

PACKER: It's true that this is my second Ridgecrest conference. I would like simply to underline and endorse all the things that Grant Osborne has said, and I think said very excellently. As a way of expressing the mind of your team of visiting firemen (May I call us that?), my perception, I think, I would focus this way; it's entirely in line with what's being said. There's a question of the total trustworthiness of the Word of God, the question of biblical inerrancy which has been before you and is being much discussed. It has in many peoples' minds been linked and linked unfruitfully with the quite different question of biblical interpretation, which is what we've been dealing with at this conference.

Inerrancy has to do with a commitment, an advance commitment as well as a present commitment to trust and obey whatever teaching the Bible proves on inspection to be giving. One will receive it as from God in its entirety, and one will be bound by it. Interpretation has to do with finding out what the text does actually teach. I have said and others have said that inerrantists may find themselves and frequently do find themselves disagreeing about the precise nuances of a text, the precise thrust and implications of the text, and, therefore, you see the kind of discussion that we've had on this panel about women, women in teaching roles. Just what is Paul saying about women in 1 Timothy 2:8-11? And we have that discussion on the basis of our common commitment to be bound by the Word of God when we understand what it means. It seems to me that in the Southern Baptist situation for quite a long time, the people who have insisted most strongly that they stand for the inerrancy of Scripture have also been standing for a particular way of interpreting Scripture, which in certain respects would seem to others of us to be less than scholarly. This style of interpretation, and I'm sorry to have to say this, is linked in the minds of some people with a commitment to inerrancy in such a way that they won't believe that anyone who doesn't handle the Bible in the way that they do really believes in the total trustworthiness of Scripture.

I think that more work has to be done in the Southern Baptist world to detach those two questions from each other and get them considered separately. I think that a conference like this one is extremely strategic from that standpoint because here you see an attempt on the part of people who would confess themselves inerrantists to do biblical interpretation in a way which, so we hope, forgive us for this, but it's what we were asked to do really, we hope will stand as something of a model for scholarly and disciplined handling of this totally trustworthy Bible, and which we know very well is not the way of handling the Bible that is found amongst all the inerrantists of the Southern Baptist Convention. I'm trying to say gently, again I ask, forgive me, I don't want to cause offense, I'm just trying to analyze something which I think I see. And there's a major area for discussion there which really it will take years, I think, fully to deal with because the intellectual habits of years are not undone in five minutes. I think that this kind of thing will have to be mounted and to go on happening, one way or another, again and again and again.

And the final thing, let me add this just as a footnote, I am sure that it will be very helpful, helpful I mean to this whole situation, if the Bible teachers in the seminaries, who after all are supposed to be modeling biblical interpretation for the whole denomination, surely that is true, do take time out to demonstrate by speech, by utterance, by illustration, the reality of their commitment to the total trustworthiness of the Bible. One of the mistrust-causing factors in the situation is that the inerrantists whose handling of the Bible is sometimes, as we may think, deficient, are quite sure, for whatever reason I don't know, that the Bible teachers of the seminaries as a body don't accept the total trustworthiness of the Bible in the final analysis. It will be very good if the Bible teachers in the seminaries are able to dispell that suspicion by public gestures and things that they say and do which show where they really stand. I am assuming that they do, shall I, well, let me just generalize, I'm assuming that they do take that view, that they would not think themselves in the proper place if they didn't, and that they would be able to rise to this invitation and make it creditable to the people on the other side, that indeed they do trust their Bibles and that the differences between the one side and the other therefore, have to do only with the style and results of interpretation.

NEWPORT: Thank you, Dr. Packer. Those are very helpful words. Can I have two brief statements here now from you Dr. Kaiser and Dr. Johnston and then we will conclude.

KAISER: Well, it's no small thing with regard to what happens to 14 million people. I'm terribly impressed with what God has done through the Southern Baptists. You have an awfully lot to be giving thanks to God for. It's such a remarkable thing that you've got to believe, as I do, that the contests of the evil one has got to in a pretty high-pitched battle for what you have. And on the other hand what happens to you is going to affect all of American church life. So, we're talking very serious things. My children are in the marrying state, they marry across denominational lines, there is total impact. And, furthermore, you have four or five of the largest seminaries in the world; that is another remarkable achievement. It is something to give thanks to God for. I think you ought to preserve it. Southern Baptists as I understand it, became great through stressing evangelism and the solid teaching of the Word of God, and people flock to be fed. I hope you never lose your evangelistic fervor. And what you've done in missions overseas I hope you'll redouble that. Don't sit back and look at the stats. Take a small denomination like mine and multiply that out in terms of where you have to be in missions right now. It'll shock you if you do that figuring. You have remarkable figures, but you've got remarkable resources too. The evangelical world in the Southern Baptist world has become wealthy too. We've got enormous wealth. That was determined recently when we saw what the televangelists could collect, they were collecting it from a lot of our people. So, I'd urge you along these lines.

I'd urge you, too, to end the famine of the Word of God. I still think we have a lot of junk food, and we're worried about that and rightfully so, but we have a lot of junk theology, too, and junk preaching. By this I mean, theology and preaching where we are talking about religious and theological topics, but I don't think we've gotten down to cutting the line of the word loose. I've been trying myself in my messages, trying to do this with my students, telling them to let the shape of the biblical passage shape both the content and the structure of the message, so it was totally biblically. I think that's true expository preaching. I long for that on the American scene again. It's here, it's in part, but it should just be spreading like wild fire.

And I think, finally, in the long run, when the end of the day comes, while I'm terribly anxious about theological definition, and I think it's really important, yet practice is going to tell me a whole lot more when it really comes down to it. We can fuss or misunderstand each others' terms, but when we open the text and get on our knees together and start praying for the Spirit of God to once again do what He did 1905, 1906; it's been over 80 years since a genuine revival went coast-to-coast in the United States. I suspect a lot of our problems which are real and important will find a lot of resolution when my heart and your heart and the hearts of all God's men and women start being affected once again by a real work of the Holy Spirit, such as we have seen in the two great awakenings, and I think in 1905, 1906. I think we ought to pray for that. I think we ought to risk that because we desperately need it. I think that all of our best men and all of our best computers and all our best conferences, while they help and while I think they are honoring God, are not going to, in the end, produce what we want because the task is too great. We're going to need a real heaven-sent revival to change all our hearts. I'm not thinking of just Southern Baptists, for I tell you as best I can, your problems are reduplicated in small or larger measure in every major denomination that I know of that is trying to point to the Scriptures. The contest and the stakes are enormous. So, thank you for letting me have an opportunity to say even these words and just to show my deep appreciation, for what you are continuing to do because we deeply love you in the Lord and respect what's being done here. It is not as if we sit on the sidelines and say, well, we don't understand the politics there and it's no concern to us. It's a matter of deep concern, and we pray that God will deal mercifully with you and therefore with us.

NEWPORT: Thank you so much, Walter. Robert, this last word and then Dr. Honeycutt will close.

JOHNSTON: Let me focus back on the seminary question rather than the larger denominational one. I echo the comments that have been made and want to thank you for putting up with my long-windedness. It was a pleasure being here. There probably are several reasons as to why it happened, but the mere reporting of the number of people that attended last year and this year is at least a small parable of the problems facing seminaries today. When you get down in the trenches and have to do the interpretive work, because there are differences and because it moves into levels of certainty rather than full certainty, as you saw us tonight here disagree, people bail out and people become suspicious. So that though we had a thousand last year, we had 300 this year.

Seminaries are in the business of trying to help people hone their interpretation. It's a risky business that demands our prayers and respect and effort. At North Park, we have tried to do one thing concretely to help with that trust, something that Jim Packer was referring to. The second year, the first year really that I came as dean, there was a gap between where our churches were and where it was perceived our seminary was. It was more perceived than real, but perception is what people act on, and so it was real. We as a seminary put in an optional tenth month to the ninth month contract in which we ask our faculty to volunteer for $22^1/_2$ extra days to be arranged with the dean for writing for laity, serving on denominational committees, preaching and teaching in local churches, and getting out there where the people were so that the seminary faculty could be sensitive to the life of the church and the church could understand where they were. We have a little tiny denomination in reference to you and, therefore, it's easier for that to be accomplished. But trust is built through relationship and interaction, so we do things like this effort. As our faculty can be out in the churches preaching, teaching, showing their respect for Scripture, much of the hard feeling will fade away.

I don't want to whitewash over real differences. I tell a story, a parable with no right answer; you can deconstruct it. Tommy Lankford, the dean at Duke Divinity School, who I wrote my dissertation under, was the Methodist representative for a consultation between Lutherans and Methodists, one each from each of the five continents, ten people dialoguing over theological matters. Tommy said that the first two or three years he was there he was always embarrassed because regardless of what issue came up, he sort of scratched his head and shifted in his chair and sort of began to create, hopefully, a biblical answer. On the other hand, his Lutheran brethren pulled out their books of creeds, opened them up, paragraph 3, point 1, subsection 4, and began their discussion from a defined entity. The one represents preEnlightment Christianity in which the major argument was intrachurch, the refining of doctrine ever more precisely. The other was postEnlightment in which the Methodist had to get on with the task of speaking to a secular pagan world the sure message of salvation.

We run the risk as evangelical churches of losing our mission to a secular world to the degree we concentrate on intrachurch warfare. We risk having nothing to say to the world to the degree we don't authorize what we say out of a clear and sure word. That surely is the horns of the dilemma that I, as an outsider, hear you struggling with, and it would be presumptuous to say on which side one should lean. Perhaps we can agree on biblical authority, we can agree on Scriptures' trustworthiness, we can agree on Scriptures' foundation and get back to the task of mission and evangelism, proclamation, witness. There's a needy world.

NEWPORT: Thank you very much. What a wonderful climax. Let's thank these persons for what they've done. (Applause)

14
WORKSHOP SUMMARY

In a series of four workshops, participants in The Conference on Biblical Interpretation were given opportunities to deal in practical ways with various issues of interpretation and to engage in dialogue with persons with different perspectives.

The workgroups, led by eight professors from the Southern Baptist Convention's seminaries, were held after the conference's plenary sessions. They focused on general issues of interpretation and a selection of biblical texts dealing with three contemporary concerns addressed in presentations by well-known theologian James I. Packer: creation, women, and eschatology. In many cases, the Scripture passages paralleled the primary texts cited by Packer and other plenary speakers.

With open Bibles in their laps, Southern Baptist pastors, other church staff members, educators, and laypersons examined the texts and then discussed possible interpretations of those texts and their practical application to the Christian life.

Leaders of the eight workgroups were:

Albert F. Bean, associate professor of Old Testament interpretation and Hebrew, Midwestern Baptist Theological Seminary;

Robert L. Cate, dean of academic affairs and professor of Old Testament interpretation, Golden Gate Baptist Theological Seminary;

M. Vernon Davis, associate professor of Christian theology, Midwestern Seminary;

John P. Newport, vice president for academic affairs and provost and professor of philosophy of religion, Southwestern Baptist Theological Seminary;

Craig P. Skinner, professor of preaching, Golden Gate Seminary;

Wayne E. Ward, Joseph Emerson Brown professor of Christian theology, The Southern Baptist Theological Seminary;

Gerald L. Borchert, professor of New Testament interpretation, Southern Seminary; and

R. Bruce Corley, associate professor of New Testament, Southwestern Seminary.

In written evaluation of the conference, participants rated the workgroups as one of the most practical and helpful dimensions of the three-day meeting.